Legali...

Editorial Advisors:
Gloria A. Aluise
Attorney at Law
Jonathan Neville
Attorney at Law
Robert A. Wyler
Attorney at Law

Authors:
Gloria A. Aluise
Attorney at Law
Daniel O. Bernstine
Attorney at Law
Roy L. Brooks
Professor of Law
Scott M. Burbank
C.P.A.
Charles N. Carnes
Prpfessor of Law
Paul S. Dempsey
Professor of Law
Jerome A. Hoffman
Professor of Law
Mark R. Lee
Professor of Law
Jonathan Neville
Attorney at Law
Laurence C. Nolan
Professor of Law
Arpiar Saunders
Attorney at Law
Robert A. Wyler
Attorney at Law

CONTRACTS

Adaptable to Seventh Edition* of Farnsworth Casebook

By Jonathan Neville
Attorney at Law

*If your casebook is a newer edition, go to www.gilbertlaw.com to see if a supplement is available for this title.

THOMSON

WEST

EDITORIAL OFFICE: 1 N. Dearborn Street, Suite 650, Chicago, IL 60602
REGIONAL OFFICES: Chicago, Dallas, Los Angeles, New York, Washington, D.C.

SERIES EDITOR
Linda C. Schneider, J.D.
Attorney at Law

PRODUCTION MANAGER
Elizabeth G. Duke

FIRST PRINTING—2009

Legalines®

**Features Detailed Briefs of Every Major Case,
Plus Summaries of the Black Letter Law**

Titles Available

Administrative Law .... Keyed to Breyer
Administrative Law .... Keyed to Schwartz
Administrative Law .... Keyed to Strauss
Antitrust .... Keyed to Areeda
Antitrust .... Keyed to Pitofsky
Business Associations .... Keyed to Klein
Civil Procedure .... Keyed to Friedenthal
Civil Procedure .... Keyed to Hazard
Civil Procedure .... Keyed to Yeazell
Conflict of Laws .... Keyed to Currie
Constitutional Law .... Keyed to Brest
Constitutional Law .... Keyed to Choper
Constitutional Law .... Keyed to Cohen
Constitutional Law .... Keyed to Rotunda
Constitutional Law .... Keyed to Stone
Constitutional Law .... Keyed to Sullivan
Contracts .... Keyed to Calamari
Contracts .... Keyed to Dawson
Contracts .... Keyed to Farnsworth
Contracts .... Keyed to Fuller
Contracts .... Keyed to Kessler
Contracts .... Keyed to Knapp
Contracts .... Keyed to Murphy
Corporations .... Keyed to Choper
Corporations .... Keyed to Eisenberg
Corporations .... Keyed to Hamilton

Criminal Law .... Keyed to Dressler
Criminal Law .... Keyed to Johnson
Criminal Law .... Keyed to Kadish
Criminal Law .... Keyed to Kaplan
Criminal Law .... Keyed to LaFave
Criminal Procedure .... Keyed to Kamisar
Domestic Relations .... Keyed to Wadlington
Estates and Trusts .... Keyed to Dobris
Evidence .... Keyed to Mueller
Evidence .... Keyed to Waltz
Family Law .... Keyed to Areen
Income Tax .... Keyed to Freeland
Income Tax .... Keyed to Klein
Labor Law .... Keyed to Cox
Property .... Keyed to Cribbet
Property .... Keyed to Dukeminier
Property .... Keyed to Nelson
Property .... Keyed to Rabin
Remedies .... Keyed to Rendelman
Securities Regulation .... Keyed to Coffee
Torts .... Keyed to Dobbs
Torts .... Keyed to Epstein
Torts .... Keyed to Franklin
Torts .... Keyed to Henderson
Torts .... Keyed to Prosser
Wills, Trusts & Estates .... Keyed to Dukeminier

All Titles Available at Your Law School Bookstore

THOMSON

WEST

SHORT SUMMARY OF CONTENTS

TABLE OF CONTENTS AND SHORT REVIEW OUTLINE

I. BASIS FOR ENFORCING PROMISES

A. INTRODUCTION

1. **Sources of Law.** The law of contracts deals with the interpretation and enforcement of promises. Much of the "black letter law" discussed in courses on contracts is found in the Restatement of Contracts, published by the American Law Institute ("ALI"), and in the Uniform Commercial Code ("U.C.C."), with which the ALI is also heavily involved.

   a. **Case law.** The law of contracts as developed through case law is fluid; it reflects the tensions between: (i) individual freedom to negotiate terms and enter binding contracts, and (ii) the public interest in various types of social control. Even though many of the cases studied are very old, the problems they raise recur regularly in our day.

   1) **Distinguishing a promise from a belief--**

Hawkins v. McGee, 146 A. 641 (N.H. 1929).

Facts. Hawkins's (P's) hand was severely burned in an accident. McGee (D), a doctor, solicited an opportunity to operate, promising that he could make the hand "100% perfect." The operation was unsuccessful. P brought an action for damages based on breach of warranty.

Issue. May a surgeon's promise of a particular surgical outcome constitute an offer to enter a contract?

Held. Yes. New trial ordered.

♦   D argues that, even if he said that he could make P's hand perfect, no reasonable man would think that he intended to enter into a contractual relationship. D contends that his words could reasonably be understood only as expressing his strong belief that he would give P a very good hand.

♦   Before the court could submit the question of the making of a contract to the jury, the court had to decide whether the words could possibly have been meant as intending to form a contract. The trial court's decision was not erroneous.

♦   Even if it is common knowledge that there is uncertainty in any surgical procedure, in this case D repeatedly sought to do the surgery. There was evidence that D wanted to experiment with skin grafting. This evidence was sufficient to allow a jury to find that D's representations induced P to consent to the operation and that there was a contract. Thus, the question of the making of the alleged contract was properly submitted to the jury.

♦   However, the court did err in instructing the jury regarding damages, so a new trial is necessary.

---

b.   **Restatement of Contracts.** The First Restatement of Contracts was published in 1932, and in 1981, a Restatement (Second) of Contracts was issued to refine the first one and to correlate with the U.C.C. The Restatement is not statutory; it is an attempt to "restate" the essence of the law after a thorough review of cases and careful analysis of the relevant legal principles. Thus, it is not binding, but it is very persuasive and highly regarded by the courts.

c.   **Uniform Commercial Code.** The U.C.C. is a model code adopted by all of the states except Louisiana (which has a civil law tradition) in one form or another. Most of the provisions relevant to the study of contracts are in Article 2 (Sales), which applies to transactions in "goods," although certain parts of Article 1 (General Provisions) and Article 9 (Secured Transactions, Sales of Accounts and Chattel Paper) are also relevant.

1)   **General product information not a warranty--**

Bayliner Marine Corp. v. Crow, 509 S.E.2d 499 (Va. 1999).

Facts. Crow (P) was invited to ride on a new sport fishing boat manufactured by Bayliner Marine Corp. (D). A sales representative from Tidewater, the dealer, gave P printed information from D's dealer's manual that gave the specifications for its boats, including a maximum speed of 30 miles per hour for a boat with a specified propeller. P purchased a boat with a smaller propeller and also purchased 2,000 pounds of optional equipment. When he piloted it for the first time, the maximum speed P could reach was 13 miles per hour. Tidewater worked on the boat and was able to temporarily increase the speed to 24 miles per hour. D wrote a letter to P, stating that the performance representations made at the time of purchase were incorrect and that 23 to 25 miles per hour was the maximum possible speed. P sued for breach of express warranties and implied warranties of merchantability and fitness for a particular purpose. The trial court entered judgment in favor of P. D appeals.

Issue. Does a manufacturer make an express warranty to a purchaser about a specific product when it provides information about the performance of products with different features?

Held. No. Judgment reversed.

♦ Only affirmations of fact or promise that relate to the goods at issue create express warranties. Here, D's dealer's manual specified performance for boats based on their propeller size. P purchased a boat that had a smaller propeller than those described in D's manual. The boats described in D's manual also did not have all of the extra equipment that P purchased. Therefore, D's manual did not constitute an express warranty as to P's boat.

♦ D's sales brochure stated that the boat would deliver "the kind of performance you need to get to the prime offshore fishing grounds." P claims that this constitutes an express warranty. However, under Va. Code Ann. section 8.2-313(2), "a statement purporting to be merely the seller's opinion or commendation of the goods does not create a warranty." The statement in the brochure did not describe a specific characteristic of the boat, but was merely D's opinion about the quality of the boat's performance. The brochure did not create an express warranty.

Comment. P claimed that D breached an implied warranty of merchantability because the boat's slow speed made it unfit for offshore fishing in his area. Under U.C.C. section 2-314, goods are merchantable if they "are fit for the ordinary purposes for which goods of that description are used." P was required to establish the standard of merchantability in the trade, but he failed to do this or to show that a significant portion of the boat-buying public would object to purchasing an offshore fishing boat with the speed capability P's boat had. Therefore, D did not breach the implied warranty of merchantability.

---

2. **Definitions.**

   a. **Promise.** A "promise" is an assurance or undertaking, however expressed, that something will or will not be done in the future. Promises enforceable by law are called contracts.

   b. **Promisor.** The "promisor" is the person who makes the promise.

   c. **Promisee.** The person to whom the promise is addressed is called the "promisee."

   d. **Beneficiary.** When performance of a promise will benefit someone other than the promisee, that person is called the "beneficiary."

   e. **Consideration.** "Consideration" is a benefit received by the promisor or a detriment incurred by the promisee.

3. **Theories of Contractual Liability.**

a. **Express contracts.** An express contract may be oral or written and consists of an offer, acceptance, and bargained-for consideration. It may be bilateral, requiring both of the contracting parties to fulfill obligations reciprocally toward each other (*e.g.,* a contract of sale where the seller becomes bound to deliver goods to the buyer and the buyer becomes bound to pay the price for them), or unilateral, where one party becomes bound to fulfill obligations toward the other without receiving any return promise of performance (*e.g.,* A promises to pay $100 for return of her dog).

   1) **Promises enforceable without consideration.** In addition to recognizing the enforceability of express contracts consisting of an offer, acceptance, and bargained-for consideration, certain types of promises are enforceable notwithstanding a lack of consideration.

      a) **Promissory estoppel.** Where one party acts to her detriment in reliance upon a gratuitous promise, the detrimental reliance of the promisee, within limits, will be deemed sufficient for estopping the promisor from asserting the defense of lack of consideration.

      b) **Promise to pay a barred legal obligation.** Subsequent promises to perform contractual obligations which had become unenforceable (i) because the promisor was discharged through bankruptcy or (ii) because of the running of the statute of limitations are enforceable without new consideration.

      c) **Promise to perform voidable preexisting duty.** Subsequent promises to perform contractual obligations which became unenforceable because of the assertion of some privilege or defense (lack of capacity, Statute of Frauds, duress, etc.) are enforceable without consideration, provided the new promise is not also subject to the same privilege or defense.

      d) **Promise to pay for benefits previously conferred.** Where no contractual liability previously existed, a subsequent promise to pay for benefits previously conferred may nonetheless be enforceable.

b. **Implied-in-fact contracts.** An implied-in-fact contract is one inferred as a matter of reason and justice from the acts, conduct, or circumstances surrounding a transaction rather than one formally or explicitly stated in words. As with express contracts, the source of the obligation in implied-in-fact contracts is the manifested intent of the parties; however, whereas in express contracts, all of the terms and conditions are expressed by the parties, implied-in-fact contracts require one or more of the terms of the contract to be inferred from the conduct of the parties. For example, an implied-in-fact contract may be found where one person renders services to another at the other's request but without an express agreement as to the compensation to be paid therefor. In such case, if the circumstances warrant (*e.g.,* both parties are businesspeople), a promise to pay the reasonable value of the services may be inferred. The Uniform Commercial Code section 1-201(3) specifically recognizes agreements arising by implication.

c. **Implied-in-law or quasi-contracts.** An implied-in-law or quasi-contract is an obligation imposed upon a person, not because of her intent to agree (and usually against her will), but because one party has conferred a benefit upon the other under such circumstances that in equity and good conscience there ought to be compensation for the benefit conferred. This avoids unjust enrichment of one party at the other's expense. For example, where one party appropriates for her benefit the inventions of another, she will be liable in quasi-contract for the benefits resulting from such appropriation.

B. REMEDYING BREACH

1. **Introduction.** When a contract which the courts recognize as enforceable is breached, the nonbreaching party often has a choice of remedies, including damages, specific performance, rescission and restitution, quasi-contract, and a tort action.

2. **Common Law.** At common law, the rules relating to the enforcement of promises developed in large part from the actions of covenant, debt, and assumpsit.

   a. **Covenant.** Promises made under seal were enforceable through an action of covenant whether or not there was consideration. Today, under the U.C.C., adopted in all states except Louisiana, the presence or absence of a seal is immaterial in contracts concerning the sale of goods. [U.C.C. §2-203] In contracts not involving the sale of goods, however, the seal generally raises a presumption that the contract was validly executed or included consideration, or acts to extend the statute of limitations.

   b. **Debt.** The action of debt was generally used to recover a certain specific sum of money when the promise to pay was unsealed. The promisor's obligation in debt was based upon her receipt of a benefit from the promisee, and the action in debt gave rise to the concept of quid pro quo on the bargain element.

   c. **Assumpsit.** The action of assumpsit was generally used by a promisee to recover damages for physical injury to person or property as a result of the failure of the promisor to perform in accordance with her promise. At first, assumpsit applied only to cases where the promisor's performance was less than promised; later, assumpsit was extended to include failure to perform at all.

3. **Enforcement Principles.** There are basic principles that guide courts in enforcing promises. Among these are the concepts that (i) contract law is intended to provide relief to the promisee to make up for the breach, not to punish the promisor for breaching; (ii) relief should put the promisee in the position she would have been in had the contract been performed, thereby fulfilling the promisee's expectations; and (iii) in most cases, relief should be substitutional (*i.e.,* a money award) and not specific (*i.e.,* ordering the promisor to perform).

4. **Focus on Injured Party's Damages--**

United States Naval Institute v. Charter Communications, Inc., 936 F.2d 692 (2d Cir. 1991).

Facts. The United States Naval Institute (P) owned the copyright to the book *The Hunt For Red October*. It granted an exclusive license to Charter Communications, Inc. (D) to publish a paperback edition of the book "not sooner than October 1985." D sent its paperback books to retail outlets early enough to allow sales to begin on September 15. The book was near the top of the paperback best seller lists by the end of September and allegedly reduced P's sales of hardback copies of the book. P sued, claiming copyright infringement and seeking all of D's profits from pre-October sales (estimated at $724,300). The district court found that D had breached the contract and that P was entitled to recover damages for copyright infringement, comprising actual damages suffered by P plus D's profits attributable to the infringement. The court calculated P's actual damages as the profits P would have earned from hardcover sales in September if D's paperback had not been for sale, based on the difference between September and August sales ($35,380). D's profits attributable to the infringement were its profits on paperback sales to buyers who would not have bought a hardcover copy in September ($7,760). D appeals.

Issue. Must a breaching party pay the profits it received through its breach to the promisee?

Held. No. Judgment reversed in part.

♦ As an exclusive licensee, D could not infringe P's copyright, so the statutory measure of damages does not apply here. P could not recover D's profits on the sale of the paperback books.

♦ Damages for breach of contract are generally measured by P's actual loss, which achieves the objective of compensating the injured party. Sometimes, D's profits may be the measure of damages, so long as they define P's loss. But awarding D's profits that far exceed P's loss would be a penalty and punitive awards are not part of contract law.

♦   The district court concluded that D's early shipment of books caused P to lose hardcover sales, and its $35,000 award for the lost profits is justified by the evidence. Even though there is no proof of what exactly the hardcover sales would have been, any such proof would necessarily be hypothetical anyway. The amount awarded was based on the previous month's sales, which is a reasonable estimate.

---

5.   **The Measure of Damages.**

a.   **Benefit of the bargain rule.** Normally, when A contracts with B for B to perform some act and B defaults, A is given a measure of damages that would place him or her in the same position as if B had performed (expectation damages). This is the "benefit of the bargain" rule, discussed further in chapter VI. However, there are many situations that arise where this rule does not provide a fair result, so the court uses some other measure of damages for breach of contract.

b.   **Unsuccessful surgery--**

Sullivan v. O'Connor, 296 N.E.2d 183 (Mass. 1973).

Facts. Sullivan (P), a professional entertainer, contracted with O'Connor (D), a plastic surgeon, for a nose job. D promised to enhance P's beauty. The parties contemplated two operations. The surgery actually required three operations and resulted in irreparable disfigurement of P's nose. P sued for breach of contract and for negligence (malpractice), but obtained a favorable verdict only on the first count. P recovered her out-of-pocket expenses, foreseeable damages flowing from D's breach (for any disfigurement of P's nose), and pain and suffering for the third operation. P did not recover pain and suffering for the first two operations nor the difference in value between the nose as promised and the nose as actually completed. D appeals, claiming that only out-of-pocket expenses should have been awarded.

Issue. Is reliance the proper measure of damages for breach of a physician's contract to produce certain results?

Held. Yes. Judgment affirmed.

♦   Contract actions based on medical services are allowed but not encouraged. The uncertainties of medical science have made the courts require clear proof in such actions.

♦ In ascertaining damages, mere restitution (an amount equal to the value of the benefit conferred on D for performing the operation) would usually be inadequate. On the other hand, expectation recovery (an amount intended to put P in the position she would have been in had the contract been performed as agreed) would be excessive. Reliance (putting P back in the position she occupied before the agreement) provides a middle ground, particularly in noncommercial settings, and adequately protects both doctors and patients.

♦ Recovery for pain and suffering for the third operation may be awarded under either an expectation or a reliance view, because P has waived her claims for pain and suffering for the first two operations.

Comment. The court declined to follow the approach of the leading case, *Hawkins v. McGee*, 146 A. 641 (N.H. 1929), where an expectation measure of damages was applied.

---

c. **Ways of measuring damages.** An award of damages in a contract action aims to put the plaintiff in the position he would have been in if the contract had been fulfilled. In a tort action, however, the objective is to restore the plaintiff to the position he would have been in had the wrong not been committed. There are three basic measures of contract damages.

1) **Compensatory or expectation damages:** An amount intended to put the plaintiff in the position he would be in if the contract had been performed as agreed.

2) **Restitution damages:** An amount corresponding to any benefit conferred by the plaintiff upon the defendant in the performance of the contract.

3) **Reliance damages:** Any expenditure made by the plaintiff and any other detriment following proximately and foreseeably from the defendant's failure to carry out his promise; *i.e.,* putting the plaintiff back in the position he occupied before the agreement.

6. **Punitive Damages in Actions for Breach of Contract--**

White v. Benkowski, 155 N.W.2d 74 (Wis. 1967).

Facts. White (P) purchased a house next to Benkowski (D) and contracted with D to share water from D's well. The relationship became hostile and on a few occasions D turned off P's water supply for a few minutes. As a result, P twice had to take the children to a neighbor's home for a bath, and once there was an odor in the bathroom.

P sued for compensatory and punitive damages and recovered $10 and $2,000, respectively, which the trial court later reduced to $1 compensatory and no punitive damages. P appeals.

Issue. Are punitive damages permitted in actions for breach of contract?

Held. No. Judgment affirmed as modified.

◆ The jury award of $10 is not merely nominal but compensatory, and the judge erred in reducing the amount awarded.

◆ Except for breach of a promise to marry, a party may never recover punitive damages for breach of contract. In certain cases, breach of a contractual duty may be a tort, and punitive damages may be awarded, but no tort was pleaded or proved by P.

Comments.

◆ *Nominal* damages are a minimal sum such as $1 that are awarded when the plaintiff has proved a technical invasion of his rights or a breach by the defendant of some duty owed to the plaintiff, but where the plaintiff cannot prove substantial loss or injury. *Compensatory* damages are awarded to compensate the plaintiff for the loss or injury suffered. *Punitive* or exemplary damages are awarded to punish the defendant for wrongful conduct and to deter such conduct in the future.

◆ Courts have awarded punitive damages against insurance companies that refuse in bad faith to settle claims or unreasonably deny coverage. One case allowed punitive damages for a bad faith rescission of a lease. [*See* Nicholson v. United Pacific Insurance Co., 710 P.2d 1342 (Mont. 1985)]

----

7. **Arbitration.** Due to the delays and expenses of litigation in the courts, many commercial contracts include provisions requiring arbitration of disputes. This is a private procedure in which, generally, the parties choose their own judges and agree to be bound by their decision. The American Arbitration Association has established rules to be followed by arbitrators which assure that principles of justice will be followed. Arbitration awards are generally not reviewed by the courts.

C. CONSIDERATION AS A BASIS FOR ENFORCEMENT

1. **Fundamental Principles of Consideration.** In order to have a legally enforceable promise, there must be adequate consideration given. Consideration is a legal term defined as a benefit received by the promisor or a

detriment incurred by the promisee. The courts will infer a legal detriment whenever a party obliges himself through a bargain to perform in a certain manner, even if the performance is not detrimental in the ordinary sense of that term. Thus, the fact that a promise is bargained for is generally sufficient to make it enforceable. The element of bargain assures that, at least when the contract is formed, both parties see an advantage in contracting for the anticipated performance.

a. Abstention from conduct--

Hamer v. Sidway, 27 N.E. 256 (N.Y. 1891).

Facts. Decedent promised his nephew that if he would refrain from drinking, using tobacco, swearing, and playing cards or billiards for money until he became 21, he, the uncle, would pay him $5,000. Upon reaching 21, the nephew informed decedent that he had kept the bargain. Decedent reaffirmed his obligation but retained the funds until the nephew would be capable of taking care of them. Decedent died without paying. The nephew assigned his claim to Hamer (P), who sued Sidway (D), the executor. The trial court held for P, but was reversed on appeal. P appeals.

Issue. Does a promisee's abstention from legal but harmful conduct constitute legal and sufficient consideration for a promise to pay money?

Held. Yes. Judgment reversed.

♦ D claims the nephew suffered no detriment or loss but a real benefit in abstaining from these vices; enforcing the contract would confer a double benefit on one party. However, a waiver of any legal right at the request of another party is sufficient consideration for a promise.

♦ The nephew clearly had a legal right to engage in these vices, and his waiver of that right, his voluntary restriction of his lawful freedom, is legal and sufficient consideration for the promise. In addition, we cannot say that decedent was not benefited in a legal sense by his nephew's abstention from these vices.

Comments.

♦ A bargain promise is not always easily distinguished from a conditional donative promise (*e.g.,* A promises to provide B a hotel room if B comes to Los Angeles; no bargain; B's coming to Los Angeles was merely a condition to fulfillment of the gift). The distinguishing test is how the parties view the condition. In *Hamer*, abstention was the price of the promise, so there was a bargain.

♦ Certain promises must be in writing in order to be enforced. (*See* discussion of the Statute of Frauds, *infra.*)

---

b. **Contract not to sue.** There is a split of authority concerning the circumstances under which a contract not to sue may be enforced (*e.g.,* A agrees not to prosecute a claim against B in return for B's paying A $100). However, the majority rule is that forbearance to sue is legally valid consideration whether or not the claim is doubtful, so long as the claim is reasonable and honestly asserted.

1) **Forbearance as sufficient consideration--**

Fiege v. Boehm, 123 A.2d 316 (Md. 1956).

Facts. Boehm (P) became pregnant and threatened Fiege (D) with a suit in bastardy. D promised to pay for expenses of P's child and provide for its support if P would forbear prosecuting the suit. D paid $480 between September 1951 and May 1953, at which time he stopped payments when he found out that blood tests indicated the child could not possibly be his. P then filed a charge of bastardy with the state's attorney. At a trial for bastardy, D was found not guilty, and P sued to enforce the promise to support. The jury was not bound by D's acquittal and found that D was liable to P. D appeals.

Issue. Is a forbearance to sue, although based on an invalid claim, sufficient consideration to make a promise to pay binding?

Held. Yes. Judgment affirmed.

♦   P's promise while pregnant that she would not institute bastardy proceedings against D was sufficient consideration for his promise to pay, even though it was not certain that D was the father. All that is required is that P act in good faith, under a reasonable belief.

Comment. Under the minority rule, where the parties bargain in good faith and the claimant honestly believes that the claim is valid, the disputed claim need not be reasonable.

---

2. **The Exchange Requirement and Past Action.**

a. **Introduction.** The cases are split as to whether a promise to pay a moral obligation is enforceable when it arises out of a benefit previously conferred upon the promisor. However, the modern tendency is to hold that such a promise is enforceable, at least up to the value of the benefit conferred.

b. **Moral obligations.** A promise is said to be given for moral or past consideration when the promisor is motivated by some past event which inspires the promisor to make his promise. Usually (but not invariably), the past event is a transaction of some sort between the promisor and the promisee which benefited the promisor and placed him under a moral obligation to the promisee. Such promise is similar to a simple donative promise, differing principally with regard to the promisor's motive; *i.e.,* in the case of moral or past consideration, the promisor's motive is to discharge a preexisting moral obligation, while in the case of a simple donative promise (*e.g.,* I will give you $100 on your next birthday), such motive need not be present.

c.   **Gratuitous pension plan--**

Feinberg v. Pfeiffer Co., 322 S.W.2d 163 (Mo. Ct. App. 1959).

Facts. Feinberg (P) worked for Pfeiffer Co. (D) for 37 years. Unknown to P, the directors of D voted to give her a raise and a guaranteed retirement income for life. After the vote, P was informed of the action and was told she was free to retire whenever she saw fit. P continued working for a year and a half, and would have continued even without these added benefits. However, the retirement plan was a major factor in her decision to retire. D paid the benefits for several years, but a new president of D determined to stop the payments. P sued to recover the payments because she had suffered severe medical problems and could no longer work. The trial court found for P, and D appeals.

Issue. Is a gratuitous pension plan enforceable if the promisee retires in reliance on continued payments?

Held. Yes. Judgment affirmed.

♦   Promissory estoppel is now a recognized species of consideration. Although the plan was originally adopted solely in recognition of P's past work and was therefore unsupported by consideration, P's retirement was a change in position made in reliance on the plan.

♦   Even though she could have been dismissed at will by D, the actual change in P's position was retirement, induced in part by D's promise. D must pay the benefits.

Comment. Promissory estoppel is one theory which permits enforcement of contracts lacking consideration without abandoning the doctrine of consideration. Other theories include treating the act of reliance itself as consideration and finding a bilateral contract (promisee, by starting to rely, impliedly promises to complete, so there are two promises).

---

d.   Traditional approach denying enforcement--

Mills v. Wyman, 3 Pick. 207 (Mass. 1825).

Facts. Mills (P) took in Wyman's (D's) 25-year-old son who was poor and had become sick on a sea voyage. P cared for him for two weeks. D subsequently promised to repay P's expenses, but then changed his mind. P sued to recover the expenses. The court granted nonsuit to D, and P appeals.

Issue. Does a moral obligation constitute sufficient consideration to make a promise enforceable?

Held. No. Judgment affirmed.

- ◆   A moral obligation is generally not sufficient consideration for an express promise. The execution of such a promise is left to the conscience of the promisor.

- ◆   The law will only give a promise validity if the promisor gains something, or the promisee loses something, as a result of the promise.

---

e.   Modern approach allowing enforcement--

Webb v. McGowin, 168 So. 196 (Ala. Ct. App. 1935), *cert. denied,* 168 So. 199 (Ala. 1936).

Facts. Webb (P) was cleaning the upper floor of a mill and was about to drop a heavy weight to the floor below. P saw McGowin there, and in the process of avoiding harm to him, P himself fell and sustained permanent injuries. McGowin promised to pay P a monthly sum for life, and made payments for eight years until he died. McGowin's executor (D) stopped the payments. P sued. D was granted a nonsuit. P appeals.

Issue. Is moral consideration sufficient to support a promise given in recognition of a past economic benefit received by the promisor?

Held. Yes. Judgment reversed.

- ◆   Where the promisor receives a material benefit, and the promisee suffers a material detriment, then moral obligation is sufficient consideration to support a promise.

- ◆   In this case, McGowin received a material benefit of not being injured, and P suffered a material detriment of permanent disability.

Comment. Note that even when the only consideration is moral obligation, the courts may enforce the contract if the promisee has detrimentally relied on the promise.

---

3. **The Bargain Requirement.**

    a. **Introduction.** Even when a promise is unenforceable when made because the promisee is not bound, it may become binding when the promisee subsequently furnishes the consideration contemplated by doing what he was expected to do. The question in many such cases is whether the promise was a gratuitous promise of a gift or a bargain for an exchange.

    b. **Early cases did not apply estoppel doctrine--**

Kirksey v. Kirksey, 8 Ala. 131 (1845).

Facts. P's deceased husband's brother (D) invited P to bring the children and he promised that he would provide a home for them on the farm until they had grown up. P moved the 70 miles to the farm; after two years, D required them to leave. P sued for breach of contract and won a judgment for damages in the trial court. D appeals.

Issue. Is a gratuitous promise legally enforceable after P has suffered loss and inconvenience in reliance on the promise?

Held. No. Judgment reversed. D gave a mere gift; there was no consideration for enforcement.

Dissent. Loss and inconvenience to P is sufficient consideration.

---

    c. **Covenant not to compete--**

Lake Land Employment Group of Akron, LLC v. Columber, 804 N.E.2d 27 (Ohio 2004).

Facts. Columber (D) worked for Lake Land Employment Group of Akron, LLC (P). D signed an agreement not to engage in any business within 50 miles of Akron that competed with P's business for three years after he stopped working for P. D continued working for P for 10 years as an at-will employee before he left. Then he started a corporation that competed with P's. P sued for damages and to enjoin further violation of the noncompetition agreement. D moved for summary judgment, claiming that the agreement was unenforceable for lack of consideration and because the restrictions imposed an undue hardship on him. The trial court granted summary judgment for D, finding a lack of consideration. The court of appeals affirmed but certified an issue to the Ohio Supreme Court because of a conflict among other Ohio district courts.

Issue. Where an at-will employee who has already been working for an employer enters a covenant-not-to-compete agreement with his employer, is the employee's continued employment alone sufficient consideration to support the agreement?

Held. Yes. Judgment reversed and case remanded.

♦   At common law, noncompetition agreements were considered against public policy because working men had few options. Modern courts recognize that economic circumstances have changed and tend to uphold these agreements to allow employers to share confidential information with employees. However, there is no consensus among the states regarding the specific issue in this case.

♦   Some courts hold that continued employment is not sufficient consideration for a noncompetition agreement. Others hold that continued employment is sufficient consideration as long as a substantial period of employment follows the signing of the agreement, especially if the employee receives raises, promotions, or other tangible benefits. The latter approach leaves parties uncertain about the enforceability of the agreement until events occur after its execution.

♦   D in this case was an at-will employee, which means either party could terminate the employment relationship at any time. When P asked D to sign the noncompetition agreement, P was proposing to renegotiate the terms of D's at-will employment. When D agreed to sign, he accepted employment on the new terms. D's acceptance of the agreement was given in exchange for P's forbearance from terminating D's employment. Accordingly, P gave consideration for D's promise not to compete following termination.

♦   Although consideration is adequate in cases like this, the courts may examine the reasonableness of noncompetition agreements, an issue that has been addressed in prior cases. On remand, the trial court must determine whether the agreement is reasonable.

Dissent (Resnick, J.). Continued employment in an at-will situation does not constitute consideration for the noncompetition agreement, because the only difference in the parties' employment relationship after D signed the agreement was the agreement itself. P relinquished nothing—it could still fire D at any time, with or without cause. And D gained nothing.

Dissent (Pfeifer, J.). P's conduct in this case constitutes coercion, not consideration. The only way there could be consideration in this case is if D's signing of the agreement altered the at-will nature of his employment, such as a promise from P of continued employment. The courts will have to determine what amount of time of continued employment is reasonable.

———————

d. **Change in employee handbook.** An employer with a written policy requiring discharge for cause may unilaterally change its policy to one of termination at will, so long as it provides affected employees reasonable notice of the change. In *In re Certified Question (Bankey v. Storer Broadcasting Co.)*, 443 N.W.2d 112 (Mich. 1989), the court noted that written personnel policies are not enforceable because they have been "offered and accepted" as a unilateral contract, but because the employer derives a benefit by establishing such policies. Thus, when the employer changes its discharge-for-cause policy to one of employment-at-will, the employer's benefit is correspondingly extinguished and there is no rationale left for the court to enforce the discharge-for-cause policy.

e. **Employer's change of policy.** In a case involving an employer who changed its termination policy from one requiring cause to permitting an at-will termination, the federal court certified the question to the Michigan Supreme Court. The question certified in *In re Certified Question (Bankey v. Storer Broadcasting Co.)*, *supra*, was whether an employer may unilaterally change its written policy statements by adopting a generally applicable policy and alter the employment relationship with existing employees to one at the will of the employer where the employer did not reserve the right to make a change in the original policy. The court held that the employer could make the unilateral change, so long as it gave the affected employees reasonable notice of the policy change. Written employment policies are enforceable not as unilateral contracts accepted by the employee's performance, but because the employer derives a benefit by establishing the policies. Where the employer's change of policy extinguishes the benefit to the employer, the rationale for judicial enforcement of the policy is also extinguished. The employee may legitimately expect that the employer will apply whatever personnel policies are in force at a given time, not that the policies will never change.

4. **Promise as Consideration.** A contract may be formed by the exchange of promises (*e.g.*, I promise to pay you $500 if you promise to paint my house), or by the exchange of a promise for performance of a specific act (*e.g.*, I promise to pay you $500 if you paint my house). The former type of contract is called bilateral; the latter type is unilateral. For a bilateral contract to be legally enforceable, each party's bargained-for promise must be legally sufficient consideration for its counter-promise. The test is whether the performance promised would be sufficient consideration. In other words, a bargain

must have mutuality of obligation; both parties must be bound or neither will be.

    a.   **Illusory promises—promises reserving to the promisor the power to determine performance.** If the promisor reserves expressly or by implication an alternative by which she can escape performance altogether, she has really not promised anything at all. Thus, the promisor's promise is "illusory," and such a promise is not sufficient consideration for the return promise. There is no mutuality, and thus, no valid contract.

    b.   **Lack of consideration and specificity renders promise illusory--**

Strong v. Sheffield, 39 N.E. 330 (N.Y. 1895).

Facts. Sheffield (D) endorsed a demand note made by her husband and delivered it to Strong (P) as security for an antecedent debt owed by her husband to P. D expected that P would forbear to collect the note; however, there was no agreement as to how long the forbearance should last. When P demanded payment two years later and D failed to pay, P brought suit on the note. From a judgment for P, D appealed. The intermediate appellate court reversed, and P appeals.

Issue. Does an agreement not to collect a debt for as long as the creditor shall elect constitute consideration?

Held. No. Judgment affirmed.

♦   No fixed time or reasonable time of forbearance was specified. It was left to the election of P.

♦   While P did not foreclose for two years, the test is what was the agreement, not what actually was done. There was no consideration given for the note through the agreement. Here, the note was payable on demand, and therefore, the agreement to forbear was illusory.

Comments.

♦   The rule of this case is reversed by U.C.C. section 3-408, which states that no consideration is required to create an enforceable obligation which guarantees an antecedent debt of any kind.

♦   An agreement by a creditor to forbear the collection of a debt presently due is a good consideration for an absolute or conditional promise of a third person to pay the debt or for any obligation he may assume in respect thereto.

---

c.   Promise conditional on promisor's satisfaction--

Mattei v. Hopper, 330 P.2d 625 (Cal. 1958).

Facts. Mattei (P), a real estate developer, unsuccessfully tried to buy property belonging to Hopper (D) until D made an offer which P accepted. The deposit receipt showed that P made a down payment and was given 120 days to consummate the purchase. However, the agreement was expressly subject to P's obtaining leases satisfactory to P. During the 120-day period, D told P she would not sell her land. P obtained the necessary satisfactory leases and tendered the balance of the price, but D failed to tender the deed. P sued, but the trial court found that the agreement was illusory and lacked mutuality because the condition depended on P's satisfaction. P appeals.

Issue. Is a promise that is conditional on the promisor's satisfaction with a related matter enforceable?

Held. Yes. Judgment reversed.

◆   When a contract is made using an exchange of promises as consideration, the promises must be mutual in obligation or the consideration fails and there is no contract. This problem has been referred to as mutuality of obligation, or alternatively as one promise being illusory, but the basic issue is whether the consideration is sufficient.

◆   Satisfaction clauses consist of either (i) satisfaction as to commercial value or usefulness, for which the standard is whether a reasonable person would be satisfied, or (ii) satisfaction based on personal taste or judgment, for which the standard is the promisor's good faith. The promise in this case falls within the second category.

◆   A promise conditional on the promisor's satisfaction is not illusory because it does not permit the promisor to arbitrarily avoid the contract. An expression of dissatisfaction is not conclusive; the promisor must actually be dissatisfied with the performance, and not with the contract itself. P could not have simply changed his mind about the contract and walked away.

----

   d.   Conditioned promises. A conditioned promise is one in which the promise to perform is conditioned on the occurrence of some event or condition. The mere fact that a promise is conditional does not make it insufficient consideration for a return promise. As long as the promisor has undertaken something of legal detriment to him, such as becoming bound if the contingency occurs, the promise is sufficient consideration.

e. **Requirements contracts.** A promise by A to "buy all I require" from B may appear illusory, but it is actually good consideration because it imposes a detriment upon A; *i.e.,* it limits his freedom of action because if he has requirements, he must buy them from B.

f. **Foreseeable quantity sufficiently binding--**

Eastern Air Lines, Inc. v. Gulf Oil Corp., 415 F. Supp. 429 (S.D. Fla. 1975).

Facts. Eastern Air Lines, Inc. (P) and Gulf Oil Corp. (D) had a long-term business relationship whereby D supplied aviation fuel to P at various locations pursuant to a series of requirements contracts. In 1972, the parties agreed to another in the series of contracts. Unlike the previous contracts, however, P agreed to bear the costs of increased crude oil prices in a direct proportional relationship of crude oil cost per barrel to jet fuel cost per gallon. As the indicator of crude oil cost, the parties agreed to use the posted price of West Texas Sour crude, the price of which was controlled by the U.S. Government. As the price was increased, P paid more for the fuel. By 1973, foreign oil was more expensive than controlled domestic oil. The U.S. Government began an unprecedented two-tier price control, whereby all production at May 1972 levels from a given oil well ("old oil") were priced at one lower level, and all production over that level ("new oil"), plus an equivalent amount of old production, was released from price controls. The posted price was the "old oil" price. D wanted P to pay higher prices for its fuel, but P insisted that the contract be adhered to. Because D threatened to shut off its supply to P, P seeks an injunction requiring D to provide fuel as agreed. D claims the contract was not a binding requirements contract.

Issue. May a contract be a valid requirements contract even if it does not specifically approximate the amounts involved, as long as the amounts are reasonably foreseeable?

Held. Yes. Judgment for P.

♦ Early cases held requirements contracts invalid for lack of mutuality or indefiniteness. These objections were resolved in later cases as courts looked to objective evidence of the volume of material required to operate the business that was buying it. U.C.C. section 2-306(1) approves requirements contracts based on good faith and reasonably foreseeable requirements.

♦ The parties in this case have acted pursuant to requirements contracts such as the one here for several years and have acted in good faith. They have discussed estimates and generally worked things out. The contract is a valid and enforceable requirements contract.

♦ Since the contract is valid and enforceable, and D has no defenses against it, P is entitled to a permanent injunction preserving the status quo.

---

g.   **Implied promises.** Even where a bilateral contract apparently contains no promise at all on one side (*i.e.,* there is a complete lack of mutuality), the contract may still be upheld if the surrounding facts and the nature of the agreement fairly imply a promise of performance by that party. For example, in *Sylvan Crest Sand & Gravel Co. v. United States*, 150 F.2d 642 (2d Cir. 1945), the court relied on the reasonable commercial expectations of the parties.

1)   **Uniform Commercial Code.** U.C.C. section 2-306(2) indicates that in an exclusive sales contract the manufacturer impliedly agrees to use his best efforts to supply the goods and the distributor impliedly agrees to use his best efforts to promote their sale.

2)   **Exclusive contract—reasonable efforts implied--**

Wood v. Lucy, Lady Duff-Gordon, 118 N.E. 214 (N.Y. 1917).

Facts. Wood (P) was given an exclusive contract to place Lucy, Lady Duff-Gordon's (D's) indorsement on the designs of other clothiers and to place D's own designs on sale and to license others to sell them. D was to receive one-half of P's profits. The contract indicated that P had an organization capable of performing the contract, but it did not expressly indicate that P would perform. P sues D here for breach of the contract on the basis that D put her indorsement on clothes of a competitor without P's knowledge and with no share of the profits to P. The intermediate appellate court reversed the trial court's denial of D's motion for judgment on the pleadings. From a dismissal of the complaint, P appeals.

Issue. Where P did not specifically promise to use reasonable efforts to promote D's goods, and all compensation to D under the contract is to come from such efforts, is there a valid promise by P?

Held. Yes. Judgment reversed.

♦   A promise that P will use reasonable efforts to promote D's goods is fairly implied.

♦   The circumstances of the contract make such an implication reasonable: It was an exclusive dealing contract D gave to P; any return to D was to come from P's profits. This meant that if D was to get anything at all, P had to perform.

D.   RELIANCE AS A BASIS OF ENFORCEMENT

1.   **Introduction.** In certain situations, detrimental action or forbearance by the promisee (A) in reliance on a promise by the promisor (B) will constitute a substitute for consideration and render the promise by B enforceable.

a. **Requirements.** The original Restatement section 90 indicates that a promisor will be estopped to deny the enforceability of his promise if the following elements appear:

1) Although the promise is gratuitous (without consideration), it is of the type that might foreseeably induce the promisee to rely on it.

2) The promisee did rely on the promise.

3) Reliance was reasonable under the circumstances.

4) As a result of reliance, the promisee suffered a substantial economic detriment.

5) Injustice can only be avoided by enforcing the promise.

b. **Gift vs. bargain promises—the general rule.** The general rule has been that promissory estoppel only applies where the reliance is on the promise of a gift. Thus, in situations where a promise is intended as part of a bargain but it is unenforceable for some reason (*i.e.,* the promise is too indefinite), then detrimental reliance would not apply (*i.e.,* if the parties were bargaining, they should be left to rely on their bargain).

c. **The modern trend.** The Restatement (Second) section 90 has moved to liberalize the doctrine of estoppel, applying it to more situations. It eliminates the requirement of "substantial reliance"; where reliance is less than substantial, partial enforcement of the contract may still be granted. Also, the doctrine is now applied to bargain situations as well as gift situations.

2. **Gratuitous Promissory Note--**

Ricketts v. Scothorn, 77 N.W. 365 (Neb. 1898).

Facts. Scothorn (P) received a note on May 1, 1891, from her grandfather promising to pay $2,000. She then quit her job on the strength of the note. On June 8, 1894, her grandfather died after paying only one year's interest and Ricketts (D), the grandfather's executor, refused to pay the note, claiming that there was no consideration for it. From a judgment for P, D appeals.

Issue. Is a gift promise enforceable if it induces the promisee to take detrimental action in reasonable reliance on the promise?

Held. Yes. Judgment affirmed.

♦ While the note was given as a gratuity, P was influenced by it and thereby changed her position to her detriment. It is therefore inequitable to permit D to resist payment on the basis of no consideration.

3. **Promissory Estoppel as Consideration.** In *Feinberg v. Pfeiffer Co., supra,* the court held that the plaintiff's retirement from her lucrative position in reliance on the defendant's promise to pay her a pension was sufficient to make the defendant's promise enforceable. Compare this with Restatement (Second) section 90:

   a. A promise which the promisor should reasonably expect to induce action or forbearance on the part of the promisee or a third person and which does induce such action or forbearance is binding if injustice can be avoided only by enforcement of the promise. The remedy granted for breach may be limited as justice requires.

   b. A charitable subscription or a marriage settlement is binding under subsection (1) without proof that the promise induced action or forbearance.

4. **Enforcement to Prevent Injustice.** The test under Restatement (Second) section 90(1) is not whether the promise should be enforced to do justice, but whether enforcement is required to prevent an injustice. In *Cohen v. Cowles Media Co.,* 479 N.W.2d 387 (Minn. 1992), Cohen had informed newspaper reporters of an arrest and a conviction of a political candidate. The reporters had promised to keep Cohen's identity confidential, but the editors published his name. Cohen was fired from his job and sued for damages. He won $200,000 in compensatory damages. After the United States Supreme Court held that promissory estoppel in this situation would not violate the First Amendment, the Minnesota Supreme Court upheld the award. The court noted that it would be unjust to allow the newspapers to break their promise, especially where the newspapers themselves believed that they generally must keep promises of confidentiality they give to their sources.

5. **Reliance Interest in Promise--**

D & G Stout, Inc. v. Bacardi Imports, Inc., 923 F.2d 566 (7th Cir. 1991).

Facts. D & G Stout, Inc. (P) was a liquor distributor. When two of its main suppliers chose another distributor, P had to either continue operating on a smaller scale or sell out. D started negotiating a potential sale and received an offer price. Bacardi Imports, Inc. (D), one of P's major remaining suppliers, knew about the negotiations and promised that P would continue to act as D's distributor. Based on this representation, P turned down the offer. A week later, D withdrew its account. When this news spread,

P lost another major account and its employees started taking jobs with other distributors. P could not continue to operate, and settled for a sales price $550,000 lower than the prior offer. P sued D for the price differential on a theory of promissory estoppel. The trial court granted D summary judgment. P appeals.

Issue. May a party who promises to maintain a business relationship become liable for damages when the promisee relies to its detriment on the promise?

Held. Yes. Judgment reversed.

♦   The relationship between P and D had always been terminable at will, and D's promise to continue to use P as its distributor did not specify any time period, so the relationship remained terminable at will.

♦   By way of analogy, a prospective employee cannot sue for lost wages on an unfulfilled promise of at-will employment, on the rationale that the employer could have terminated the employee at any time after the employment began, so the employee could have no reasonable expectation of any determinable period of employment or pay. But even if lost wages cannot be recovered in such a case, damages for expenses incurred in moving for a job can be recovered. In that case, the employer could have expected the prospective employee to move in reliance on the promise of employment.

♦   P could recover if its damages were more like moving expenses than lost future wages. The distinction is between expectation damages and reliance damages. An employee has only an expectation interest in future wages that cannot be recovered through promissory estoppel. Moving expenses, however, are incurred in reliance, not expectation, and are recoverable.

♦   In this case, P's loss of income from future sales of D's products is lost future income expected from an at-will relationship, and is no more recoverable under promissory estoppel than lost future wages would be. But P is not seeking lost profits. Instead, P seeks the lost value of its sale opportunity. P rejected an offer based on D's promise, and the extent of the devaluation of the sale opportunity represents a reliance injury. P could reasonably rely on D's promise under these circumstances.

Comment. On remand, the trial court awarded P damages of nearly $400,000, representing the difference between the original offer and the final sales price.

———————————————

E.   RESTITUTION AS AN ALTERNATIVE BASIS FOR RECOVERY

1.   **Introduction.** When the defendant receives a benefit from the plaintiff under such circumstances that the defendant ought to compensate the plaintiff

for the benefit received, the law implies a promise by the defendant to pay the reasonable value of the benefits conferred. The plaintiff recovers on a theory of "quasi-contract" or restitution.

a. **Definition.** A "quasi-contract" is *not* a true contract, since there is no mutual assent bargained for and received by the parties (no bargain consciously made between A and B). Rather, the law creates or implies a contract. This is normally done where a benefit has been received by the defendant (B) from the plaintiff (A) under such circumstances that in equity the defendant (B) ought to compensate the plaintiff (A) therefor. Thus, the law implies a promise by the defendant (B) to pay the reasonable value of the benefit which has been conferred on him by A. The purpose of the implied promise is to avoid unjust enrichment of the defendant (B) at the plaintiff's (A's) expense.

b. **Elements of a quasi-contract recovery.**

1) A has rendered services or expended property which confers a benefit on B.

2) A rendered such performance with the expectation of being paid.

3) A was not acting as an intermeddler or "volunteer."

4) To allow B to retain the benefits without paying A would result in the unjust enrichment of B at A's expense.

c. **Alternative to contract remedy.** Quasi-contract is often available as an alternative to enforcement of the express contract.

1) For example, where A has built a house for B and B refuses to pay, A may sue for the reasonable value of the benefits conferred on B, *or* A may sue for damages under the contract between A and B.

2) Also, suppose A is in breach of the contract with B, having performed in part and then breached the contract (as in a contract for the delivery of goods, where only part of the goods have been delivered). A cannot sue in contract for damages (he is in breach); but he can sue in quasi-contract for the value of the part performance (of course, B can offset any damages he has suffered from A's breach of the contract).

a) Note that the quasi-contract action is governed by equitable principles. Hence, it may not be allowed where D's breach of a contract after part performance has been willful (intentional).

2. **Measure of Recovery.**

a. **Unjust enrichment.** Normally, the recovery is measured by the reasonable value of the benefit conferred on the defendant.

b. **Detriment to plaintiff.** But modern courts have also recognized that in some instances the proper recovery is the detriment suffered by the plaintiff (and hence the recovery is the reasonable value of the services or property expended by the plaintiff). This may be critical in situations where the defendant has really received no benefit, although the plaintiff has suffered a detriment. Note that normally where the action is brought by a plaintiff who is in default under a contract, or where the suit is barred by the Statute of Frauds and the plaintiff is suing for the benefits conferred under such an unenforceable contract, then the measure of recovery is limited by the contract price, no matter what the detriment has been to the plaintiff.

3. **Emergency Services--**

Cotnam v. Wisdom, 104 S.W. 164 (Ark. 1907).

Facts. Harrison was mortally injured in a streetcar wreck. A third party summoned Wisdom (P), a physician, to attempt to save Harrison's life. P later brought this action against Cotnam (D), Harrison's administrator, to recover the reasonable value of services rendered. The judge instructed the jury that if P rendered the services in an attempt to save decedent's life, then P should recover, and that in awarding compensation, the jury should consider the character and importance of the operation, the responsibility of the surgeon, his experience and training, and the ability of the injured to pay. D appeals from a judgment for P.

Issue. May courts find an implied contract to pay for medical services provided to a person who is incapable of contracting?

Held. Yes. Judgment reversed as to measure of damages.

♦ Here, decedent was unconscious and therefore unable to consent to the rendering of the medical services by P. The theory of recovery by P thus was not based on an implied-in-fact contract, since there could be no conscious assent, but was based on implied-in-law or quasi-contract. Although the medical help did not avert Harrison's death, it was nonetheless competent professional service for which compensation was due.

♦ Services are the same in value be the patient prince or pauper. P is entitled only to fair compensation for services rendered and not allowed unjust enrichment simply because the decedent may have been wealthy or his estate may have been left to collateral heirs.

---

4. Indirect Benefit--

Callano v. Oakwood Park Homes Corp., 219 A.2d 332 (N.J. Super. Ct. 1966).

Facts. Callano (P) planted shrubbery for Pendergast, who was the purchaser of a home under a contract of sale with Oakwood Park Homes Corp. (D). Pendergast died before paying P for the shrubbery. D had no knowledge that P was not paid by Pendergast, though it had knowledge of the planting. After Pendergast's death, his estate canceled the contract of sale with D. D then resold the property, including the shrubbery, to a third party. From a judgment of $475 for P for the reasonable value of the shrubbery on the theory of quasi-contractual liability (*i.e.,* that D was unjustly enriched through the cancellation and resale), D appeals.

Issue. Is D, with no direct contractual relationship to P, obligated to pay for the benefit received on the theory of quasi-contract?

Held. No. Judgment reversed.

♦   To prove liability in quasi-contract, P must show that D was enriched and that the retention of the benefit by D would be unjust under the circumstances. Here, while D clearly received a benefit, the retention of such benefit does not appear unjust. P had no dealings with D and did not expect remuneration from it when the shrubbery was provided; there was no mistake involved. P's remedy is against the estate of Pendergast and not against D.

Comment. P cannot use the fiction of quasi-contract to substitute one promisor or debtor for another.

5.   **Restitutionary Claims Between Spouses.** In *Pyeatte v. Pyeatte,* 661 P.2d 196 (Ariz. 1982), the court held that although restitution is not normally a proper remedy for services provided during a marital relationship, it may be appropriate where one spouse took advantage of another by not performing his part of an agreement between the parties. In that case, the parties had agreed that the wife would put the husband through law school, and that after graduation, the husband would put the wife through graduate school. A year after the husband graduated, and before the wife started graduate school, the husband asked for a divorce. The wife sued for breach. The trial court awarded the wife $23,000 for breach of contract. The court of appeals granted the wife's alternate claim for restitution. The Arizona Supreme Court remanded, holding that restitution may be appropriate where the wife's unilateral effort inured solely to the benefit of the husband by the time of dissolution.

6. **Gratuitous Services Not Consideration.** In *Dementas v. Estate of Tallas*, 764 P.2d 628 (Utah Ct. App. 1988), Dementas had provided personal assistance to Tallas, who left a memo stating that he owed Dementas $50,000 for his help. Tallas had notarized the document but died without changing his will. Dementas claimed $50,000 from the estate of Tallas, but the trial court held that the memo was merely an expression of appreciation and was not enforceable. On appeal, the court of appeals affirmed, holding that Tallas's promise to pay was for services already performed by Dementas, which cannot constitute legal consideration. Noting that some courts may recognize past consideration as sufficient under a "moral obligation" theory, in this case, Dementas's services were gratuitous. Dementas had not provided the service with the expectation of being compensated, so there was no moral obligation on Tallas's part.

II. CREATING CONTRACTUAL OBLIGATIONS

A. THE NATURE OF ASSENT

1. **Introduction.** The most characteristic type of contract is the bargain, which is typically formed by the mutual assent of the parties, through an offer by one and acceptance by the other. This section deals first with some basic concepts of mutual assent, and then treats problems with offers and acceptance.

2. **Objective Theory of Contracts.** In determining whether there is mutual assent, the usual test to be applied is the objective theory of contracts; *i.e.,* what a reasonable person in the position of each of the respective parties would be led to believe by the words or conduct of the other party. This means that words or conduct are interpreted not according to what the speaker or actor subjectively meant to convey, nor what the person to whom the words or conduct were addressed subjectively understood them to mean (the subjective theory of contracts), but rather what a reasonable person, standing in the place of the respective parties, would understand them to mean.

   a. **Rationale.** Courts today have rejected the requirement that there be any actual, subjective meeting of the minds. Demands for security and certainty in business transactions, and the fundamental objective of protecting a party's reasonable expectations in relying on a promise, make it imperative that each contracting party be able to rely on the other party's apparent intentions without regard to his secret thoughts or mental reservations.

   b. **Contract made in subjective jest--**

Lucy v. Zehmer, 84 S.E.2d 516 (Va. 1954).

Facts. Lucy (P) sued Zehmer (D) to obtain specific performance of an alleged land sales contract. The contract was written, specified a price of $50,000, and was signed by D and his wife. D had declined several previous offers to sell the land, but one night, at D's restaurant, P offered $50,000. There was a dispute over what was actually said and done, but the signed document resulted. D claimed it was only signed in jest and that he had been drinking. The trial court dismissed P's action. P appeals.

Issue. Is a contract enforceable if one of the parties mentally agreed to it only in jest?

Held. Yes. Judgment reversed.

- The extent of the negotiations and the rewriting of the initial contract indicate that the contract was a serious business transaction. P was justified in actually believing that the contract represented a good faith sale and purchase of the farm.

- The mental assent of the parties is not required for the formation of a contract; a person's undisclosed intention is immaterial if his words and acts have but one reasonable meaning. Whether both P and D were serious or only P was serious and D acted in secret jest, the contract is binding and specific performance is available.

Comment. The court's holding is likely influenced by the equal bargaining position of the parties, the absence of fraud or misrepresentation, and the admitted fairness of the price. D also stated that the contract was made to force P to admit that he did not have the $50,000.

---

   c. **Measure of damages.** In *Sullivan v. O'Connor, supra*, the court pointed out that expectancy damages are primarily appropriate for breach of contracts in the business context. For example, if the court had awarded damages to Sullivan based on expectancy, it would have had to inquire into her subjective expectation of what her improved nose would have meant to her.

B. THE OFFER

1. **What Constitutes an Offer.**

   a. **Definition.** An offer is a proposal by one party to the other manifesting a willingness to enter into a bargain and made in such a way (by words or conduct) that the other person is justified in believing that her assent (*i.e.,* acceptance) to that bargain is invited and, if given, will create a binding contract between the parties. The person making the offer is often called the "offeror," and the party to whom the offer is made is often called the "offeree." An offer creates the power in the offeree to make a contract between the parties by an appropriate acceptance. [Restatement (Second) §24]

   b. **Requirements for a valid offer.**

      1) Manifestation of present contractual intent.

      2) Certainty and definiteness of terms.

      3) Communication to the offeree. The offer must be communicated to the offeree; in no other way will it create a power of acceptance

in him. [Restatement (Second) §24] Thus, there is no valid offer where A prepares an offer to B, intending to mail it, but never does.

c. **Requirement of manifestation of present contractual intent.** The words or conduct used in the proposal must be words of offer rather than mere words of preliminary negotiation.

1) **The test.** The test is based on the objective theory of contracts. Would a reasonable person in the shoes of the offeree feel that if he accepted the proposal, a contract would be complete? Factors considered:

a) **The words used.** Some words strongly suggest that an offer has been made, while others suggest a mere invitation to make an offer. "I bid" suggests an offer. "Are you interested?" suggests preliminary negotiation.

b) **Surrounding circumstances.** The surrounding circumstances may alter the normal meaning of words. For example, words may sound like an offer but be made as a jest.

c) **To whom made.** A proposal made to the public or a large group of persons (such as in advertisements) is more likely to be construed as a mere invitation to make an offer.

d) **Definiteness and certainty of terms.** The more definite, the more likely an offer. This is a separate requirement for finding a valid offer.

e) **Written contract contemplated.** Some courts hold that where a proposal contemplates a subsequent written memorandum of the agreement, there is a presumption that there is no contract until the written instrument is signed. Other courts, however, resolve this issue based on the intent of the parties, which is determined from all of the surrounding circumstances.

2. **Price Quotations.** A simple quotation of a price is usually construed merely as an invitation to the buyer to make an offer.

a. **Stating minimum price--**

Owen v. Tunison, 158 A. 926 (Me. 1932).

Facts. Owen (P) sued Tunison (D) for breach of contract, claiming that D agreed in writing to sell property to P but later refused, causing P to suffer damages. P offered to purchase D's property for $6,000. D responded to P by letter saying that he could not sell the property unless he received $16,000. P then replied that he accepted D's offer, whereupon D decided not to sell.

Issue. Does a statement specifying a minimum price for the sale of property constitute an offer to sell?

Held. No. Judgment reversed.

♦ D's letter at most may have indicated an intent to open negotiations, but it was not a proposal to sell.

Comment. In *Harvey v. Facey*, 1893 A.C. 552 (Privy Council, Jamaica), the court held that a communication regarding only a price term is inadequate to constitute an offer. Facey was negotiating to sell certain property to the town of Kingston for £900. Harvey, a solicitor in Kingston, sent Facey a telegraph, asking if Facey would sell to Harvey and what his lowest price was. Facey answered that the lowest price was £900. Harvey answered that he agreed to buy the property for £900. Harvey then sued for specific performance. The trial court held that there was no contract. The appellate court reversed. Facey appealed to the Privy Council, which held that there was no contract because Facey had provided only a price term. Facey never stated whether he would sell to Harvey, and Harvey's last telegram was actually an offer that Facey never accepted.

---

b. "For immediate acceptance"--

Fairmount Glass Works v. Crunden-Martin Woodenware Co., 51 S.W. 196 (Ky. Ct. App. 1899).

Facts. Crunden-Martin (P) asked for the lowest price at which Fairmount Glass Works (D) would sell to P 10 carloads of mason jars. D replied with a quote and terms for immediate acceptance and shipment. P replied by telegraph with an order and included an additional clause requiring the "jars and caps to be strictly top quality goods." The same day, D telegraphed that its output was sold out and that it could not fill the order. P then brought an action for breach of contract. From a judgment for P, D appeals.

Issue. Does a quotation of prices for immediate acceptance constitute an offer to sell?

Held. Yes. Judgment affirmed.

♦ D's quotation of prices "for immediate acceptance" was more than a quotation and constituted an offer. Here, the correspondence taken as a whole indicated that the seller intended to create in the buyer the power to accept or reject the seller's proposal.

---

3. **Advertisements.** Advertisements are generally deemed invitations to deal, rather than offers.

    a. **Rationale.** There are three basic reasons for this rule:

        1) Advertisements are usually indefinite as to quantity and other terms;

        2) Sellers ought to be able to choose with whom they deal; and

        3) Advertisements are typically addressed to the general public, so that if they were considered to be offers, a seller might find her offer overaccepted; *i.e.,* the number of people who "accept" might exceed the number of items that the advertiser has available for sale.

    b. **Exception to the general rule--**

Lefkowitz v. Great Minneapolis Surplus Store, 86 N.W.2d 689 (Minn. 1957).

Facts. Great Minneapolis Surplus Store (D) advertised in a paper that it would sell a fur stole for $1 on Saturday, "first come first served." Lefkowitz (P) was the first to present himself and demanded the stole for $1, but D refused, saying that a "house rule" limited the offer to women only. From a judgment for P, D appeals.

Issue. Can an advertisement to the general public be a binding obligation requiring the seller to sell the advertised merchandise?

Held. Yes. Judgment affirmed.

♦   Advertisements addressed to the public are considered binding if the facts show that some performance is definitely promised for something requested. Here, the advertisement offered specific merchandise at a stated price to the first person to present himself. There was no room for negotiation as the offer was clear, explicit, and definite. Further, once the offer was published, D had no right to impose new or arbitrary conditions such as the alleged "house rule."

---

    c. **Bait-and-switch advertisements.** Unscrupulous sellers sometimes employ the bait-and-switch technique to attract customers by advertising a product at an exceptionally low price (the bait), which the seller has no intention of selling, in order to sell the customer another product (the switch) that will bring the seller a higher profit. The Uniform Deceptive Practices Act makes it a deceptive practice to advertise goods or services with the intent not to sell them as advertised or with the intent not to supply reasonably expected public demand unless the advertisement discloses a limitation of quantity. In addition, unfair or deceptive practices are unlawful under the Federal Trade Commission Act.

d. Mistaken bidder--

Elsinore Union Elementary School District v. Kastorff, 353 P.2d 713 (Cal. 1960).

Facts. Kastorff (D), a contractor, submitted a bid for construction work on a school. Elsinore School District (P) opened the bid and, finding that it was substantially less than the others, asked D if his figures were correct. D said "Yes," although D did not have his worksheets to refer to. After a vote by P to accept D's bid, D discovered that he had not included $6,500 for plumbing work; D promptly notified P and asked to withdraw his bid. P refused and asked D to sign the written contract. D refused. P sues; judgment for P, and D appeals.

Issue. Where P had an irrevocable option to accept D's bid but learned of D's mistake of computation before accepting, is D entitled to rescission?

Held. Yes. Judgment reversed.

♦ P knew or had reason to know before it accepted D's bid that there had been a unilateral mistake by D. D was not guilty of negligence in preparing the bid; D informed P promptly. Furthermore, it would be unconscionable to enforce the contract in these circumstances. The error was material since $6,500 is a substantial portion of D's total bid of $89,990.

Comment. The nature of construction contract bidding leads to many potential types of mistakes. A general contractor may make a mistake as in this case; any of the several subcontractors can make similar mistakes. Frequently, bids are prepared under time pressures that make verification and qualification of subcontractor bids difficult.

C. THE ACCEPTANCE

In order for a contract to exist, there must be an acceptance of the offer. The acceptance (assent to the offer) must be in the same manner requested or authorized by the offeror.

1. Requirements for a Valid Acceptance.

a. **Who may accept.** The general rule (there are exceptions) is that the offer may be accepted only by the person to whom it is made.

b. **Acceptance must be unequivocal.** The acceptance must be unequivocal and unqualified. If it is qualified, then it is not an acceptance but a counteroffer, which works as a rejection of the offer.

c. **Unilateral vs. bilateral contracts.** The rules for acceptance differ depending on whether the offer is for a unilateral or bilateral contract.

    1) **Bilateral contracts.** Here, the mere giving of the counter-promise to the offeror is all that is required. The objective theory of contract prevails, and whether or not an acceptance has been given depends on how a reasonable person would interpret the words or conduct of the offeree. But the offeree must have knowledge of the offer, and notice of acceptance to the offeror is generally required (there are exceptions, such as where the offeror indicates that no notice is required).

    2) **Unilateral contracts.** A unilateral contract may be accepted only by doing the act requested by the offeror, with knowledge of the offer and with the intent to accept it. Normally, notice to the offeror of acceptance is not required. (There are exceptions, such as where the offeror requires that notice be given or where the offeror has no reasonable means of knowing that the requested performance has been rendered; in such a case there is a requirement that notice that the requested performance has been rendered be given within a reasonable time after performance.)

2. **Methods of Acceptance.**

a. **Unilateral vs. bilateral contracts.** While the legal distinction between the two types of contracts is easy to state, making the distinction in true factual situations is difficult. Whether a contract is found to be unilateral or bilateral makes a big difference in the mode of acceptance which is permissible. The distinction is also important in regard to revocation (*i.e.,* if all the offeror wants is a return promise, then if such a promise is given, revocation becomes impossible; but if the offeror requests an act as acceptance, then the act itself must be performed or the offeror can still revoke the offer). Note that the Restatement (Second) does not distinguish between the two.

    1) **Policy.** Where the offer is unclear as to whether a bilateral or unilateral contract is contemplated, it is the policy of the law to construe it as an offer for a bilateral contract rather than unilateral. [Restatement (First) §31]

    2) **Rationale.** A bilateral contract affords immediate rights and complete protection to both parties, since a contract arises as soon as the offeree promises to perform, whereas an offer for a unilateral

contract does not ripen into a binding contract until the performance is actually rendered.

3) **U.C.C. position.** The U.C.C. accepts this same policy. The U.C.C. states that unless an offer to buy goods expressly limits acceptance to shipment of the goods, it is to be construed as inviting acceptance either by shipment or by a prompt promise to ship the goods. [U.C.C. §2-206]

b. **No notice requested--**

International Filter Co. v. Conroe Gin, Ice & Light Co., 277 S.W. 631 (Tex. 1925).

Facts. International Filter Co.'s (P's) salesman submitted a letter to Conroe Gin, Ice & Light Co. (D), offering to sell water purification machinery. The letter provided that a contract would arise when the proposal was (i) accepted by D and (ii) approved by an executive officer of P. D's manager signed the letter "Accepted, Feb. 10, 1920 . . ." and specified delivery for March 10. The letter was then sent to P's home office where its president indorsed "O.K. Feb. 13, 1920, P.N. Engel." On February 14, 1920, P sent an acknowledgment of the order to D. On February 28, D tried to cancel the order but P insisted on performance. When D refused, P brought suit. D claimed that the "O.K." indorsement was insufficient as an acceptance, that notification to D from P of approval or acceptance was required, and that the letter of February 14 was insufficient acceptance or notification. From a judgment for D, P appeals.

Issue. Must notice of an acceptance be given if the offeror does not require it?

Held. No. Judgment reversed and case remanded.

♦   A contract was formed when Engel indorsed the paper sent to him with D's signature on it. An offeror may include any terms or conditions in the offer which he desires. Here D, although using a form prepared by P's salesman, was the offeror and made no stipulation as to notice of acceptance and therefore none was required. On the contrary, the agreement specifically provided that it would become a binding contract when approved by an executive officer of P.

♦   Even though no notice was required, the letter of February 14 to D acknowledging the order fairly communicated P's acceptance. Generally, the form and manner of notice of acceptance need only be such as to convey by word or fair implication the fact of acceptance itself.

Comment. Restatement (Second) sections 54 and 56 requires that in a bilateral contract where the offeror requests a promise, that promise must be actually communicated or attempted to be communicated (*e.g.,* by mailing an acceptance) to the offeror.

---

c. Communication of acceptance to offeror.

1) Implied acceptance--

White v. Corlies & Tift, 46 N.Y. 467 (1871).

Facts. White (P) gave an estimate of costs to fix up a suite of Corlies & Tift's (D's) offices; the next day D's bookkeeper sent a note to P indicating that he could begin immediately if he would agree to finish within two weeks and that the bookkeeper would "call again between 5 and 6 p.m." P never answered but immediately purchased lumber and began work. The next day, D canceled the order. P sued for breach. The court charged the jury that there was a contract. D appeals.

Issue. Where the offer requests a promise, will P's beginning of performance be sufficient to create a binding contract?

Held. No. Judgment reversed; new trial ordered.

- ♦ D's note was an offer to P and requested his return promise, which had to be manifested by some objective words or conduct of acceptance. Purchasing the lumber was insufficient since it could have been purchased to perform on any job. Thus, there was no indication of P's return promise before D's revocation.

Comment. The court held that this was an offer of a bilateral contract. The Restatement (Second) provides that in this situation the offeree's return promise must be expressly or impliedly given. [*See* Restatement (Second) §§30, 50, 60, 62] An implication of a promise can be given by commencement of performance, but here D had no awareness of such commencement when it canceled the order.

---

2) Intention to accept. Under the objective theory of contracts, subjective intent of the offeree is immaterial. If a reasonable offeror would be justified in relying upon the apparent intent of the offeree as manifested by his conduct, then "acceptance" will be deemed to have occurred, irrespective of the actual intent of the offeree. Further, if the offeree intends to accept the offer but fails to communicate such intent in a manner which a reasonable offeror would understand as an acceptance, no contract is formed.

3) Time for acceptance. In *Ever-Tite Roofing Corp. v. Green*, 83 So. 2d 449 (La. App. 1955), the court held that the offeror must allow a reasonable time for the offeree to accept by commencing performance. There, the plaintiff attempted to begin work on the defendant's roof nine days after the parties agreed that the plaintiff's performance would make the contract binding.

d. Suggested method of acceptance--

Allied Steel & Conveyors, Inc. v. Ford Motor Co., 277 F.2d 907 (6th Cir. 1960).

Facts. Allied Steel & Conveyors, Inc. (D) received a purchase order form from Ford Motor Co. (P), which stated that the contract would not be binding until accepted and stated that acceptance should be executed on the "acknowledgment" copy which should be returned to P. The purchase order contained a provision requiring D to indemnify P against the negligence of D's and P's employees in connection with the work D was to perform in P's facility. During the course of performing the work called for by the purchase order, an employee of D was injured through the negligence of an employee of P. The injured employee sued P, which impleaded D. From judgments for the employee against P and P against D, D appeals, claiming that it did not formally execute the contract in the manner specified in the purchase order and that therefore no contract existed and P has no right to indemnity against D.

Issue. When an offeree fails to comply with the suggested method of acceptance, but instead begins performance, is a contract formed?

Held. Yes. Judgment affirmed.

♦ The suggested method of acceptance was not the only method since the words of the purchase order said "should." Here, D manifested its intent to accept by beginning performance with the knowledge of P and in accordance with the material terms of the offer. Thus, a contract was formed.

Comment. In *White, supra*, the offeree failed to communicate its acceptance through commencement of performance to the offeror, whereas in *Allied*, performance was commenced with the full knowledge, consent, and acquiescence of the offeror.

---

e. Accommodation as a counteroffer--

Corinthian Pharmaceutical Systems, Inc. v. Lederle Laboratories, 724 F. Supp. 605 (S.D. Ind. 1989).

Facts. Corinthian Pharmaceutical Systems, Inc. (P) distributed pharmaceutical products to physicians. P regularly purchased DTP vaccine from the manufacturer, Lederle Laboratories (D). D's price list included a statement that prices were subject to change and that any changes would take immediate effect on unfilled orders. In response to product liability lawsuits, D decided to self-insure and increased the price of DTP vaccine from $64.32 to $171 per vial. The price increase was effective as of May 20, but P learned about the increase on May 19 by obtaining a copy of D's internal price memorandum and immediately ordered 1,000 vials of DTP vaccine through D's computer system. P received a tracking number for its order from D's computer, then sent a written confirmation of the order to D. On June 3, D sent P an invoice for 50 vials priced at $64.32 per vial. D then sent P the vials, accompanied by a letter stating that the shipment normally would be priced at the new price of $171, but that D had made an exception for this partial shipment. Subsequent shipments would be priced at $171. P brought an action seeking specific performance for the 950 vials that D did not ship. D moves for summary judgment.

Issue. Does a seller's shipment of nonconforming goods constitute an acceptance of the buyer's offer to purchase?

Held. No. Summary judgment granted for D.

♦ The first step in the analysis is determining when the first offer was made. D's price lists and its internal price memorandum were merely quotations, which are invitations to make an offer. Therefore, P's May 19th order for 1,000 vials at $64.32 was the first offer between the parties.

♦ P claims that D accepted P's offer prior to sending the 50 vials. However, D did nothing prior to shipping the 50 vials that can be considered an acceptance. It issued a tracking number for P's order, but this is an automated, ministerial act, not an acceptance.

♦ Under U.C.C. section 2-206(b), the shipment of nonconforming goods does not constitute an acceptance if the seller seasonably notifies the buyer that the shipment is offered only as an accommodation to the buyer. Here, P offered to buy 1,000 vials at $64.32. D shipped only 50 vials at $64.32 and informed P that the balance of its order would be priced at $171 per vial. D's shipment did not conform to P's offer, so it could not be considered an acceptance. It was merely an accommodation. D had no duty to make the partial shipment, but did so merely to help P. The accompanying letter spelled out the terms of the accommodation and gave P the opportunity to cancel the balance of the shipment if P did not accept the higher price.

♦ D satisfied the requirements of U.C.C. section 2-206(1)(b). D's shipment of nonconforming goods should be treated as a counteroffer, which P could choose to accept or reject.

---

f. **Silence as acceptance.** The basic rule is that an offeror cannot force the offeree to reply by wording his offer: "Your silence will be an acceptance of my offer." [Restatement (Second) §69] A person has no duty to pay for or return unsolicited merchandise in most situations. A course of dealing may modify this rule, however. In *Hobbs v. Massasoit Whip Co.,* 33 N.E. 495 (Mass. 1893), Hobbs sent eelskins to the Massasoit Whip Co. Massasoit had not ordered the skins, but it paid for them. The parties followed this practice four or five times. The last time, Massasoit retained the skins without communicating with Hobbs and eventually destroyed them. Hobbs sued. The court held that although Massasoit did not order the skins, its past dealings created a duty for Massasoit to act when it received them. By remaining silent and retaining the skins, Massasoit justified Hobbs in assuming that Massasoit had accepted the skins.

D. TERMINATION OF THE POWER OF ACCEPTANCE

An offer may no longer be effectively accepted if the offeree's power of acceptance has been terminated by an act of the parties or by operation of law.

1. **Revocation of the Offer by the Offeror.** Where the offeror communicates a revocation before an acceptance by the offeree, the offer is terminated.

    a. **Requirements of effective revocation.** Assuming the offer can be revoked, the following are required to make an effective revocation:

        1) **Words or conduct.** The offeror's words or conduct must be sufficient for a reasonable person to interpret as a revocation.

        2) **Communicated to the offeree.** The revocation must be communicated to the offeree (at least the offeror must make reasonable efforts to communicate the revocation).

        3) **Effective when received.** The revocation is generally held to be effective when received. [Restatement (Second) §42] A minority (California, Montana, North Dakota, and South Dakota) holds that it is effective when dispatched.

    b. **Offer to the public.** Where an offer has been made to the public, then it may be revoked by publicity equivalent to that given the offer.

    c. **Option contracts.** An offer is revocable even if the offeror expressly promises not to revoke or gives a definite period when the offer is to remain open. There are a number of exceptions to this rule, however.

        1) **Firm offers under the U.C.C.** A signed, written offer to buy or sell goods, which states that it will be kept open for a definite time (or if no time is stated, for a reasonable period of time), may not be revoked for this period (as long as the period is no longer than three months). [U.C.C. §2-205]

2) **Offers for consideration.** If the offeree has given any consideration (even nominal consideration) for the offer, it then becomes an option and is not revocable for the period stated therein. [Restatement (Second) §25]

3) **Recitals of consideration.** Where there is a recital that consideration has been received for the option, the general rule has been that this recital is not conclusive (the courts reserve the right to see if the consideration was actually paid). But the Restatement (Second) section 87 provides that an offer is binding as an option if it is in writing, signed by the offeror, and recites a purported consideration.

2. **Termination by Operation of Law.**

   a. **By the lapse of time.** The offer lapses by operation of law after expiration (and before acceptance) of whatever period of time was specified in the offer.

      1) **Computation of time.** The period begins to run from the date of actual receipt by the offeree.

      2) **Where no time period specified.** Where no specific time period is specified, then the offer lapses after a reasonable period of time.

         a) Consideration is given regarding the subject matter involved and all other relevant circumstances in determining what is a reasonable time.

      3) **Offers revocable where specified to remain open.** Note that just because the offer says it will remain open until some date does not mean that the offeror cannot validly revoke the offer before acceptance.

   b. **By death or destruction of the subject matter of the offer.**

   c. **By death or insanity of the offeror or the offeree.** [Restatement (Second) §§37, 48]

   d. **By the intervening illegality of the proposed contract.** A offers to loan B $1,000 at 10%; a state law is passed that 8% interest is the maximum rate that can be charged.

3. **Revocation of Offer Prior to Specified Term--**

Dickinson v. Dodds, 2 Ch. Div. 463 (Cal. 1876).

Facts. Dodds (D) offered to sell property to Dickinson (P), indicating that the offer was to remain open until 9:00 a.m. on June 12. On June 11, P made up his mind to buy the property. In the afternoon, however, P was informed by a third party that D had offered or agreed to sell the property to another person. In the evening, P delivered his acceptance to D's mother-in-law and D finally received it at 7:00 a.m. on June 12. D refused the acceptance because he had already sold the property on June 11. P sued for specific performance or damages. The trial court found for P. D appeals.

Issue. If an offeror says he will hold his offer to sell open for a given time period, may he sell the property to a third party prior to the expiration of the specified time period?

Held. Yes. Judgment reversed.

♦ Although D originally agreed to keep his offer open until June 12, D could revoke the offer at any time prior to acceptance by P.

♦ Before accepting D's offer, P learned that D was going to sell to another person. This is a sufficient communication of D's retraction of the offer.

Comment. The court held that D was not bound by the option because there was no consideration for it. The common law requirement for consideration has been modified by U.C.C. section 2-205, which allows a merchant offeror to make an irrevocable offer by using a signed writing.

---

4.   **Revocation Prior to Acceptance by Performance--**

Ragosta v. Wilder, 592 A.2d 367 (Vt. 1991).

Facts. The Ragostas (Ps) discussed purchasing "The Fork Shop" from Wilder (D), but the parties never reached an agreement. When Ps later heard that D was considering the sale of the shop, Ps sent D $2,000 with a letter offering to buy the shop. D returned the check with a letter declining to accept the proposal, but also offered to sell the Fork Shop for $88,000 at "anytime up until the 1st of November" if Ps would come to D's bank with the cash. Ps obtained financing and made arrangements to travel to D's bank to close the deal, but two days before the scheduled date, D called Ps and stated that he was no longer willing to sell the shop. Ps appeared anyway with the money as scheduled. When D did not appear, Ps sued for specific performance. The trial court held that D could not revoke his offer because Ps, relying on the offer, had already begun performance and D was estopped from revoking the offer on a theory of equitable estoppel. D was ordered to convey the shop as agreed. D appeals.

Issue. May an offeror revoke an offer at any time before the other party accepts by performing, so long as there is no consideration for the promise to keep the offer open?

Held. Yes. Judgment reversed.

♦ D's offer could only be accepted by performance prior to the deadline, and D's promise to keep the offer open was not supported by consideration so it was not enforceable. Therefore, D could revoke the offer to sell the property at any time before Ps accepted it.

♦ Ps claim that their effort to obtain financing was detrimental to them and could constitute consideration for the promise to keep D's offer to sell open. While a detriment may be consideration in some circumstances, it can only be consideration if it is bargained for. Here, Ps' financing efforts were not in exchange for D's promise to keep the offer to sell open.

♦ Under the Restatement (Second) of Contracts, section 45, an offer that invites an offeree to accept by rendering a performance creates an option contract when the offeree tenders or begins the invited performance or tenders a beginning of it. Ps' financing efforts were not performance of the contract, however; these efforts were merely preparation for performance. Ps never tendered, nor began to tender, the money to D, so they never accepted the contract.

♦ The court applied equitable estoppel, which requires that the party being estopped know facts that the other party does not know. D did not know any facts that Ps did not know in this case. Ps started getting financing even before D made the offer, and they understood that they were assuming a risk that they would not be able to buy the property even if they did get financing.

——————————————————

5. **Rejection by the Offeree.** An offer may also be terminated by act of the parties by a rejection by the offeree. A rejection by the offeree terminates the offeree's power to accept. If the offeree later attempts to accept the offer notwithstanding the prior rejection, her "acceptance" is a mere counteroffer.

   a. **How effected.** A rejection may occur by either words or conduct, or by a qualified acceptance (which amounts to a counteroffer and therefore a rejection of the offer).

   b. **Equivocation.** As stated above, an acceptance by the offeree must be unequivocal and unqualified. If a purported acceptance is qualified, it is legally insufficient as an acceptance. Instead, a qualified acceptance will act as a counteroffer and will operate as an implied rejection of the original offer. However, the line between a "qualified" and an "unqualified" acceptance is not always clear.

      1) **Conditional acceptance.** An acceptance which includes any term or condition which was not part of the original offer is ordinarily

considered a "qualified" acceptance and thus an implicit rejection of the offer. However, if the condition was implicit in the offer or if the offeree had a legal right to insist upon the condition under the terms of the offer, the acceptance will be considered an "unqualified" acceptance. For example, X accepts Y's offer to sell land but includes a condition that Y give X good title.

2) **"Grumbling" acceptances.** Acceptances which express dissatisfaction but place no condition on the acceptance generally are considered "unqualified." For example, "Ship the goods on the 10th, although I wish you could deliver sooner." When a change or modification suggested in the offeree's reply is a demand for more favorable terms, then it goes beyond the mere "grumbling" acceptance and operates as an implied rejection of the offer.

3) **Inquiries and requests.** Acceptances which include inquiries or requests by the offeree for a better deal generally do not impair the original offer.

4) **U.C.C. section 2-207.** In a contract for the sale of goods, the inclusion of different terms by the offeree in the acceptance will not operate as a rejection of the offer unless the offer expressly limits acceptance to its terms. The additional terms included in the acceptance are treated as proposals for modifications to the contract. However, if the transaction is between "merchants," the additional terms included in the acceptance become part of the contract unless they *materially* alter the contract or are promptly objected to by the offeror.

c. **When effective.** Normally, a rejection is effective only when received by the offeror.

6. **The "Mailbox Rule."**

a. **Introduction.** When parties are not negotiating orally, it becomes important to determine when a communication (*e.g.*, offer, acceptance, revocation, rejection) takes effect. The general rule is that an acceptance is effective on dispatch, but all other communications are effective on receipt. The reason is that at the moment of dispatch the offeree has done all that he reasonably can to manifest assent; this is the safest and fairest point at which to hold that a contract is binding.

b. **Acceptance.** To be effective, the dispatch must be timely and made in a proper manner. Unless otherwise specified, an offer is deemed to invite acceptance in a reasonable time and by any medium reasonable in the circumstances.

c. **Revocation.** Under the common law rule, a revocation by the offeror is effective only upon receipt, although a few state statutes have changed this rule.

d. **Rejection.** A rejection of the offer by the offeree is effective only upon receipt. If an offeree sends a rejection and then an acceptance, there is no contract even though the rejection arrives after the acceptance was dispatched.

e. **Withdrawing acceptance.** The general rule is that the power to withdraw a letter of acceptance from the mail does not affect the formation of a contract when the letter is deposited in the mail, properly addressed with postage prepaid.

E. THE BATTLE OF THE FORMS AND THE UNIFORM COMMERCIAL CODE

1. **Battle of the Forms.** Modern business transactions are often conducted primarily through forms. Typically, the buyer sends a purchase order to the seller. The purchase order form contains the basic terms of the sale, such as price, quantity, and a description of the goods, but it also contains printed terms drafted by the buyer's attorney in favor of the buyer. After receiving the order, the seller sends a written acceptance or confirmation to the buyer. The acceptance contains the basic terms of the sale but also a series of printed terms drafted by the seller's attorney in favor of the seller. These terms may conflict with the terms printed on the purchase order.

a. **Common law.** Standard contract law principles require that the offeree's acceptance be in the precise terms of the offer (the mirror image rule) and that any variance therefrom, material or not, constitutes a rejection of the original offer. It becomes a counteroffer.

b. **U.C.C.** On the premise that both parties recognize a contract despite their clashing forms, the U.C.C. establishes a general rule that a contract can be formed under such circumstances, unless the responding offeree (the seller) specifically states that there shall be no contract unless his set of terms is accepted by the original offeror, in which case the offeree's response is treated merely as a counteroffer. [U.C.C. §2-207] In the absence of such a specific limitation, the existence of a contract and its terms is determined by U.C.C. rules.

1) **Proposed additional terms.** If the offeree's response contains terms additional to those contained in the original offer, a contract exists consisting of the terms on which the offer and acceptance agree. The additional terms are deemed a proposal for additions to the contract. Where the parties are merchants, the proposals become part of the contract unless:

a) The offeror's original offer expressly limited acceptance to the offered terms (take it or leave it); or

b) The additional terms are a material alteration of the contract.

2) **Proposed inconsistent terms.** If the offeree's response contains terms which are actually inconsistent with those contained in the original offer, the courts look at the parties' conduct to determine whether they acted as though a contract had been formed. If so, the contract consists of those terms on which the writings agree; the conflicting terms cancel each other out and necessary terms are provided by the U.C.C. or by custom.

2. **Requirement to Expressly Communicate Conditional Acceptance--**

Dorton v. Collins & Aikman Corp., 453 F.2d 1161 (6th Cir. 1972).

Facts. Dorton (P), a partner in The Carpet Mart, bought carpet from Collins & Aikman Corp. (D) in a series of transactions. P or one of D's salesmen would telephone D's order department and order carpet listed in D's catalogue. D would then type the information on its preprinted acknowledgment forms which contained a provision that all claims arising out of the contract would be submitted to arbitration. P never objected to the forms. P subsequently learned that some of the carpets were made of a cheaper and inferior fiber than that contracted for. P sued for damages due to D's fraud, deceit, and misrepresentation. D moved for a stay pending arbitration. Finding that the arbitration agreement was not binding, the court denied the stay. D appeals.

Issue. Does a form that states that acceptance is subject to all the terms printed on the form satisfy the "expressly made conditional" requirement of U.C.C. section 2-207(1)?

Held. No. Judgment reversed and case remanded for decision under section 2-207(2).

♦ The district court relied on section 2-207(3) to find that the arbitration clause was ineffective. Since the parties' conduct showed that a contract existed, but the writings of the parties did not agree, the court determined that the U.C.C. would supply any needed additional terms. But the U.C.C. does not impose an arbitration clause.

♦ The court first should have determined whether the forms were acceptances or confirmations under section 2-207. The evidence on this issue is conflicting, and the question must be resolved on remand.

♦ If the forms are acceptances under section 2-207(1), the question becomes whether the arbitration provision was additional to or different from P's oral offers, and, if so, whether D's acceptances were expressly made conditional on assent to the additional terms under section 2-207(1).

- The form did include a statement that the acceptances were subject to all the terms, including arbitration. This alone was insufficient to make the acceptance expressly conditional on P's assent to the terms. To reach that level, it must have been clear that D was unwilling to proceed with the transaction unless it was assured that P assented to the additional or different terms. Yet the acceptances by their own terms provided that P could be bound by simply retaining the form for 10 days without objection.

- Since P's assent to D's terms was not necessary, the additional terms must be treated as proposals under section 2-207(2). The court must determine whether the arbitration provision materially altered the oral offer.

- If the court finds that the acknowledgment forms were confirmations of the prior oral agreements, the court would have to determine whether the arbitration clause was additional to or different from the oral agreement, and if so, it should treat the clause as a proposal under section 2-207(2).

- If the court finds that the arbitration clause is a term of the contracts, D's motion for a stay pending arbitration should be granted.

---

3. **Contract Based on Performance--**

C. Itoh & Co. (America) Inc. v. Jordan International Co., 552 F.2d 1228 (7th Cir. 1977).

Facts. C. Itoh & Co. (America) Inc. (P) ordered steel coils from Jordan International Co. (D). D's acknowledgment included a provision that its acceptance was expressly conditional on P's assent to the additional terms printed on the reverse side. These provisions included a requirement for mandatory arbitration. P received, accepted, and paid for the steel, then discovered it was defective. P sued, but D moved for a stay pending arbitration. The trial court denied the motion, and D appeals.

Issue. When no contract is formed because acceptance is expressly made conditional on assent to additional or different terms and the offeror does not assent, is a contract formed instead by performance governed by the gap-filling provisions of the U.C.C.?

Held. Yes. Judgment affirmed.

- Under U.C.C. section 2-207(1), no contract was created by the exchange of forms. Because the parties did perform, however, they do have an enforceable contract under section 2-207(3).

- At common law, the contract formed by performance would be governed by D's acknowledgment form, which was in effect a counteroffer. However, un-

the box-top license permits the return of the product if the purchaser does not agree to the terms. However, TSL did not satisfy the requirement of U.C.C. section 2-207(1) regarding the clear expression of its unwillingness to proceed with the sale unless P accepted the terms of the box-top license. Therefore, the box-top license did not constitute a conditional acceptance.

♦ TSL also asserts that the parties' course of dealing bound P to the terms of the box-top license. However, a party cannot establish a course of conduct by simply repeatedly sending a writing, the terms of which would otherwise be excluded under U.C.C. section 2-207.

♦ In effect, the box-top license is a written confirmation containing additional terms. Under U.C.C. section 2-207, an additional term included in the box-top license is not incorporated into the parties' contract if the term's addition to the contract would materially alter the parties' agreement. The disclaimer of warranties that were otherwise part of the agreement is, as a matter of law, a substantial alteration and therefore cannot become part of the agreement.

---

6. Acceptance when Terms Are Not Disclosed Before Purchase--

ProCD, Inc. v. Zeidenberg, 86 F.3d 1447 (7th Cir. 1996).

Facts. ProCD, Inc. (P) compiled a database that was marketed on CD-ROM. The user license limited use of the program and database to noncommercial purposes. The license was packaged inside the shrinkwrap covering the box the CDs came in. Zeidenberg (D) purchased one of P's products and resold the information in P's database over the Internet. P sued to enjoin further dissemination of its database. The trial court held that P's licenses were ineffective because their terms did not appear on the outside of the package. P appeals.

Issue. May a seller enforce restrictions on the use of its product if these restrictions are not disclosed prior to the purchase of the product, so long as the buyer can return the product for a refund if the restrictions are unacceptable?

Held. Yes. Judgment reversed.

♦ Licenses are ordinary contracts accompanying the sale of products and are governed by contract law and the U.C.C. D claims P made an "offer" by putting its software on the shelf, and that D "accepted" P's offer by paying the asking price and leaving the store with the goods. The trial court agreed on the ground that a contract can only include the terms that the parties agree to, and if terms are hidden, they cannot be part of the contract. But one of the terms D agreed to by purchasing the software is that the transaction was subject to a license.

- D's theory would require P to put the entire license on the package, which would require microscopic type and elimination of other, possibly more useful information from the box. It is more commercially valuable to allow sellers to provide notice on the outside, terms on the inside, and a right to return the software for a refund if the terms are unacceptable.

- There are many transactions in which the exchange of money precedes the communication of detailed terms, including insurance contracts, airplane tickets, concert tickets, and so forth. It would be impractical to require the vendors in each of these situations to provide the full terms of the contract before the buyer pays the money, and in each case, the buyer is entitled to a refund if the full terms are unacceptable. Most consumer goods are purchased the same way, with the warranty contained inside the packaging.

- Software in particular is often purchased over the Internet or over the phone, where there is no way to provide the buyer in advance with the full terms of the license.

- There have been proposals to explicitly validate standard-form user licenses, but these proposals to the law's text do not change the law's effect. The U.C.C. allows a vendor to invite acceptance by conduct. P's offer proposed acceptance by the buyer's use of the software after reading the license. Also, under U.C.C. section 2-606(1)(b), an acceptance occurs when, after an opportunity to inspect, the buyer fails to make an effective rejection under section 2-602(1). The U.C.C. allows the parties to structure their relationship so the buyer can make a final decision after a detailed review.

- Under the U.C.C., certain types of terms must be agreed to in particular ways, such as the requirement that a disclaimer of implied warranty of merchantability be "conspicuous." [U.C.C. §2-316(2)] However, other terms need not receive special treatment. There is nothing in the U.C.C. that suggests that the ordinary terms included in a shrinkwrap license require any special prominence. The terms of the license in this case are identical to the contents of the product, including the size and speed of the database, and a buyer cannot pick and choose among the terms.

7. **Purchase by Phone--**

Hill v. Gateway 2000, Inc., 105 F.3d 1147 (7th Cir. 1997).

Facts. The Hills (Ps) purchased a computer from Gateway 2000, Inc. (D). Ps ordered the computer over the phone and received it by mail. The computer was accompanied by a list of terms that stated that they applied to the transaction unless the customer returned the computer within 30 days. One of the terms was an arbitration clause. More than 30 days after they received the computer, Ps complained about the computer. Ps filed suit in federal court, claiming mail and wire fraud, leading to treble damages under the RICO statute. D asked the court to enforce the arbitration clause. The court refused on the ground that Ps had not been given adequate notice of the arbitration clause. D appeals.

Issue. When a product is purchased by telephone, do the terms of the writing that accompanies the product when it is shipped become contract terms as long as the customer has the option of returning the product within 30 days?

Held. Yes. Judgment vacated and case remanded.

♦ In *ProCD, Inc. v. Zeidenberg, supra*, the court held that the terms inside a box of software are binding on consumers who use the software after having an opportunity to read the terms and return the product if they disagree with the terms. The vendor is the master of the offer and may invite acceptance by conduct. The buyer may accept by performing the acts the vendor proposes to treat as acceptance.

♦ The rule of *ProCD* should not be limited to the software industry. This approve-or-return type of transaction, where payment is made before all the terms are revealed, is common for air transportation, insurance, and other commercial dealings. It would be impractical to require order-takers, store clerks, or cashiers to read the terms of a sales agreement to customers before allowing customers to take possession.

♦ *ProCD* is also not limited to executory contracts, as Ps contend. The issue here is formation of the contract, not performance. Furthermore, the transaction in *ProCD* was no more executory than the one here—both contracts were incompletely performed. ProCD did not complete performance when Zeidenberg purchased the software, and D did not complete performance when Ps' box was delivered. Because Ps invoked D's warranty, they cannot now say that D's obligations were fulfilled when the box was delivered. Moreover, ProCD and D promised to help customers to use their products after purchase.

♦ Ps contend that *ProCD* is limited to cases involving a "merchant" buyer. However, the buyer in *ProCD* bought the product at a retail store and was not a software merchant. A vendor may propose that a contract of sale be formed, not with the payment of money or a request to send a product, but after the customer, whether a merchant or a consumer, has had a chance to inspect the item and the terms.

♦ Ps also argue that there is another distinction between this case and *ProCD*. The box containing the software in *ProCD* displayed a notice that additional terms were inside, but the box containing D's computer did not. However, D's box was not on display in a store; it was a shipping carton with information on its sides for the handlers.

◆ D indicated in its ads that its products came with limited warranties. To determine how limited the warranty is, buyers have three ways to discover a seller's terms: (i) ask for an advance copy of the warranty terms; (ii) consult public resources (*e.g.*, magazines, websites); and (iii) inspect documents after delivery. Ps took the third option and kept the computer beyond 30 days, thereby accepting D's offer that included the arbitration clause.

F. PRECONTRACTUAL LIABILITY

1.   **Introduction.** Traditionally, neither party is bound until the contract is final. An exception is the situation in which one party, in reliance on the expectation of a contract, confers a benefit on the other party and can seek restitution to prevent unjust enrichment. In some circumstances, however, a party who relies on an offer but does not confer a benefit on the other party may still have a claim.

2.   **Promissory Estoppel.** Within limits, detrimental action or forbearance by the promisee, in reliance on a promise, constitutes a substitute for consideration and renders the promise enforceable to some extent. The promisee's detrimental reliance is deemed sufficient reason to estop the promisor for asserting the lack of consideration. For similar reasons, a growing number of courts hold that an offeree's foreseeable, detrimental reliance on an offer will serve as a substitute for consideration, so as to create an option and prevent the offeror from thereafter revoking the offer for at least a reasonable time.

3.   **Restatement (Second) Approach.** Section 45 of Restatement (Second) provides that an option contract is created when the offer invites acceptance by performance and the offeree tenders or begins the invited performance. The offeror's duty of performance under such an option contract is conditional on completion or tender of the invited performance according to the terms of the offer.

4.   **Liability of Subcontractor--**

Drennan v. Star Paving Co., 333 P.2d 757 (Cal. 1958).

Facts. Star Paving Co. (D), a subcontractor, submitted a bid to Drennan (P), a general contractor, for paving work on a school building project. In his bid, P had to provide all of the subcontractors' names. P used D's bid to calculate the overall bid. P's bid was accepted. The next day, D told P that D's bid was underestimated, and refused to perform. P then contracted with another paving company at a higher price and sued D for the difference. P won a judgment. D appeals.

Issue. When a general contractor relies on a subcontractor's bid but the subcontractor later declines to perform, does that refusal constitute a breach of contract?

Held. Yes. Judgment affirmed.

♦ D did not offer to make its bid irrevocable, nor was P's use of D's bid an acceptance which bound P to award the subcontract to D. Thus, there was neither an option supported by consideration nor a bilateral contract binding on both parties.

♦ However, D's bid also did not expressly state that it was revocable at any time before acceptance. Thus, we must determine whether there are conditions to the right of revocation imposed by law or reasonably inferable in fact.

♦ D made P a clear and definite offer. D had reason to expect that P would use its bid if it were the lowest, and by bidding, D induced such action on P's part. P's reliance was reasonable and foreseeable by D, and P relied to his detriment. This is sufficient to imply a subsidiary promise by D not to revoke its offer.

♦ P and D shared an interest in the contract. Given this interest and the fact that P was bound by its own bid, P must be allowed to accept D's bid after receiving the general contract.

♦ D claims that it should be able to revoke because of its mistake. However, D's mistake misled P so that P bid too low. Between P and D, D should incur the loss resulting from the mistake because D made the mistake.

Comment. Modern cases hold that if the reliance was reasonable and foreseeable, and if the reliance produced detriment, then the subcontractor will be bound to his bid. This is a distinct change from the old rule which required the general contractor to formally accept the sub's bid before a binding contract existed.

---

5. **Liability of General Contractor.** In *Holman Erection Co. v. Orville E. Madsen & Sons, Inc.*, 330 N.W.2d 693 (Minn. 1983), the court held that the listing of a subcontractor in a general contractor's bid does not constitute acceptance of the sub's bid. This is true even though the sub is bound to his bid as submitted on the theory of promissory estoppel. A general contractor relies on the subcontractor's bid when it makes its own bid. This detrimental reliance supports the rule that the sub is bound. On the other hand, the subcontractor does not rely on a particular general contractor. The sub gives its bid to several general contractors and does not incur any further expense unless and until it reaches agreement with the winning general contractor. Promissory estoppel does not apply to the subcontractor's situation.

6. **Failed Negotiations.**

   a. **Introduction.** While contract law generally allows parties freedom to negotiate without risk of liability in the event negotiations fail, many negotiations involve considerable time and expense by the parties. Where one party confers a benefit on the other while working toward a formal contract, the beneficiary may be required to make restitution in the event the negotiations fail.

   b. **Estoppel.** During negotiations, one party may make representations that induce the other party to incur expenses. In such cases, the party making the representations may be estopped from disclaiming liability for the natural consequences of his conduct. For example, in *Goodman v. Dicker*, 169 F.2d 684 (D.C. Cir. 1948), distributors for Emerson radios told the applicant for a franchise that the application had been accepted and the franchise would be granted. In reliance on these statements, the applicant spent money preparing to do business as a franchisee. When no contract was actually entered, the applicant was allowed to recover actual damages incurred in reliance on the representations.

   c. **No estoppel under written agreement.** In *Prince v. Miller Brewing Co.*, 434 S.W.2d 232 (Tex. App. 1968), the court did not allow a recovery for cancellation of a distributorship. For 18 months, Prince had developed the territory until it became profitable, sustaining losses in the interim. When Miller Brewing Co. canceled the distributorship, Prince sued for the losses. The court directed a verdict for the defendant on the ground that the parties had a written agreement which specifically provided for cancellation at will. Promissory estoppel was deemed inapplicable where there was a valid contract which the parties followed.

   d. **Calculation of damages.** In *Grouse v. Group Health Plan, Inc.*, 306 N.W.2d 114 (Minn. 1981), the court allowed a prospective employee to recover when, after being offered a job by Group Health Plan, Inc., he quit his existing job and declined a separate job offer, only to discover someone else had been hired for his position. The court noted that the prospective employment was at-will, so the measure of damages would not be what he would have earned on the job, but what he lost in quitting his existing job and declining the other job offer.

   e. **Promissory estoppel vs. part performance.** In *Ragosta v. Wilder, supra,* the court noted that the trial court had relied on a part performance theory to allow the plaintiffs to recover the cost of obtaining financing. While this theory was inapplicable to the case, promissory estoppel might have justified a recovery. Under this theory, the plaintiffs are entitled to enforcement of the defendant's promise if (i) the promise induced them to take action of a definite and substantial character, and (ii) injustice can be avoided only by enforcement of the promise. The case was remanded for consideration of promissory estoppel.

7. Promise Incomplete as an Offer--

Hoffman v. Red Owl Stores, 133 N.W.2d 267 (Wis. 1965).

Facts. Red Owl Stores, Inc.'s (D's) agent promised Hoffman (P) that D would give P a supermarket franchise for $18,000. P purchased a small store to gain experience; it was profitable. After three months, D advised P to sell the store just before the profitable summer months began. Then P was advised to put up $1,000 for an option on land to build the store. Next P was told he would get the franchise as soon as he sold his bakery (which he did). Subsequently, the amount was raised to $24,100; then an additional $2,000 was required. Some of P's money was a loan from P's father-in-law; D then required that the loan be changed to a gift. P brought an action for damages based on his reliance and D's nonperformance. Judgment for P; D appeals.

Issue. Where P relies to his detriment on a promise made by D, and such detrimental reliance is foreseeable to D, can P recover damages even though all details of the proposed transaction are not included in the promise?

Held. Yes. Judgment affirmed.

♦   The doctrine of promissory estoppel applies here. It applies even though the promise which is relied on by P does not contain all of the necessary essential elements to form a contract (here the plans for construction, etc., had not been decided on). The required elements are a promise, substantial reliance, detriment, injustice unless damages are granted, and foreseeability of reliance by P.

Comment. This is an important decision; it extends the promissory estoppel doctrine since it does not rationalize it in terms of reliance as a substitute for consideration. Here, there is not even an offer. There is simply negotiation. The implication is that parties must bargain in good faith; where they do not, and where the one party relies to its detriment, promissory estoppel will apply and damages will be awarded to prevent injustice from the detrimental reliance.

8. Estoppel to Avoid Injustice--

Cyberchron Corp. v. Calldata Systems Development, Inc., 47 F.3d 39 (2nd Cir. 1995).

Facts. Cyberchron Corp. (P) provided customized computer hardware for its customers. Calldata Systems Development, Inc. (D) negotiated with P to purchase certain equipment that was to be used for a military contract. The parties never agreed to the weight of the equipment or to the penalties P would incur for exceeding the weight. D gave P a purchase order specifying a maximum weight of 145 pounds. P never agreed to the terms, but commenced production despite the lack of an agreement. In July, D directed P to proceed with production as if there had been an agreement on the weight issue, on the understanding that they would resolve the purchase order terms in the future. P submitted a progress payment request for $495,000, which represented 80% of its incurred costs. D didn't pay the progress payment due to separate litigation. In September, D directed P to show cause why the purchase order should not be terminated. D rejected P's detailed response and terminated the purchase order on September 25. P sued. The trial court found that D had started negotiating with alternate suppliers in August and, the day after terminating P's purchase order, contracted with another supplier for inferior equipment that weighed more than P's. The trial court also found that the parties never entered an enforceable contract because they did not agree to the essential weight term. The court awarded P $162,824 for out-of-pocket labor and materials costs incurred after July and before September 25, based on promissory estoppel. Both parties appeal.

Issue. Where the parties never agreed to a material term of a contract, but the buyer induces the seller to incur development costs in the hope that an agreement would be reached, is the seller entitled to damages under promissory estoppel?

Held. Yes. Judgment affirmed but case remanded for redetermination of damages.

♦ The three elements for promissory estoppel in New York are: (i) a clear and unambiguous promise; (ii) a reasonable and foreseeable reliance by the party to whom the promise is made; and (iii) an injury sustained by the party asserting the estoppel by reason of the reliance. Some courts require an unconscionable injury or an injustice to justify application of the doctrine.

♦ In this case, P's injury is unconscionable and injustice can be avoided only by applying promissory estoppel on P's behalf. Starting in July, D pressured P to produce the equipment and assured P that if it did the work, the negotiation problem could be resolved. The parties had several meetings and discussions about this.

♦ The trial court found that D's behavior, especially its abrupt termination of P's purchase order to purchase heavier, inferior equipment from another party, was unconscionable. While pressuring P to produce, D was actually negotiating with another company to do the work.

♦ The trial court denied P's claim for overhead and shutdown expenses. Overhead expenses should be allowed if P can show that such costs are normally allocated to specific projects in P's cost accounting practices. Shutdown expenses should be allowed so long as they were incurred in reliance on D's promises.

9.   Obligation to Negotiate in Good Faith--

Channel Home Centers, Division of Grace Retail Corp. v. Grossman,
795 F.2d 291 (3d Cir. 1986).

Facts. Grossman (D) was planning to purchase a shopping mall. P approached Channel Home Centers, Division of Grace Retail Corp. (P), to see if P was interested in leasing space in the mall. When P showed interest, D requested a letter of intent that D would use to help secure financing. P provided the letter of intent, which provided that D agree to withdraw the space from the market and that P obtain the necessary zoning permits. P had its legal department prepare the lease. P sent D a copy of the draft lease, and P and D continued negotiations. A competitor of P's, Mr. Good Buys, contacted D about the space in the mall and D began discussing a possible lease. Later, D told P that negotiations were terminated because P did not provide a mutually acceptable lease within 30 days of the letter of intent. The next day, D signed a lease with Mr. Good Buys for a higher rent than P had negotiated. P sued for breach of contract. The trial court held that there was no enforceable agreement. P appeals.

Issue. May a property owner's agreement to negotiate in good faith and to withdraw the premises from the market during the negotiation bind the owner for a reasonable period of time?

Held. Yes. Judgment reversed.

♦   Preliminary negotiations and agreements to enter a binding contract in the future are not contracts. However, parties may agree to negotiate in good faith, and this agreement may constitute a binding contract. The test is whether (i) both parties manifested an intention to be bound by the agreement; (ii) the terms of the agreement are sufficiently definite to be enforced; and (iii) there was consideration.

♦   In this case, the letter of intent and the activities of both parties, including planning by P and D's efforts to obtain zoning variances, show that both parties intended to be bound by an agreement to negotiate in good faith. D's promise to withdraw the space from the market and negotiate with P is sufficiently definite to be enforced.

♦   D claims there was no consideration given, but in reality the letter of intent P gave D was valuable to D. D requested it and used it to help with financing. D made his promise to negotiate in return for this valuable letter of intent. This consideration is sufficient.

♦   At trial, the court must evaluate D's claim that P orally agreed to provide a draft lease within 30 days of the letter of intent, and if there was no such agreement, the court must determine what a reasonable time for the negotiations was under the circumstances.

G. THE REQUIREMENT OF DEFINITENESS

1. **The Requirement of Definiteness and Certainty of Terms.** The terms of the offer must be sufficiently clear and complete so that the court can determine what the parties intended and can fix damages in case of nonperformance. [Restatement (Second) §33]

2. **The Essential Terms.** A contract must cover (expressly or impliedly) the following four essential terms:

    a. Parties to the contract;

    b. The subject matter of the contract;

    c. Time for performance; and

    d. Price.

3. **Implication of Reasonable Terms.** The essential terms must either be expressly stated in the contract or be capable of reasonable implication from the agreement. The general trend of the courts is to adopt a policy of liberal construction so as to uphold the reasonable expectations of the parties; thus, the court will usually imply reasonable terms (*i.e.,* implied-in-fact terms from the dealings and relationship of the parties) where none are expressly covered by the parties. For example, failure to specify price may not invalidate the contract.

    a. **Where price is completely omitted.** Where the parties have made no provision for price but a charge was intended, the court will normally imply a "reasonable price" (*i.e.,* fair market value for the goods, etc.).

    b. **Where the price stated is indefinite.** Often, however, where the parties have made some attempt to include terms on the price but it is stated in such a vague way as to be unintelligible, the courts will refuse to imply a reasonable price, and the contract will be unenforceable due to lack of certainty on an essential term (*i.e.,* A agrees to employ B "at a rate not exceeding $300 per week").

4. **The Uniform Commercial Code.** In contracts for the sale of goods, the omission of one or more essential terms does not render an offer invalid, as long as it appears that the parties intended to make a contract and there is a reasonably certain basis for giving an appropriate remedy. [U.C.C. §2-204] In effect, the Restatement (Second) section 33 takes this same approach with respect to all contracts.

5. **Method of Determining Terms.** Courts faced with challenges based on indefiniteness may conclude that the contract is adequate as long as the lan-

guage sets forth a definite, ascertainable method of determining what the challenged provision should be.

6. Conditional Exercise of Option--

Toys, Inc. v. F.M. Burlington Co., 582 A.2d 123 (Vt. 1990).

Facts. F.M. Burlington Co. (D) owned a shopping mall and leased space to Toys, Inc. (P) for an initial five-year term ending in February, with an option to renew for an additional five years. P was required to provide D one year's written notice of intention to exercise the option. P sent D the required notice on February 7 in a timely manner, and D confirmed, stating the prevailing rental rate as specified in the option agreement. P then wrote that its notice of renewal was based on a different understanding of the prevailing rental rate and suggested the parties could renegotiate a rent structure. D responded that P's rights under the option were based on the prevailing rate, but that another rate could be negotiated. The parties agreed to a different rent structure, and D wrote to P saying that if the new offer was accepted, P should execute an acknowledgment prior to August 1. P asked for more time and D extended the date to August 15. On August 15, P asked for another extension. D never responded. P found another building to move into. D notified P that it was listing P's space for lease effective March 1. P informed D that such a lease would be a breach of D's lease with P. P moved into its new location and then sued D for breach. The court awarded P summary judgment. D appeals.

Issue. Where an optionee gives notice of exercising the option but later disputes the terms of the agreement, may the optionee enforce the option agreement?

Held. No. Judgment reversed.

♦ There was no genuine issue of fact regarding the validity of the option, so the court properly granted summary judgment on that issue. However, an option must be accepted according to its terms to create a binding contract.

♦ An acceptance that varies from the offer does not create a contract. A reply may exceed the terms of the proposal without qualifying the acceptance, however, where the addition is merely a request instead of a condition. All the circumstances must be considered as well as reasonable inferences.

♦ In this case, P claims that both parties were bound by the February 7 letter, but P subsequently refused to agree to terms that were more favorable than those that would have applied had the February letter been binding. Rather than accept the terms of the contract under the option, P told D that its notice of intent to renew was based on a substantially different understanding of the prevailing rental rate. This suggests that the February 7 letter was merely an expression of intent, with the actual exercise of the option contingent on a determination of the prevailing rental rate. Under these circumstances, it cannot be said as a matter of law that P accepted the option according to its terms, and summary judgment should not have been granted.

♦ The facts also suggest that P may have waived its acceptance of the option because P's conduct after the February 7 letter was inconsistent with the intent to renew. As a fact finder could find a waiver on these facts, summary judgment was inappropriate.

Comments.

♦ In this case, P clearly had notified D of its intention to exercise the option. The subsequent dispute about the rental rate could be construed as an agreement by the parties to a withdrawal of P's notice of intention to exercise.

♦ In *Lee v. Joseph E. Seagram & Sons, Inc.*, 552 F.2d 447 (2d Cir. 1977), the court held that a jury could properly find that the parties to an oral agreement intended that the purchase price for a new distributorship would be roughly the same as the sales price of the old distributorship, and that this finding was sufficient to satisfy the price term, making the agreement enforceable.

---

7. Omission of Specific Price Term in Long-Term Contract--

Oglebay Norton Co. v. Armco, Inc., 556 N.E.2d 515 (Ohio 1990).

Facts. Armco, Inc. (D) and Oglebay Norton Co. (P) entered a long-term contract in 1957 whereby P would reserve shipping capacity and D would use the capacity to ship iron ore from the Lake Superior district to D's steel plants in the lower Great Lakes region. The contract required D to pay the "regular net contract rates" as recognized by leading iron ore shippers, but if there was no such rate, the parties would mutually agree upon a rate. The parties modified the contract four times by 1980, extending the term through 2010 and requiring P to upgrade and expand its fleet through significant capital expenditures. P had a seat on D's board of directors and owned a portion of D's stock. Until 1983, the parties determined the shipping rate by reference to a published rate. In 1983, D objected to P's quoted rate and the parties negotiated a lower rate for 1984. The parties were unable to agree to a rate for 1985; P billed $7.66 per ton, but D changed the invoice amount to $5 and only paid $5. The previous reference rate was no longer published. The parties failed to reach an agreed rate for 1986, and P sought a declaratory judgment as to the proper rate to be charged. P continued to ship ore, for which D paid as little as $3.85 per ton. D then sought a declaration that the contract was no longer enforceable because of the breakdown of the rate-pricing mechanism. The trial court held that the parties intended to be bound even though the rates were not fixed, that a reasonable rate should be paid, that the parties should consider rates charged for similar services by other leading iron ore vessel operators, and that the court would mediate any failure to agree to a rate and determine the applicable rate. For 1986, the court found that a reasonable rate was $6 per ton. D appeals.

Issue. May a party enforce a long-term service contract when the price is not specified and the parties must periodically resort to the court to determine a reasonable price?

Held. Yes. Judgment affirmed.

♦ D claims it never consented to be bound by a contract once the specified pricing mechanisms had failed, and that the contract was therefore unenforceable. However, the evidence of a long-standing and close business relationship, including D's participation on P's board and ownership of P's stock, supports the court's finding that the parties intended to be bound, even in the event the pricing mechanisms failed.

♦ If the parties intend to conclude a contract but the price is not settled, the price is a reasonable price at the time of delivery if the contract requires the price to be set by some standard and it is not so set. [*See* Restatement (Second) of Contracts, §33; U.C.C. §2-305(1)] In this case, the court determined that $6 per ton was reasonable, based on the parties' course of dealing and comparisons of market price. The evidence of rates charged by other companies, as well as P's quotation for 1987, supports this determination.

♦ A trial court has authority to fill an open price term when the parties intend to be bound by the contract. A term which appears to be indefinite may be supplied by factual implication. This fulfills the intention of the parties.

♦ D asserts that the court could not force the parties to negotiate, or mediate any failure to negotiate, each year through 2010. Normally, specific performance is not granted unless the terms of the contract are sufficiently certain to provide a basis for the order. Certainty may be provided by the addition of a term otherwise lacking or incomplete, however. In this case, the trial court properly determined that specific performance was necessary due to the speculative nature of any award of damages based on the length of the contract and the economic uncertainties of this type of shipping.

III. STATUTES OF FRAUDS

A. OVERVIEW

1. **History.** In most instances oral contracts are valid. However, by statute, a few types of contracts are required to be in writing, or at least evidenced by a signed, written memorandum of the essential terms. These statutory requirements stem from the English Statute of Frauds of 1677.

2. **Purpose.** The purpose of the Statute of Frauds is to prevent fraud and perjury as to the actual terms of the contract and to provide better evidence of the contract terms in the event of dispute. Failure to comply with the statute renders the contract voidable but not void. Thus, the Statute relates only to the remedy and not to the substantive validity of the contract.

B. WRITING AND SIGNING THE AGREEMENT

1. **The Required Writing.** When a contract is required to be in writing, it ordinarily must be in a permanent, written form and signed by the party to be charged. However, this does not mean that the writing must be a fully integrated, formal contract.

    a. **Memorandum of essential terms.** A memorandum of the essential terms of the agreement (*e.g.*, letters, telegrams, or even mere notations in the private books of one of the parties which were never communicated to the other) will satisfy the Statute if the memorandum contains the following:

        1) Identity of the contracting *parties*;

        2) Description of the *subject matter* of the contract;

        3) *Terms and conditions* of the agreement;

        4) Recital of the *consideration*; and

        5) *Signature* of the party sought to be charged. A party's initials, seal, etc., may be sufficient.

    b. **Integration of documents.** The requisite writing may be composed of several documents, provided each document refers to or incorporates the others, or they are otherwise integrated (*i.e.,* are physically attached).

        1) **Implementation of requirements.** The traditional rule requires that the writing contain the essential terms of the agreement. The

U.C.C. has modified this rule, but it still requires at least a quantity term. Where multiple documents are involved, oral testimony may be used to establish a connection between them to show the terms of the contract. A signed writing may also refer to extrinsic circumstances that are part of the essential terms. The signature requirement may be satisfied by a corporate logo or other symbol so long as it is intended to authenticate a writing.

    c.   **The U.C.C. position.** Under the U.C.C., even less completeness is required in contracts for the sale of goods. There need only be some writing sufficient to indicate that a contract for sale has been made and which specifies the quantity terms, even though it omits or incorrectly states other terms agreed upon. However, the contract is only enforceable as to the quantity of goods specified in the writing. [*See* U.C.C. §2-201] Note also that if one "merchant" sends a written confirmation of a contract to another (in a form sufficient to bind the sender), the requirement of a writing is thereby satisfied and the other merchant is bound thereby unless he objects within 10 days following receipt, even though he never signed anything. [*See* U.C.C. §2-201(2)]

2.   The Signature. The signature on a requisite writing need not be handwritten to satisfy the Statute of Frauds; it can be typed or printed. A party's initials may also be a sufficient signature if so intended.

C. STATUTORY SCOPE

1.   Contracts that Are Incapable of Being Performed Within One Year. This refers only to contracts which, by their terms, cannot by any possibility be performed within one year from the making thereof. The one-year period begins from the date the contract is made, not when performance is promised.

    a.   **Contracts where performance within one year is possible but unlikely.** Some contracts will probably take more than one year to perform—but performance is theoretically possible within one year. These contracts are not within the Statute. For example, A enters a contract with B to have B supply his requirements of raw materials. No time limit is stated. This contract is not within the Statute, since it is possible that A could go out of business within one year and no longer have requirements.

    b.   **No express terms regarding time for performance--**

C. R. Klewin, Inc. v. Flagship Properties, Inc., 600 A.2d 772 (Conn. 1991).

Facts. Flagship Properties, Inc. (D) was the developer of a large construction project involving the University of Connecticut. In March 1986, D orally agreed that C. R. Klewin, Inc. (P) would be construction manager for the project. In May 1987, the parties signed a formal written agreement for the first phase of the project. In March 1988, D hired another party to manage the second phase. P sued, claiming that D had agreed that P would be the manager for the entire project. D moved for summary judgment based on the Statute of Frauds. The district court granted the motion on the ground that the contract could not be performed within one year. P appealed. The appellate court certified two issues to the Connecticut Supreme Court.

Issues.

(i) Under Connecticut law, if an oral contract fails to specify explicitly the time for performance, is it a contact of "indefinite duration" and therefore outside of the Statute of Frauds?

(ii) If an oral contract contemplates performance over a period in excess of one year but does not explicitly negate the possibility of performance within one year, is the contract unenforceable?

Held. (i) Yes. (ii) No.

♦ The Statute of Frauds has been criticized because it does not serve its intended functions very well. The one-year provision is the most difficult to rationalize, and historians are not sure why it originated. At this point, the one-year provision arbitrarily prevents adjudication of possibly meritorious claims and is therefore disfavored by the courts.

♦ The courts in Connecticut have taken a narrow view of the provision. Contracts of indefinite duration are excluded from the Statute, and there is no distinction under the Statute between contracts of uncertain or indefinite duration and contracts that have no express terms regarding the time for performance.

♦ The Statute applies only to contracts whose performance cannot possibly be completed within one year. To construe the Statute narrowly, this provision must be interpreted so that "possibly" means only contracts whose completion within a year would be inconsistent with the express terms of the contract. It does not matter whether performance within a year is realistically impossible, as long as the terms of the contract would allow performance within a year.

♦ Accordingly, when a contract contains no express terms about the time for performance, courts should not inquire whether, when the contact was formed, it was realistically possible that performance would be completed within a year.

c. Contracts to make a will and contracts to be performed after death. In some states the Statute of Frauds is also applied to all contracts not to be performed during the lifetime of the promisor (even though this performance could occur within one year) and to agreements to make a will or devise or bequeath property.

d. Exception. Even if a contract cannot be performed within one year, most courts hold that if it is fully executed on one side, this will take the entire contract out of the Statute and make the oral promise enforceable. For example, A orally promises B $5,000 for which B promises to work for A for two years. A pays the money. B's promise to work for A for two years, although oral, is enforceable. The basis for the exception is fairness.

2. Contracts for the Sale of an Interest in Land. A contract for the sale of land or any interest therein must be in writing.

a. Leases. Leases are normally covered by the Statute of Frauds; however, many states provide by statute that leases for one year or less do not have to be in writing.

b. An "interest" in land. It is often difficult to determine what is included under the term an "interest in land." Fixtures, liens, growing timber, etc., have all been held to be an "interest" in land.

c. Part performance doctrine. When the plaintiff brings an action for specific performance (and not an action at law for damages), part performance of the land sale contract may take it out of the Statute of Frauds.

1) Partial performance in reliance on oral agreement--

Richard v. Richard, 900 A.2d 1170 (R.I. 2006).

Facts. Gregory Richard and his wife (Ps) lived as tenants on property owned by Gregory's father, Norman Richard (D). D agreed to sell the property to Ps, but no one wrote down the agreement. Ps began paying monthly amounts in excess of the rent toward the purchase price. The parties disagreed about the terms of the agreement. Ps sued. The trial court found that D had agreed to sell the property for $70,000, which was only one-third of its fair market value. D appeals, based on the Statute of Frauds.

Issue. May an oral agreement to sell real estate be enforced where the buyers have partially performed in reliance on the enforceability of the agreement?

Held. Yes. Judgment affirmed.

♦   Part performance is an exception to the Statute of Frauds when repudiation of the oral contract would lead to an unjust or fraudulent result. Part performance may consist of conduct taken in reliance on the contract, including possession of property, improvements made, or payment of a substantial part of the purchase price.

♦   D claims that Ps took possession of the property pursuant to a rental agreement. A continued possession by a purchaser already in possession may still relate to a parol contract of sale and therefore constitute part performance, as long as there is evidence that refers the possession to the purchase contract. In this case, D kept a ledger showing that Ps' monthly payments were deducted from a figure of $70,000 starting at the time Ps claim that D agreed to sell the property for that amount.

♦   The trial court also relied on improvements Ps made to the property. Improvements made in reliance on an oral contract ordinarily must be permanent to constitute part performance. Ps added doors and a banister, replaced floors, and renovated bedrooms after the alleged agreement with D. Such improvements would have been improvident without the contract of sale.

♦   The combination of Ps' possession, the improvements Ps made, and their periodic extra payments, deducted from the $70,000 figure in D's own ledger, is sufficient to constitute part performance of D's oral agreement to sell the property.

━━━━━━━━━━━━━━━━

3.   **Contracts for the Sale of Goods.** A contract for the sale of any goods for the price of $500 or more must be in writing. [See U.C.C. §2-201] The floor price above which a writing is required exceeds $500 in several jurisdictions. *[Note: A proposed revision to section 2-201, if approved, would change the amount required for a writing to $5,000. At press time, this revision was still under consideration.]*

   a.   **Goods defined.** "Goods" includes all tangible movable property. It does not include intangibles, securities, or labor and services.

      1)   Note that often a contract requires that goods be supplied as part of rendering services. The issue is whether the contract is primarily one for the sale of goods or for the rendering of services.

      2)   Thus, an oral contract for the service of constructing a building might be one primarily for services and, even though materials worth more than $500 are supplied as part of the job, the contract would be enforceable.

b. **Exceptions.** Oral contracts for the sale of goods of more than $500 will be enforced in the following situations:

(i) The buyer receives and accepts all or part of the goods (the contract is enforceable as to the goods accepted);

(ii) The buyer gives something in part payment for the goods (the contract is enforceable as to the goods paid for);

(iii) The contract calls for the manufacture of special goods for the buyer and the seller has made a substantial beginning in the manufacture thereof;

(iv) The contract is between merchants and within a reasonable time a written confirmation is sent and the party receiving it does not send a written objection within 10 days; and

(v) The contract is admitted by the party against whom enforcement is sought (in court pleadings or testimony).

1) **Reasonable time determined by parties' course of dealing--**

St. Ansgar Mills, Inc. v. Streit, 613 N.W.2d 289 (Iowa 2000).

Facts. St. Ansgar Mills, Inc. (P) was a grain dealer that purchased corn from grain farmers and sold it to livestock farmers such as Streit (D), who raised hogs. P and D had a long-time business relationship. D would call P for price quotes, and if the parties verbally agreed, P would prepare written confirmations that P would mail to D or keep for D or his father, as D's agent, to sign when one of them went to P's place of business. On July 1, D called to order 60,000 bushels of corn for delivery in December and May. P covered the sale in the futures market. P prepared the written confirmation and set it aside for D to sign, but neither D nor his father came to P's business for over a month. On August 10, D's father stopped by the business, and P gave him the confirmation. Subsequently, the price of corn dropped below the quoted prices and D refused delivery of the corn. P sued for $152,100, the difference between the contract price and the market price at the time D refused delivery. D moved for summary judgment, relying on the Statute of Frauds. The trial court granted summary judgment, finding that the written confirmation did not satisfy the Statute of Frauds because P did not deliver it to D or his father within a reasonable time after the oral contract. P appeals.

Issue. If a written confirmation for the sale of goods for $500 or more is not delivered to the buyer for over a month, may it satisfy the writing requirement of the Statute of Frauds if such a delay is consistent with the parties' course of dealing?

Held. Yes. Judgment reversed and case remanded.

♦ Section 2-201(2) of the U.C.C. modifies the traditional Statute of Frauds for merchants by specifying that the writing requirement is satisfied if a written confirmation is provided within a "reasonable time" and the merchant receiving it has reason to know of its contents. This means that the writing need not be signed by the party disputing the contract.

♦ The written confirmation exception includes a 10-day requirement for a merchant's objection to the writing, but it applies a flexible standard of reasonableness for the time in which the confirmation must be received. This permits the expansion of commercial practices through the custom and practice of the parties.

♦ A determination of the reasonableness of the parties' conduct is a jury question. The question of whether P gave the written confirmation to D in a reasonable time is an issue a jury must decide as a question of fact. Each case has particular facts and circumstances that must be considered.

♦ In granting summary judgment, the trial court focused on the large amount of the sale, the volatile market conditions, and P's lack of explanation for not sending the confirmation to D. These factors are relevant to the reasonableness of P's conduct, but other factors are relevant, especially the parties' course of dealing.

---

c. **Related provisions.** The U.C.C. also has separate provisions which require a written contract for transactions involving "intangibles" and "securities."

4. **Guarantee Contracts.** Promises to answer for or discharge the debts of another must be in writing to be enforceable. This applies only to promises made (i) by one who is not presently liable for the debt, (ii) to a creditor, and (iii) in order to discharge the present or future obligations of a third person.

   a. **Promises to debtor.** Note that if the promise is made to the debtor ("I'll pay your obligation to X") and is supported by consideration, it is enforceable even though it is oral. [Restatement (Second) §112] Novations are not within the Statute of Frauds either. [Restatement (Second) §115]

   b. **Primary debt by promisor.** The Statute does not apply to "primary promises." This means that if the underlying contract was between the promisor and the creditor, the promise is enforceable although oral. [Restatement (Second) §114] Thus, if A orally tells C to send $100 of goods to B and "send the bill for $100 to me," the primary contract is between A and C. B is merely a third-party beneficiary and the contract is enforceable.

c. **Exception—where the guarantor's main purpose is to benefit herself.** Even where the promise is "collateral," if it appears that the promisor's main purpose in guaranteeing the obligation of another was to secure an advantage or pecuniary benefit for herself, her promise is enforceable even though not in writing. [Restatement (Second) §116]

d. **Assumption of mortgage payments pursuant to unsigned deed--**

Langman v. Alumni Association of the University of Virginia, 442 S.E.2d 669 (Va. 1994).

Facts. Langman and Stowe (Ps) owned an arcade that they conveyed to the Alumni Association of the University of Virginia (D). The property had been appraised for $775,000 and was subject to a mortgage of $600,000. The deed specified that D assumed payment of the mortgage and agreed to hold Ps harmless from further liability on the mortgage. D acknowledged the gift and had the deed recorded, but did not sign it. When the arcade lost money, Ps made the payments on the mortgage and then sued D for reimbursement. The trial court found that D did not knowingly accept the conditions in the deed and therefore the assumption clause was unenforceable. Ps appeal.

Issue. Where a real estate deed specifically includes an assumption of debt, may the grantee later disavow the terms of the deed?

Held. No. Judgment reversed.

♦ A grantee who accepts a deed becomes contractually bound by its provisions, including a promise to assume an existing mortgage. The trial court's findings were based on parol evidence which should not have been admitted.

♦ D claims that the "suretyship" provision of the Statute of Frauds requires that D have signed the agreement to be bound to assume the mortgage. But a grantee who assumes an existing mortgage is not a surety. By promising the grantor to pay to the mortgagee the debt the grantee owes to the grantor, the assumption becomes an original undertaking. Unlike the normal surety or guarantor, D in this case received a direct benefit and did not merely act as surety for the grantors.

e. **The main-purpose rule--**

Central Ceilings, Inc. v. National Amusements, Inc., 873 N.E.2d 754 (Mass. App. Ct. 2007).

Facts. Central Ceilings, Inc. (P) was a subcontractor on a project to build a theater complex for National Amusements, Inc. (D). When the prime contractor was having financial difficulties, P met with D and received D's verbal guarantee that it would pay P what the prime contractor owed P. P continued working. Later, when D discovered it did not owe the prime contractor any more money, D refused to pay P. P sued D and won a judgment for $600,000. D appeals, asserting that P's claim was barred by the Statute of Frauds.

Issue. In the absence of a writing, may a project owner's guarantee to pay a subcontractor if the prime contractor fails to pay be enforceable if the project owner's main purpose was to secure performance and not to satisfy the prime contractor's obligation?

Held. Yes. Judgment affirmed.

♦ In lawsuits brought to charge a party upon a special promise to answer for the debt of another, the Statute of Frauds requires a writing signed by the party to be charged under the contract. D claims that under this rule, it could only be liable to P if the alleged agreement was a novation that released the prime contractor from its obligation to P and substituted D for the prime contractor. While novation is a valid exception to the Statute, it does not apply in this case.

♦ The trial court applied the "leading object" or "main purpose" exception to the Statute of Frauds. Under this exception, an oral agreement that is not a novation is still enforceable if the promise was given primarily or solely to benefit the promisor.

♦ In this case, D wanted to have its project completed in time for the Labor Day weekend, which was a tight time frame when P and D were discussing the prime contractor's financial problems. P was a core subcontractor on the project. Therefore, the jury could reasonably find that D's promise was made to secure P's continued and timely performance. The satisfaction of the prime contractor's obligation was merely incidental to D's promise. Under the leading object exception, the contract was enforceable.

D. RELIANCE AND OTHER EQUITIES

1. **Introduction.** Some courts will permit restitution or even reliance recovery for a person who is injured by relying on a promise which turns out to be unenforceable under the Statute of Frauds. [*See* Restatement (Second) §375]

2. **Estoppel--**

Monarco v. Lo Greco, 220 P.2d 737 (Cal. 1950).

Facts. Natale and Carmela Castiglia had three children, John, Rosie, and Christie. Rosie married Nick Norcia. The Castiglias invested $4,000 in a one-half interest in agricultural land; the Norcias acquired the other one-half interest. At this time, Christie desired to leave home. However, his parents promised him that if he would stay and work in the family venture, they would keep the property in joint tenancy so that it would pass to the survivor who would in turn leave it to Christie. Wills were drafted accordingly. Out of consideration for this promise Christie stayed. At the time of Natale's death, the Castiglia venture was worth $100,000. However, just before his death, Natale, unbeknownst to Carmela or Christie, terminated the joint tenancy and devised all his property to his grandson, Monarco (P). This will was probated, and the Natale property was distributed to P. P then brought this action for partition and accounting of the properties. By cross-claim, Carmela asked that P be declared a constructive trustee of the property he received as a result of Natale's breach of his agreement to keep the property in joint tenancy. The trial court held for defendant and cross-complainant, and P appeals.

Issue. Is plaintiff estopped from relying upon the Statute of Frauds to avoid the enforcement of the oral contract to not change the property from joint tenancy?

Held. Yes. Judgment affirmed.

◆   The doctrine of estoppel to assert the Statute of Frauds is applied to prevent fraud. Such fraud may inhere in the unconscionable injury that would result from denying enforcement of the contract after one party has been induced by the other to change his position in reliance on the contract, or in the unjust enrichment that would result if a party who has received the benefits of the other's performance were allowed to rely upon the Statute. Often both elements are present; both elements are present in this case.

◆   Furthermore, the estoppel to plead the Statute of Frauds is *not* dependent upon a misrepresentation that a writing is not necessary, as long as one or both of the above elements is present.

Comment. In *Warder & Lee Elevator, Inc. v. Britten*, 274 N.W.2d 339 (Iowa 1979), the court allowed Lee Elevator to recover cover damages against Britten, a farmer. The parties had an oral agreement for Britten to sell Lee Elevator corn and beans, but when prices rose, Britten refused to deliver. Lee Elevator had already committed to sell the goods to a third party. The court applied promissory estoppel to defeat Britten's Statute of Frauds defense, noting that the U.C.C. does not eliminate equitable and legal principles traditionally applicable in contract actions.

IV. POLICING THE BARGAINING PROCESS

A. CAPACITY

1. **General Rule.** Legal capacity of both the offeror and offeree is essential to formation of a contract. If the parties lack legal capacity, they cannot give the required legally binding mutual assent. Legal capacity, however, must be distinguished from physical capacity. While a person may be physically able to perform the acts necessary to otherwise create a binding contract, if that person possesses certain legal disabilities, the purported contract will either be void or voidable. Typically, contracts entered into by the following persons will be void or voidable: infants (those not having yet reached the age of majority); insane persons; convicts deprived of their civil rights; and drunken persons.

2. **Minority.**

   a. **General rule.** The contracts of a minor are voidable at the option of the minor, but a minor may nevertheless enforce the contract against the adult. However, a minor is always liable for the reasonable value of necessaries furnished to him. This liability is quasi-contractual, rather than based on the contract; hence, minority is no defense.

   b. **Emancipated minor--**

Kiefer v. Fred Howe Motors, Inc., 158 N.W.2d 288 (Wis. 1968).

Facts. Kiefer (P), 20 years old, married and a father, misrepresented his age as 21 and purchased a five-year-old station wagon from Fred Howe Motors, Inc. (D). After turning 21, P sought to return the vehicle claiming that it had a cracked block. D refused to accept the return of the vehicle, and P sued to recover the purchase price, claiming that his contract was voidable since he was a minor at the time he entered into it.

Issue. Is the contract voidable?

Held. Yes. Judgment affirmed.

♦ The general rule is that the contract of a minor, other than for necessaries, is either void or voidable at his option. The general rule is not affected by the minor's status as emancipated (*i.e.,* free from parental control and self-supporting) or unemancipated. With respect to the representation of majority on the part of P, the court held that D had not established by the evidence that P had intended to deceive D or D's justifiable reliance on the representation.

Dissent. The age of 21 years no longer has a basis in fact or in public policy as an indication of contractual maturity.

Comment. Many jurisdictions have lowered the age of majority to 18 years of age following the adoption of the amendment to the United States Constitution lowering the voting age to 18.

---

3. **Mental Infirmity.**

   a. **Mental illness--**

Ortelere v. Teachers' Retirement Board, 250 N.E.2d 460 (N.Y. 1969).

Facts. Ortelere (P) quit his job to care for his wife, a New York City school teacher, who suffered a nervous breakdown involving "involutional psychosis, melancholia type" and was diagnosed as suffering from cerebral arteriosclerosis. She had participated in the public retirement system for 40 years and had a reserve of $70,925. While on leave for mental illness, she borrowed the maximum amount from the retirement system and made an irrevocable election to take the maximum retirement benefits of $450 a month during her lifetime, revoking her earlier election to receive $375 a month during her lifetime with the unexhausted reserve in her retirement account to go, on her death, to her husband and her two grown children. Under the subsequent election, her husband and children would receive no benefits on her death. Two months after her election, she died and her husband (P) sued to set aside her election on the basis of mental incompetence. P appeals a judgment for Teachers' Retirement Board (D).

Issue. When one party to a transaction has knowledge of the mental incompetence of the other party, is the contract between them voidable?

Held. Yes. Judgment reversed.

♦   As stated in the Restatement (Second) section 18C, a person incurs only voidable contractual duties by entering into a transaction if by reason of mental illness or defect he is unable to act in a reasonable manner in relation to the transaction and the other party has reason to know of his condition. Here the court held that the retirement system was or should have been fully aware of decedent's condition, since she was on leave of absence for medical reasons known to the Board of Education.

Dissent. Decedent sent a detailed letter with eight questions to the retirement system prior to her election, thus evidencing a mind fully in command of the salient features of the retirement system.

---

b.   Weakness vs. incapacity--

Cundick v. Broadbent, 383 F.2d 157(10th Cir. 1967).

Facts. Cundick (P) agreed to sell certain ranch land and an interest in a development company to Broadbent (D). A one-page handwritten agreement between P and D was later refined by P's lawyer to an 11-page document, and P executed documents and received the agreed-upon purchase price over a period of six months following the initial agreement. The prices set forth in the contract turned out to be less than half the appraised values, and shortly before the transaction was to be completed, P's wife, who had been appointed guardian ad litem, brought an action on behalf of her husband against D to set aside the agreement, asserting that her husband had been mentally incompetent to contract and that D was aware of this condition and had intentionally overreached him. The trial court dismissed P's action and P appeals.

Issue. Is the contract voidable?

Held. No. Judgment affirmed.

♦   The modern rule is that the contractual act by one claiming to be mentally deficient but not under guardianship, absent fraud or knowledge of such asserted incapacity by the other contracting party, is not a void act but at most only voidable at the instance of the deficient party, and then only in accordance with certain equitable principles. Mental capacity to contract depends upon whether the disabled person possessed sufficient reason to enable him to understand the nature and effect of the act in issue.

♦   While there was evidence that P suffered from premature arteriosclerosis and underwent a change in his personality and attitude toward his business affairs prior to the time of the transaction in question, it does not appear that P was incapable of transacting his own business affairs, and the facts do not support a finding that D deceived or overreached P.

Dissent. The undisputed medical testimony indicated that P was not a mentally competent person.

B. OVERREACHING

1.   **Introduction.** If a contract results from unfairness in the bargaining process, it is generally voidable. Such circumstances as duress, fraud, and mistake are the usual things the courts look at to find unfairness.

2.   **Preexisting Duty.** When A and B have a contract under which A is contractually obliged to perform some act, neither A's new promise to perform that

same act nor his actual performance of that act constitutes consideration for a promise by B to pay a greater amount for the performance than that set by the original contract. This prevents A from taking advantage of B's inability to contract with someone else to perform the consideration.

    a.   **Exceptions.** The general rule is inapplicable where:

        1)   A agrees to perform an act similar to, but different from, the action he was contractually obligated to perform.

        2)   A owes the preexisting contractual duty to someone other than B.

        3)   A had a valid defense under the original contract.

        4)   Unanticipated circumstances arise that make modification of the terms of the first contract fair and equitable.

    b.   **Threat of nonperformance--**

Alaska Packers' Association v. Domenico, 117 F. 99 (9th Cir. 1902).

Facts. In San Francisco, Domenico and other seamen (Ps) entered into a contract with the Alaska Packers' Association (D) to work as seamen and fishermen in a remote area of Alaska for $50 for the season plus two cents per salmon caught. Ps sailed to Alaska, but when they arrived at D's canning factory, they stopped work as a group and demanded $100 each. D's superintendent signed an agreement to pay the $100 because he could not get substitute workers. At the end of the season, D paid Ps according to the original contract. Ps sued in admiralty for the additional money. The court found for Ps. D appeals.

Issue. Is a contract to pay a higher salary than originally agreed, entered into under threat of nonperformance, enforceable?

Held. No. Judgment reversed.

♦   The supervisor's consent to Ps' demands was without consideration because it was based solely upon Ps' agreement to render the exact services they were already under contract to render.

♦   A party who refuses to perform, thereby coercing the other party to promise to pay him more for doing what he was already legally bound to do, takes unjustifiable advantage of the other party. There is no consideration for the promise of the other party, and it cannot be legally enforced. This is true even when the first party has completed his duty in reliance on the second contract.

Comment. Some courts find new consideration for a modified employment contract in the employee giving up his right to breach the first contract.

---

c. **Rescission and modification.** If the parties agree to rescind the original contract, a subsequent contract calling for the same performance at a higher price is enforceable. In *Schwartzreich v. Bauman-Basch, Inc.,* 131 N.E. 887 (N.Y. 1921), Schwartzreich had agreed to work for Bauman-Basch, Inc. for one year at $90 per week. Before Schwartzreich had started working, he received an offer for a higher salary elsewhere. The parties tore their signatures off the old contract and executed a new one, word for word with the old one, except that Schwartzreich was to receive $100 per week. Two months later, Bauman-Basch, Inc. discharged Schwartzreich. Schwartzreich sued under the second contract and won, the jury finding that the parties had mutually agreed to rescind the original contract before signing the second one.

d. **Economic adversity--**

Watkins & Son v. Carrig, 21 A.2d 591 (N.H. 1941).

Facts. Watkins & Son (P) contracted to excavate a cellar for Carrig (D) but found hard rock instead of the expected dirt. D then agreed to pay more for the labor involved in performing the excavation. Upon completion of the work, D refused to pay the additional sum, claiming that P was obligated under the initial contract and therefore the new contract had no consideration. P sued on the contract and won. D appeals.

Issue. May economic adversity be sufficient consideration to support a second contract?

Held. Yes. Judgment affirmed.

♦   D released his right as a creditor under the first contract and made a new one with P. This is analogous to the idea of a gift. There was an effective release of the obligation of P under the first contract. The promise of a special price for excavating rock necessarily imported a release or waiver of any right under the contract to hold P to the lower price that the contract stipulated. In mutual understanding the parties agreed that the contract price was not to control.

Comment. The contract could have been rescinded since something still was left to do. However, the court allowed what amounted to a partial rescission.

---

3. **Accord and Satisfaction.** An accord is a contract between a creditor and debtor for the settlement of the claim between them by some performance other than that which was originally contracted for. Satisfaction occurs upon performance of the accord. Payment of part of an undisputed debt is not a discharge. But where the claim is in dispute and the amount owed is uncer-

tain, a compromise in which the creditor accepts a partial satisfaction of the amount claimed is sufficient to discharge the claim. However, in order for there to be a discharge, the creditor must know he is being offered a full settlement. Generally, such compromises will be set aside only for fraud, mistake, or duress.

4. **Duress.** Duress is any wrongful act or threat by one contracting party that compels or induces through fear the other party to enter into a transaction against his will. While the courts look only at whether the victim exercised free will in entering into or assenting to the transaction, factors such as age, emotional nature, surrounding circumstances, etc., are considered.

    a. **Economic duress--**

Austin Instrument, Inc. v. Loral Corp., 272 N.E.2d 533 (N.Y. 1971).

Facts. Austin Instrument, Inc. (P) was a subcontractor to Loral Corp. (D) on a government contract under which D agreed to supply certain radar sets requiring precision gear components to be manufactured by P. During the course of the contract, D obtained a second contract and requested bids on additional gear components. When D notified P that it would receive a subcontract only for those items on which it was low bidder, P responded that it would cease deliveries of parts due under the existing subcontract unless D consented to substantial increases in the prices provided for by that agreement (both retroactively for parts already delivered and prospectively on those not yet shipped) and placed the order for the additional parts with P. When D was unable to locate a second source, it notified P, who had stopped deliveries, that it would consent to P's demands. D failed to pay P all amounts called for by the increased prices and P brought suit against D for such amounts. D also sued P for the excess charges and the suits were consolidated. From a judgment for P, D appeals.

Issue. Is a contract modification executed under threat of economic duress enforceable?

Held. No. Judgment reversed.

♦   A contract is voidable on the ground of duress when one party is forced to agree to the modification by means of a wrongful threat precluding the exercise of its free will. The existence of economic duress or business compulsion is demonstrated by proof that immediate possession of needful goods is threatened or that one party to a contract has threatened to breach the agreement by withholding goods unless the other party agrees to some further demand.

♦   However, threatened breach, without proof that the threatened party cannot obtain the goods from another source of supply, is inadequate to constitute economic duress. Here, P's threat to stop deliveries unless the prices were increased deprived D of its free will and constituted economic duress.

Dissent. The facts do not support D's contention in that, viewed most favorably to P, the "threat" was really only a request to accommodate the closing of its plant for a customary vacation period.

---

b.   Undue influence--

Odorizzi v. Bloomfield School District, 54 Cal. Rptr. 533 (Cal. Ct. App. 1966).

Facts. Odorizzi (P) was arrested for homosexual activities on June 10. On June 11, he resigned from his position as an elementary school teacher in response to statements from the school officials that if he did not resign, he would be dismissed and the charges against him would be publicized. In July, the criminal charges were dismissed. P sued the Bloomfield School District to rescind his resignation because it was obtained by duress and undue influence. The trial court dismissed P's complaint. P appeals.

Issue. May a threat of termination for cause, made to obtain a resignation, constitute undue influence?

Held. Yes. Judgment reversed.

♦   There was no duress in this case because D had a legal right to threaten to dismiss P, and even had a positive duty to do so. So long as D acted in good faith, it could properly start dismissal proceedings, regardless of the impact on P's reputation.

♦   Unlike duress, undue influence is persuasion that is coercive in nature, characterized by high pressure that works on mental, moral, or emotional weakness. Misrepresentation of law or fact is not essential to a determination of undue influence. Most reported cases of undue influence involve confidential relationships, but this is not an essential element where the undue influence involves unfair advantage taken of another's weakness or distress.

♦   A critical element of undue influence is a lessened capacity of one party to make a free contract. It involves an unfair advantage attributable to a mismatch between the parties. It is not merely hindsight that makes one party wish to escape a bad bargain.

♦   The elements of undue influence include: (i) discussion of the transaction at an unusual or inappropriate time; (ii) consummation of the transaction in an unusual place; (iii) insistent demand that the deal be done at once; (iv) extreme emphasis on serious consequences of delay; (v) the use of multiple persuaders by the dominant side against a single servient party; (vi) absence of third-party advisors to the servient party; and (vii) statements that there is no time to consult advisors. The more of these factors that are present, the more likely the persuasion may be characterized as excessive.

♦ In this case, D sought to secure P's signature on the resignation, not his consent to his resignation. It assured P it was trying to help him, that he should rely on its advice, and that there was not time to consult a lawyer. D also advised P that dire consequences would immediately follow if he did not sign, and that if he resigned, the incident would not prevent him from getting a teaching job somewhere else. These elements were sufficient to raise a question about whether D had used undue influence to secure P's resignation.

---

5. Concealment--

Swinton v. Whitinsville Savings Bank, 42 N.E.2d 808 (Mass. 1942).

Facts. Swinton (P) purchased a house from Whitinsville Savings Bank (D). The house was infested with termites at the time of purchase, and D did not disclose this fact to P. P did not ask about the termites. P was forced to repair the house at considerable expense and sued for damages. D demurred, and the demurrer was sustained. P appeals.

Issue. Is a seller liable for bare nondisclosure of material facts which affect the value of the property sold?

Held. No. Judgment affirmed.

♦ The rule placing the burden of discovery and inquiry on the buyer is affirmed. As long as D does not make affirmative representations relating to the defect, he is not liable for failure to disclose the defect.

Comment. There is substantial authority contrary to this case with regard to a seller's duty to give information to a purchaser about termite infestation. Also, some state laws provide, and institutional lenders generally require, a structural pest control clearance (or waiver thereof) in sales of personal residences.

---

6. Misrepresentation--

Kannavos v. Annino, 247 N.E.2d 708 (Mass. 1969).

Facts. Annino (D) purchased a residence and converted it into an eight-unit apartment in violation of city zoning restrictions. She decided to sell the property and listed it with a realtor who advertised the property as income property. Kannavos (P) contacted the realtor and received expense and income figures provided by D and purchased the property without the aid of a lawyer. The city began an action to abate the nonconforming use of the property, and P sued D for rescission. The trial court allowed rescission, and D appeals.

Issue. When a seller makes a representation, does he incur a responsibility to disclose the entire truth about the matter represented?

Held. Yes. Judgment affirmed.

♦ D's misrepresentation about the use of the property implied that the apartments could continue to be used as such in the future. D's representation created the confusion, and D cannot take advantage of that confusion at the expense of P. P did not use due diligence in discovering the defect, but this is no bar to an action for rescission based on fraud.

---

7. **Misrepresentation of Opinion as Fact--**

Vokes v. Arthur Murray, Inc., 212 So. 2d 906 (Fla. Dist. Ct. App. 1968).

Facts. Vokes (P), a widow without family, desired to become a dancer. She attended a "dance party" at a studio franchisee of Arthur Murray, Inc. (D). The owner praised P's skills and sold her eight introductory lessons for a total of $14.50. Subsequently, P purchased a succession of additional dance courses that totaled over $31,000, even though she had hundreds of unused lessons. D was influenced during her dance lessons by a constant barrage of flattery, false praise, and excessive compliments, and she was told that additional lessons would make her a beautiful dancer. In reality, P did not progress in her dancing ability and even had difficulty hearing the musical beat. P sued for rescission on the grounds of fraud and misrepresentation. The trial court dismissed P's claim for failure to state a cause of action. P appeals.

Issue. May a party's misrepresentation about its opinion of a customer's progress constitute actionable misrepresentation as if it involved a fact?

Held. Yes. Judgment reversed.

♦ To rescind a contract for misrepresentation, the misrepresentation normally must be one of material fact and not opinion. However, where there is a fiduciary relationship between the parties, where one party has tricked the other, where the parties do not deal at "arm's length," or where one party has greater opportunity to learn the truth or falsity of the fact represented, a statement of opinion may be treated as a statement of fact.

♦ In this case, a factfinder may conclude that D had superior knowledge regarding P's dance potential and the amount of her progress. D should have known that P's payment for hundreds of additional hours of instruction was not justified by her slow progress. In this situation, D's statements of opinion about these matters may be treated as statements of fact for purposes of misrepresentation.

———————————

V. DETERMINING THE PARTIES' OBLIGATIONS UNDER THE CONTRACT: ASCERTAINING, INTERPRETING, AND SUPPLEMENTING THE AGREEMENT

A. THE PAROL EVIDENCE RULE

1. **Statement of the Parol Evidence Rule.** Where an agreement has been reduced to writing which the parties intend as the final and complete expression of their agreement, evidence of any earlier oral or written expressions is not admissible to vary the terms of the writing.

2. **The Rationale.** The law favors written contracts (as more reliable). Note that the rule works as a law of evidence (indicating what evidence may be admitted) and as a rule of contract law (indicating what constitutes the contract between the parties).

3. **Determining Whether a Written Contract Is a Final and Complete Expression (*i.e.*, an "Integration").**

   a. **Tests used.** The parol evidence rule applies only where the parties intended the writing as a final expression of their agreement. There are two tests used.

      1) **Face of the agreement test.** The old view was that the parties' intent must be determined from the face of the agreement itself. Thus, if the written agreement appeared to be complete and final, no parol evidence could be admitted.

      2) **Any relevant evidence.** Many courts now hold that any evidence may be admitted to determine whether the parties intended the contract as a final and complete expression of the agreement.

   b. **Prior oral agreement excluded--**

Gianni v. R. Russell & Co., 126 A. 791 (Pa. 1924).

Facts. Gianni (P) operated a concession shop in an office building. R. Russell & Co. (D) acquired the property and signed P to a lease whereby P was allowed to sell "only fruit, candy, soda water, etc." but was prohibited, on the "penalty of instant forfeiture of the lease," from selling tobacco. D then leased an adjoining room to a drug company without a restriction on the sale of soda water and soft drinks. P, claiming that D had agreed to give P the sole right to sell soda in the building at the time of the lease negotiations, though such alleged agreement was not incorporated in the written lease, brought suit against D for breach of the alleged oral agreement in that D allowed the drug store to sell soda water. From a judgment for P, D appeals.

Issue. Is P allowed recovery on an oral agreement when no mention of the oral agreement is made in the subsequent written agreement?

Held. No. Judgment reversed.

♦ The writing, which was subsequent to the oral negotiations, and admittedly read by P and two others before P signed it, constitutes the entire contract. Here, it appears that P is attempting to reform the written document. The only instances in which the parol evidence rule may not apply to exclude prior oral agreements not incorporated in the subsequent writing are those in which fraud, accident, or mistake are involved.

Comment. Whether a prior oral agreement becomes a part of a contract is a question for the court.

---

c.   **Partially integrated agreement--**

Masterson v. Sine, 436 P.2d 561 (Cal. 1968).

Facts. Dallas and Rebecca Masterson (Ps) transferred real property to the Sines (Dallas's sister and her husband) (Ds) by deed, reserving an option to repurchase for the same consideration for a period of 10 years and to pay the depreciated value of the improvements. Dallas filed for bankruptcy, and his trustee and Rebecca brought this declaratory action to determine their right to exercise the option. The trial court admitted parol evidence to explain the meaning of consideration and depreciated value but excluded evidence indicating that the option was intended to keep the property in the family and was therefore nonassignable and not exercisable by the trustee in bankruptcy. Ds claimed that the option was too uncertain to be enforced and that extrinsic evidence as to its meaning should not have been admitted. The court entered judgment for Ps, and Ds appeal.

Issue. When a term is such that it must necessarily be included in the agreement, is the contract integrated with respect to the term?

Held. No. Judgment reversed in part.

♦ The parol testimony as to the limitation of assignment should have been admitted since that term would not necessarily have been included. The parol testimony as to the other terms was properly admitted to explain the meaning of terms not clear on the face of the instrument.

Dissent. California law implies the term that an option is assignable unless the contract expressly provides to the contrary. The restraint on assignment must therefore necessarily be included in the contract or be barred by the integration doctrine.

Comments.

♦ Chief Justice Traynor, in the above case, points out that the parol evidence rule must accommodate several policies. One policy is based on the assumption that written evidence is more accurate than human memory, though this policy can be adequately served by excluding parol evidence of agreements that directly contradict the writing. Another policy is based on the fear that fraud or unintentional invention by witnesses interested in the outcome of the litigation will mislead the finder of facts. Traynor further states that evidence of oral collateral agreements should be excluded only when the fact finder is likely to be misled and that the rule should therefore be based on the credibility of the evidence.

♦ The U.C.C. excludes such evidence in fewer instances. Comment 3 to section 2-202 provides that consistent additional terms not reduced to writing may be proved unless the court finds that the parties intended the writing to be a complete and exclusive statement of their agreement. Comment 3 further states that if the court finds the additional terms are such that, if agreed upon, they would *certainly* have been included in the document, then evidence of their alleged making must be kept from the trier of fact.

---

4. **Fraud, Duress, or Mistake.**

    a. **General rule.** Parol evidence may be admitted to show fraud, duress, or mistake in the formation of the contract.

    b. **Mutual mistake--**

Bollinger v. Central Pennsylvania Quarry Stripping and Construction Co., 229 A.2d 741 (Pa. 1967).

Facts. Bollinger (P) contracted to allow the disposal of waste from the construction of the Pennsylvania turnpike on their property. They alleged that the original oral agreement required Central Pennsylvania (D) to remove the topsoil, deposit the waste, and replace the topsoil. D followed this procedure for a while and then ceased doing it. P protested and was informed that the written contract did not require D to follow the sandwich procedure. P filed an action in equity to reform the contract and to enforce it as reformed. The trial court granted P relief, and D appeals.

Issue. May a court of equity reform a written contract when a provision is excluded by mutual mistake?

Held. Yes. Judgment affirmed.

♦ Evidence of the practice of D initially in removing and replacing the topsoil indicates that the provision was initially intended to be included. The fact that one of the parties changes his mind after the mistake is made is immaterial to P's right to reformation.

B. THE USE OF EXTRINSIC EVIDENCE OF THE PARTIES' INTENT

1. **Introduction.** Courts struggle with the appropriate determination of when a term is ambiguous. Most courts follow a two-stage approach, first determining whether the contract language is ambiguous. If it is not ambiguous, extrinsic evidence is not admissible, but if it is ambiguous, extrinsic evidence may be used to show the meaning. Some courts take a more liberal view so as to admit parol evidence more frequently, such as evidence of prior negotiations to show that the contract language is ambiguous.

2. **Ambiguity.** The subject of ambiguity is related to that of mistake. Ambiguity issues arise where the parties' expressions are susceptible to more than one interpretation, and thus there is uncertainty as to the meaning of the expressions.

3. **Types of Ambiguity.**

   a. **Latent ambiguity.** Here the terms appear certain, but because of extrinsic facts, more than one interpretation is possible.

   b. **Patent ambiguity.** Here the uncertainty is obvious. *Example*: A agrees to sell "my property" to B. Since the uncertainty is too great, there is no contract.

4. **Rules Governing Latent Ambiguity Problems.**

   a. **Where both parties are unaware of the ambiguity.** This is like a mutual mistake concerning a material fact. Since each party has a reasonable interpretation, and neither party knows of the other's interpretation or has reason to know of it, there is no contract.

    b.   **Where both parties are aware.** If both parties are aware of the ambiguity, then there is a contract only if they both agree on the same interpretation.

    c.   **Where only one party knows.** If one party knows or has reason to know that the words used are ambiguous, but the other party does not know, then there is a binding contract according to the interpretation of the innocent party.

  5.   **Extrinsic Evidence to Define Contract Terms--**

Pacific Gas & Electric Co. v. G. W. Thomas Drayage & Rigging Co., 442 P.2d 641 (Cal. 1968).

Facts. D contracted to replace a metal cover on P's steam turbine, agreeing to perform all of the work at its own risk and to indemnify P against all loss or liability arising from performance. D agreed to obtain an insurance policy covering liability for injury to property. The liability clause indicated that only third-party property was covered, but P argues that the intention was to cover its property as well. During the work, P's property was damaged; P sues to recover. D argues that its prior contracts with P indicate that only third-party property was to be covered and that admissions of P's agents indicate that this was to be the case. The trial court found for P and denied admission of D's evidence.

Issue. May D offer parol evidence to show the meaning of terms of a contract where the language of the contract is susceptible to the interpretation argued for by D?

Held. Yes. Judgment reversed for D.

♦   Evidence as to the meaning of a term of a contract must be admitted if the language of the contract is reasonably susceptible to the meaning argued for by the evidence.

♦   Extrinsic evidence may only be excluded when it is feasible to determine the meaning of words from the instrument itself; this is seldom the case since language is often inexact in conveying the intention of the parties.

Comment. In *Delta Dynamics, Inc. v. Arioto*, 446 P.2d 785 (Cal. 1968), the court allowed extrinsic evidence to show whether a termination provision was an exclusive remedy. A separate contract provision allowed recovery of attorneys' fees "in any action for damages."

---

6. Extrinsic Evidence Not Considered Where Contract Is Unambiguous--

Greenfield v. Philles Records, Inc., 780 N.E.2d 166 (N.Y. 2002).

Facts. Ronnie Greenfield, her sister, and her cousin (Ps) formed "The Ronettes," a singing group. They signed an exclusive five-year music recording contract with Phil Spector's production company, Philles Records, Inc. (D), that gave D ownership rights to Ps' recordings, free of any claims by Ps. Despite recording a song that sold over a million copies, "Be My Baby," Ps never received any royalties, only an initial advance of $15,000. Greenfield and Spector married but later divorced and executed mutual releases. D licensed master recordings of Ps' vocal performances for use in movie and television productions, a process known as "synchronization," including the song "Be My Baby" for use in the movie "Dirty Dancing." D also licensed master recordings to third parties for production and distribution in the United States (known as domestic redistribution) and sold compilation albums containing performances by Ps. Again, D did not pay royalties to Ps. Ps sued, claiming that the original agreement did not give D the right to license the master recordings for synchronization and domestic redistribution, and demanding royalties from the sales of compilation albums. The trial court awarded Ps $3 million in damages and interest. The appellate division affirmed, finding that the contract did not specifically give D the right to issue synchronization and redistribution licenses, and the court allowed Ps to assert a claim for unjust enrichment. D appeals.

Issue. If a recording contract conveys ownership of recordings "free of any claims" by the artist but does not explicitly authorize use of master recordings in new markets or mediums, is the contract ambiguous enough to require extrinsic evidence to determine the parties' intent?

Held. No. Judgment affirmed as modified and case remanded.

♦　　D claims that although the contract did not specifically refer to synchronization and domestic redistribution, the contract did grant full ownership rights to the vocal performances. Therefore, the only restriction on D's rights should be those explicitly enumerated by the artist. Since Ps did not reserve any rights, D should have no restrictions on the use of the recordings.

♦　　The fundamental principle of contract interpretation is that agreements must be construed in accord with the parties' intent. If a written agreement is complete, clear, and unambiguous on its face, it must be enforced according to the plain meaning of its terms. In this case, the contract is not ambiguous. The advent of unanticipated technological innovations does not make the contract ambiguous. Therefore, the contract must be enforced as written. D may exercise complete ownership rights, subject to paying Ps the royalties specified in the contract.

♦　　D claims that Greenfield's release in connection with the divorce bars her from receiving royalties, but that release is governed by California law, where the release was executed and the divorce was finalized. California does not apply the New York "four corners" rule, but considers all credible evidence of the parties' intent, in addition to the language of the contract. The lower courts accepted Greenfield's extrinsic evidence that the recording contract was not an intended subject of the release she signed with Spector, so she is entitled to recover on the same basis as the other members of the group.

---

7. **Extrinsic Evidence Not Admissible to Create Ambiguity.** *W.W.W. Associates, Inc. v. Giancontieri*, 566 N.E.2d 639 (N.Y. 1990), involved a reciprocal cancellation provision in a contract to sell real property. The contract clearly manifested an intention that both the plaintiff and the defendant had the right to cancel. There was no ambiguity as to the cancellation clause. The plaintiff claimed that extrinsic evidence should have been considered to create an ambiguity in the agreement. The court stated that the rule excluding use of extrinsic evidence for this purpose is well settled. Other provisions in the contract gave the plaintiff certain options, but the cancellation provision gave both parties the right to cancel. The court reasoned that resorting to extrinsic evidence to create an ambiguity would denigrate the contract and unsettle the law.

8. **California Rule--**

Trident Center v. Connecticut General Life Insurance Co., 847 F.2d 564 (9th Cir. 1988).

Facts. Trident Center (P), a partnership created by two law firms and an insurance company, obtained a loan of $56 million from Connecticut General Life Insurance Co. (D). The promissory note bore interest at 12.25% and specified that P "shall not have the right to prepay the principal amount hereof in whole or in part" for the first 12 years. In the event of default, D had the option of accelerating the note and adding a 10% prepayment fee. After a few years, market interest rates dropped and P sought to refinance the loan. D refused to allow early prepayment. P sued, claiming that it was entitled to prepay the loan subject only to the 10% prepayment fee. D removed the suit to federal court and brought a motion to dismiss. The federal district court dismissed P's complaint and sanctioned P for filing a frivolous lawsuit. P appeals.

Issue. Can parties in California draft a contract that precludes use of parol evidence to determine its terms?

Held. No. Judgment reversed and case remanded.

♦ P claims that the contract is ambiguous, despite the clear language, because of the prepayment penalty clause connected with a default. However, the contract is clear on the issue of prepayment and is unambiguous on the point that P cannot prepay the principal.

♦   P claims that under California law, as set forth in *Pacific Gas & Electric Co. v. G.W. Thomas Drayage & Rigging Co.*, *supra*, even contracts that appear unambiguous cannot be rendered impervious to attack by parol evidence. Under traditional contract law, extrinsic evidence is not admissible when the contract is unambiguous, as this one is. However, California courts have rejected the traditional rule in favor of a rule that a contract is not based on the words of the contract, but on the intention of the parties. The California Supreme Court has concluded that words do not have absolute and constant referents, and a judicial belief in the possibility of perfect verbal expression is erroneous.

♦   Therefore, in California, courts must consider extrinsic evidence of possible ambiguity. Once such evidence raises the possibility of ambiguity, the parties may offer evidence of their intentions, despite the contract language. On remand, the court must give P an opportunity to present extrinsic evidence of the parties' intentions when they drafted the contract.

Comment. The Ninth Circuit was highly critical of the California rule. "While this rule creates much business for lawyers and an occasional windfall to some clients, it leads only to frustration and delay for most litigants. . . . It also chips away at the foundation of our legal system."

C. THE USE OF EXTRINSIC EVIDENCE FROM COMMERCIAL CONTEXT

Parol evidence is admissible to show any special meanings attached to words used in the written agreement which derive from custom or usage in a particular industry. The U.C.C. also provides that parol evidence may be admitted to interpret special meanings attached by virtue of previous dealings between the parties under other contracts or by virtue of their course of performance under the current contract.

1.   Subjective Meaning of Contract Term--

Frigaliment Importing Co. v. B.N.S. International Sales Corp., 190 F. Supp. 116 (S.D.N.Y. 1960).

Facts. B.N.S. International Sales Corp. (D) contracted to sell "chicken" to Frigaliment Importing Co. (P). D shipped stewing chicken ("fowl") under both contracts instead of the broiling and frying chicken desired by P. P sues for breach of warranty.

Issue. To enforce a particular meaning of a common term used in a contract, must P prove either D's actual knowledge of the particular meaning or a widespread, universal usage in the particular manner asserted?

Held. Yes. Judgment for D.

♦   The making of a contract depends not on the agreement of two minds on one intention, but on the agreement of two sets of external signs. What the parties said, not what they meant, is the essence of the contract.

♦   P produces substantial evidence that its narrow usage of the word "chicken" is common. D, however, shows that it is relatively new in the business, did not know of this trade usage, and that in fact "chicken" is commonly used in the trade in its broadest sense, covering broilers, fryers, and stewing chickens or "fowl." Furthermore, D shows that by comparing the market price and the contract price, D would have incurred a loss by shipping broilers. Thus, D believed it could properly send "fowl." P believed it would receive broilers, but P fails to meet its burden of proving that "chicken" was to be used in the narrower rather than the broader sense.

---

2.   **Interpretation of Contract Terms--**

Hurst v. W. J. Lake Co., 16 P.2d 627 (Or. 1932).

Facts. Hurst (P) supplied 350 tons of horse meat scraps to W.J. Lake Co. (D) under a written agreement that called for the price to be $50 per ton for scraps analyzing 50% protein and $45 per ton for scraps analyzing less than 50% protein. One hundred forty tons analyzed between 49.53% and 49.96% protein, for which D paid only $45 per ton. P claims trade usage imputes 49.5% to be 50% and demands $50 per ton for the 140 tons analyzing above 49.5%. D claims 50% means 50%. From a judgment for D, P appeals.

Issue. May trade custom or usage be used to interpret the meaning of contract terms?

Held. Yes. Judgment reversed.

♦   In dealings between tradesmen, the meanings of the terms of the trade should take precedence. Parol evidence is admissible in order to explain the trade meanings. It was established in the pleadings that 49.5% was used in the trade as the lowest percentage included within the 50% protein term.

D. THE USE OF EXTRINSIC EVIDENCE TO SUPPLEMENT OR QUALIFY THE AGREEMENT: COURSE OF DEALING, USAGE OF TRADE, AND COURSE OF PERFORMANCE

1. Implied Duty to Act in Accordance with Trade Usage--

Nanakuli Paving & Rock Co. v. Shell Oil Co., 664 F.2d 772 (9th Cir. 1981).

Facts. Nanakuli Paving & Rock Co. (P) was an asphalt paver that bought all of its asphalt requirements from Shell Oil Co. (D). The supply contracts between P and D specified that the price would be D's posted price at the time of delivery. However, all material suppliers to the asphalt paving industry followed a trade practice of price protection, whereby suppliers would charge pavers the price in effect when the pavers bid on the particular project involved. Most contracts were with government agencies that did not permit escalation clauses. On two prior occasions, D in fact provided price protection for P by extending the old price for four months and then three months. However, D suddenly raised the price of asphalt from $44 to $76 after P already had a contract for which it needed 7,200 tons of asphalt. P sued, claiming D breached its contract. The jury found for P, but the trial court granted judgment n.o.v. P appeals.

Issue. May a contract term that specifically provides for a price to be established as of the date of delivery be modified by the trade usage and course of performance of the parties?

Held. Yes. Judgment reversed and jury verdict reinstated.

♦ The evidence presented at trial showed that asphalt suppliers routinely protected pavers from price changes. The suppliers would give advance notice of price increases, and would charge the old price for work committed at that price. The system worked because the market was so small.

♦ D claims that the trade usage should extend only to sellers of asphalt, of which there were only two: D and Chevron. However, usage of trade is not limited to one practiced by members of the party's own trade, if it is so commonly practiced in a locality that a party should be aware of it. D constantly dealt with P in a small market and should have been aware of P's practice of making fixed price bids based on price protection from suppliers. The definition of trade to include all suppliers was not incorrect. In addition, the practice was virtually universal and D could not show one instance of a supplier's failing to price protect a paver before its own failure to do so.

♦ D also claims that its two instances of giving P price protection do not constitute a course of performance. While it is a general rule that one instance does not constitute a course of performance, two instances may do so, especially when they were the only two occasions that necessitated such conduct. Nor were these two instances waivers as a matter of law. The jury could determine whether they were simply waivers of the contract terms or actually a course of performance of the contract. The jury's findings are supported by the evidence.

♦ D argues that the express terms are inconsistent with the usage in course of performance. Under the U.C.C., the parties' agreement may go beyond the written words; it may be found by implication from other circumstances such as course of dealing and usage of trade. The latter are not binding only if they cannot be reasonably reconciled with the express contract terms. The price protection usage was not a total negation of the price-setting term, as would be, for example, a usage that the buyer set the price. While the usage is a broad exception to that term, it does not eliminate it entirely. For that reason, the jury could have found that price protection was reasonably consistent with the express price term.

♦ D had a duty to act in good faith, specifically a duty to fix a price in good faith. [U.C.C. §2-305(2)] While a posted price normally satisfies this requirement, D's manner of carrying out the price increase did not comply with commercially reasonable standards. D did not give appropriate advance notice and did not price protect P.

Concurrence. The practice of price protection was a well-established one which the parties knew, or should have known, about. This case does not stand for a general rule that good faith requires price protection.

---

2. **Usage of Trade to Supplement a Contract--**

Columbia Nitrogen Corp. v. Royster Co., 451 F.2d 3 (4th Cir. 1971).

Facts. Royster Co. (P) contracted to sell a minimum of 31,000 tons of phosphate each year for three years to Columbia Nitrogen Corp. (D). The contract stated the price per ton, subject to an escalation clause related to production costs. The market price of phosphate soon dropped greatly, and D ordered less than one-tenth of the contract amount, although it would have ordered the full amount at the current market price. P sold the phosphate elsewhere at a price significantly below the contract price, and sued for breach of contract. D tried unsuccessfully to introduce evidence on usage of trade and course of dealing between the parties, and the district court gave P a judgment for $750,000. D appeals.

Issue. May evidence of usage of trade and course of dealing be admitted to show that a specific contract price was not to be binding on the parties?

Held. Yes. Judgment reversed.

♦ Although the general rule is that extrinsic evidence may not be used to explain an unambiguous contract, U.C.C. section 2-202 authorizes evidence of usage of trade and course of dealing between the parties to explain or supplement a contract. Therefore, a finding of ambiguity is not a prerequisite to the admission of such extrinsic evidence.

♦ P claims the evidence should be excluded because it is inconsistent with the express terms of the complete contract. The test of admissibility is not completeness but whether the evidence can reasonably be construed as consistent. The contract does not prohibit use of such extrinsic evidence. Adherence to the U.C.C. provisions reflects the reality of the marketplace and avoids overly legalistic interpretations.

Comment. *See* U.C.C. §§1-205, 2-208, and 2-209.

E. OBJECTIVE INTERPRETATION AND ITS LIMITS

1. Latent Ambiguity--

Raffles v. Wichelhaus, 159 Eng. Rep. 375 (Ex. 1864).

Facts. D agreed to buy 125 bales of cotton to be shipped by P to England from India aboard the ship "Peerless." There were two ships named "Peerless," which set sail from Bombay, one in October and one in December. When the cloth did not arrive on the first ship, D refused to accept delivery, indicating he meant the "Peerless" leaving Bombay in October, not the different ship "Peerless" leaving in December. P sues for breach of contract.

Issue. Where the contract is subject to two equally possible interpretations and the parties contracted with different interpretations in mind (neither knowing of the other's interpretation, nor having reason to know thereof), is there mutual assent?

Held. No. Judgment for D.

♦ When a term used to express an agreement is ambivalent and the parties understand it differently, and neither of them is aware of the other's understanding, there can be no contract.

♦ There was a latent ambiguity in the contract; the contract did not indicate which "Peerless" was intended, each party had a different interpretation, and neither knew of the other's interpretation. Here, there is no contract because there is no meeting of the minds.

Comments.

- In determining whether there is mutual assent, the test to be applied (with a few exceptions noted *supra*) is the objective theory of contracts—*i.e.,* what a reasonable person in the position of each of the respective parties would be led to believe by the words or conduct of the other party. Whenever there is a dispute concerning whether a contract exists (*i.e.,* whether there has been assent by each party), the issue must be decided on the basis of objective events; *i.e.,* how the actions and words of each party would appear to an objective, reasonable observer. This is necessary because no one can really tell what is in the mind of another person; if subjective intent were the test, then whenever a contract did not work out as anticipated by a party, that party would claim he had no intent to contract (in order to get out of the contract). Contract law is designed, therefore, to uphold the reasonable expectations of a party in relying on another's apparent promise. Reasonableness is determined by what the other party apparently meant to communicate (without regard to his secret thoughts or intent).

- The rule of *Raffles v. Wichelhaus* was followed in a case where one party desired not to go through with the deal. In *Oswald v. Allen*, 417 F.2d 43 (2d Cir. 1969), Oswald was a coin dealer who examined Allen's coin collections. He first examined Allen's "Swiss Coin Collection," then looked at valuable Swiss coins from Allen's "Rarity Coin Collection." Oswald did not realize these coins were from a separate collection. Oswald offered to purchase what he thought were all of Allen's Swiss coins, but what she thought was only her Swiss coin collection. Subsequently, Allen decided not to complete the sale. The court held that the agreement was not enforceable under *Raffles v. Wichelhaus* because there was no sensible basis for choosing between the conflicting understandings of the parties.

---

2.   Risk of Contrary Interpretation--

Colfax Envelope Corp. v. Local No. 458-3M, 20 F.3d 750 (7th Cir. 1994).

Facts. Colfax Envelope Corp. (P), an envelope manufacturer, had 17 employees who did the printing of its envelopes, all of whom were represented by Local No. 458-3M (D). P had two printing presses. One printed 78-inch-wide sheets in four colors. The other printed 78-inch-wide sheets in five colors, but P usually printed only four-color sheets. The collective bargaining agreements specified minimum manning requirements for the presses. P was required to have four workers on each of its presses (five men on the rare occasions when it printed five-color sheets). D submitted a summary of a new agreement that listed "4C 60 Press—3 Men" and "5C 78 Press—4 Men." Because P understood this to mean that its four-color presses would only require three workers to man them, P signed the summary. The actual agreement was later sent to P, and it contained a typo that verified P's interpretation. A subsequent corrected version required that all four-color presses over 60 inches, which P's were, be manned by four workers. P refused to sign the agreement. P then sued under the Taft-Hartley Act for a declaration that it had no collective bargaining contract with D because the parties had not agreed on an essential term. The district court granted summary judgment for D on the ground that the summary referred unambiguously to 60-inch presses and therefore could not apply to P's 78-inch presses. The court ordered arbitration of the dispute as required by the contract. P appeals.

Issue. If parties agree to contract terms containing a latent ambiguity, may the court or the arbitrator find that there was no meeting of the minds and rescind the contract?

Held. Yes. Judgment affirmed for submission to arbitration.

♦   If a contract contains an arbitration clause, disputes over the meaning of a contractual term is a matter for the arbitrator to decide. However, if the dispute between the parties is deep enough, they may have never agreed and therefore do not even have a contract to interpret.

♦   In this case, the parties disagree about the meaning of the term "4C 60 Press—3 Men." P claims that it means four-color presses, 60 inches and over, while D claims that it means four-color presses, 60 inches and under. This is like *Raffles v. Wichelhaus*, *supra*, in which the parties did not know there were two ships named Peerless, and each was thinking of a different ship when they wrote the contract. The court in that case held that there was no contract because there was no "meeting of the minds."

♦   Contract disputes usually arise because the parties did not provide for a contingency, so there was no meeting of the minds. These are treated as disputes over contractual meaning, not as grounds for rescinding the contract. But in a case such as *Raffles*, there is no basis for choosing between conflicting understandings of the language in the contract. Neither party can be assigned the greater blame for the mistake. There is no reasonable resolution short of abandoning the contract without liability.

♦   The difference between this case and those like *Raffles* is that P should have realized the contract was unclear. The expression "4C 60 Press" does not on its face refer to P's 4C 78 Press. P could hope that its interpretation was the same as D's, but it could not accept the offer on the premise that either P's interpretation was correct or else it could repudiate the contract. In effect, P gambled on being able to convince an arbitrator that its meaning was correct, and D gambled on being able to persuade an arbitrator that its meaning was correct.

♦   When parties include a patently ambiguous term in a contract, they subject themselves to having disputes resolved by interpretation by an arbitrator or court. But when parties agree to terms in which the ambiguity is buried, the possibility of rescission on grounds of mutual misunderstanding, or latent ambiguity, arises. Here, the arbitrator is responsible for interpreting the contract and deciding if the contract should be rescinded because there was no meeting of the minds between P and D regarding the manning requirements.

Comment. Judge Posner later wrote that rescission is appropriate when neither party is blamable or both parties are equally blamable, except where rescission would result in a windfall to one party.

F. SUPPLEMENTING THE AGREEMENT WITH TERMS SUPPLIED BY LAW: GAP FILLERS, WARRANTIES, AND MANDATORY TERMS

1. **Introduction.** Often a contract, even when interpreted in accordance with the applicable rules, will leave gaps in expressing the rights and duties of the parties. In such cases, courts may supply the missing terms. In *Wood v. Lucy, Lady Duff-Gordon, supra*, a promise to use reasonable efforts was implied, although it was not expressly included in the relevant writings. Terms supplied by a court are implied in law, in contrast to terms that are supplied through interpretation of the parties' words or conduct (implied in fact).

2. **U.C.C. Implied Warranties.** Under the implied warranty of merchantability, a merchant seller warrants, by implication, that goods sold are "merchantable," meaning that they meet basic standards, including fitness for their ordinary purposes. [U.C.C. §2-314] Under the implied warranty of fitness for a particular purpose, if a seller has reason to know that the buyer intends to use the good for a particular purpose and that the buyer is relying on the seller to select suitable goods, the seller warrants by implication that the goods are fit for a particular purpose. [U.C.C. §2-315]

   a. **Reasonable expectations of ordinary user--**

Koken v. Black & Veatch Construction, Inc., 426 F.3d 39 (1st Cir. 2005).

Facts. Black & Veatch Construction, Inc. (P1) was the general contractor on a construction project that was insured by Reliance Insurance Co. (P2) (with Koken acting on its behalf as liquidator). A torch-cutting operation led to a fire that was quickly extinguished, but chemicals in the extinguisher caused $9 million in damage to a generator. A fire blanket, which was manufactured by Auburn Manufacturing, Inc. and distributed by Inpro, Inc. (Ds), had been used to protect the area beneath the welding. Ps sued Ds for breach of warranty. The district court granted summary judgment for Ds. Ps appeal.

Issue. In a claim for breach of the implied warranty of merchantability, must the plaintiff prove that the product did not perform according to the reasonable expectations of an ordinary user?

Held. Yes. Judgment affirmed.

♦ Ps appear to base their claim against Ds on a breach of the implied warranty of merchantability. Ds are merchants of fire blankets, but Ps bear the burden of establishing the ordinary purpose of the fire blanket.

♦ Austin, the welder who was doing the cutting, testified that he was surprised the blanket melted. This is merely the subjective expectation of a particular user and is not on point. Ps had the obligation to prove the reasonable expectations of an ordinary user. Ps failed to meet their burden. In fact, other witnesses testified that the blanket performed as expected. The district court found that Ps offered no evidence regarding the expectations of an ordinary user. Therefore, the district court properly granted summary judgment.

---

b. Implied warranty of fitness for a particular purpose--

Lewis v. Mobil Oil Corp., 438 F.2d 500 (8th Cir. 1971).

Facts. Lewis (P), a sawmill operator, purchased a used hydraulic system for his mill. As a long-time customer of Mobil Oil Corporation (D), P asked Rowe, his Mobil dealer, for the proper hydraulic fluid for his equipment. Rowe provided straight mineral oil with no chemical additives. The system broke down, but Rowe assured P that he was using the right oil. P installed a new system and continued using D's oil. P continued having problems until another representative of D came and recommended an oil containing chemical additives. P sued D for breach of the warranty of fitness. The jury found for P and awarded $89,250 in damages. D appeals.

Issue. Does an implied warranty of fitness for a particular purpose arise when a buyer relies on a seller's expertise in specifying and supplying products for the buyer's equipment?

Held. Yes. Judgment affirmed.

♦ D claims that there was no warranty of fitness in this case. However, Rowe knew that P was using a hydraulic system and repeatedly assured P that the oil was the right kind. Rowe testified that he did not know what oil was correct and relied on his superior in D's organization, who recommended the oil Rowe sold to P.

- Under the U.C.C., there are two requirements for an implied warranty of fitness: (i) the seller must have "reason to know" the use for which the goods are purchased, and (ii) the buyer must rely on the seller's expertise in supplying the proper product. These requirements were met by the facts in this case. Rowe knew that P was purchasing D's oil for P's specific hydraulic system and was relying on Rowe's expertise.

- D claims that P did not specify that he needed an oil with additives and that he did not provide enough information for D to know that an additive oil was required. However, if a seller has reason to know the purpose intended for a product and that the buyer relies on the seller's skill and judgment, the buyer does not have to reiterate this. P made it clear that the oil was purchased for his system, that he did not know what oil he should use, and that he was relying on D to supply the proper product. If D needed further information to make a recommendation, D should have sought such information.

- Finally, D asserts that even if there was an implied warranty of fitness, it would not apply here because P's system included abnormal features such as an inadequate filtration system. However, there is no evidence that P's system was abnormal. It operated satisfactorily under the prior owner, and the new system has operated satisfactorily with the additive oil. Furthermore, even if there were peculiarities in P's system, the reason for an implied warranty of fitness is that a product be suitable for a specific purpose.

---

c. **Warranty disclaimer--**

South Carolina Electric and Gas Co. v. Combustion Engineering, Inc., 322 S.E.2d 453 (S.C. Ct. App. 1984).

Facts. South Carolina Electric and Gas Co. (P) purchased a boiler unit from Combustion Engineering, Inc. (D). The sales contract included a warranty that the equipment was free from defects in material and workmanship for a period of one year. Other provisions disclaimed any other warranties, express or implied. P began operating the boiler in March 1973. In May 1975, a flexible metal hose ruptured and caused a fire that caused P more than $350,000 in damages. P sued for breach of implied warranties and negligence. The trial court granted D summary judgment, holding that the disclaimer excluded an implied warranty of merchantability and an implied warranty of fitness for a particular purpose. P appeals.

Issue. Where a warranty disclaimer does not satisfy the statutory requirements of South Carolina Code of Law section 36-2-316(2) (U.C.C. section 2-316(2)), may it still be effective if the evidence shows that the buyer was made aware of the exclusion of warranties?

Held. Yes. Judgment affirmed.

♦   The disclaimer in this case does not satisfy the requirements of South Carolina Code of Law section 36-2-316(2). The disclaimer does not mention the word merchantability, so it is not effective in excluding an implied warranty of merchantability. It is not conspicuous, as it must be to exclude implied warranties of merchantability and fitness for a particular purpose. Also, the heading for the provision is "WARRANTY," which suggests a grant of warranty instead of a disclaimer.

♦   Despite these defects in the contract, D points to correspondence between the parties that discussed the warranty issue. P requested implied warranties, but D wrote that it could not accept such warranties and that it required a limitation on the warranty period. P responded that it agreed that implied warranties would be limited to the warranty in the original proposal.

♦   The warranty language in the contract is unambiguous in excluding all warranties other than the express one-year warranty and the warranty of title, so there is no reason to decide whether the correspondence is part of the contract. However, the correspondence does help the determination of whether the language of the disclaimer was unbargained for and unexpected. Under South Carolina Code of Law section 36-2-316(3), implied warranties may be excluded if the circumstances surrounding the transaction are sufficient to call the buyer's attention to the fact that no implied warranties are made or that a certain implied warranty is excluded.

♦   In this case, the correspondence shows that the disclaimer in the contract was bargained for and expected by P. The disclaimer was not a surprise to P, and P bargained with D for seven months over it. Therefore, even though the disclaimer does not satisfy the requirements of section 36-2-316(2), it does satisfy the requirements of section 36-2-316(3).

---

      d.   Disclaimer of implied warranty--

Henningsen v. Bloomfield Motors, Inc., 161 A.2d 69 (N.J. 1960).

Facts. Henningsen (P) bought a new car from Bloomfield Motors, Inc. (D), a dealer. P's wife was injured shortly thereafter when the car veered and crashed into a brick wall. P sued D and Chrysler Corporation for damages on the theory of implied warranty of merchantability. D defended based on small print in the purchase contract which stated that there were no warranties except as to defective parts. Judgment for P. D appeals.

Issue. Will a provision in the sales contract exculpating D from liability under implied warranty be upheld?

Held. No. Judgment affirmed.

♦ Normally there is freedom of contract between parties. However, courts will declare void as against public policy any contractual provision that tends toward injury of the public.

♦ Here the disclaimer was insufficient to indicate to a reasonable person that he was giving up personal injury claims if the car had a defect. The parties occupied totally unequal bargaining positions, and P could not go to a competitor since all car dealers had similar contract provisions.

♦ Further, the state legislature has passed a law granting an implied warranty of merchantability for cars. Here D's contract provision is an attempt to avoid such public policy. This attempt is void since it is against the public policy of protection of consumers in the purchase of a dangerous instrument.

———————

VI. LIMITS ON THE BARGAIN AND ITS PERFORMANCE

A. UNFAIRNESS

1. **Requirement of Good Faith.** Courts read all contracts as containing an implied condition that the parties will act in good faith and will not hinder or prevent the other party from performing under the contract. Thus, if A has a duty to perform under a contract with B and B in bad faith hinders A from performing, the condition of "good faith" means that A's duty to perform is excused, since the implied condition precedent to A's duty to perform (that B will act in good faith) has not been performed; thus, A's duty to perform has not become absolute.

   a. **U.C.C. section 1-203.** Every contract or duty within the U.C.C. imposes an obligation of good faith in its performance or enforcement.

   b. **Restatement (Second) section 231.** Under the Restatement, every contract imposes upon each party a duty of good faith and fair dealing in its performance.

2. **Consideration.** In order for a valid contract to exist, there must be a mutual agreement (an offer and acceptance) and consideration (or some substitute for consideration). There are two essential factors in consideration:

   a. **The bargain element.** In order for there to be sufficient consideration, each party to the contract must have intended to secure something from the other party that he was otherwise not legally entitled to—that is, each must be bargaining for something from the other party (an act, a promise to act, etc.).

   b. **The value element.** The second requirement for valid consideration is that the bargained-for element be legally sufficient.

      1) **Tests for legal sufficiency.**

         a) **Legal detriment.** The majority view is that the bargained-for act, forbearance, or return promise must impose a legal detriment on the party (A) who is to perform the act or who gives the return promise. If the act or return promise merely confers a benefit on the promisor (B), the majority holds that this is not sufficient consideration for B's promise.

         b) **Legal benefit.** However, some courts hold that if either a legal detriment is laid on the promisee (A) or a benefit is conferred on the promisor (B), there is sufficient consideration for the promisor's (B's) promise.

2) The adequacy of consideration.

a) General rule.
The exchange need not be fair; that is, what is given by one party (A) need not be of the same value as what is given by the other party (B).

(1) Legal consideration.
The courts are only interested in whether or not there is a "legal detriment" or a "legal benefit" (something of adequate legal value).

(2) Commercial value.
Normally a court will not inquire into the adequacy of consideration in terms of commercial value since it wants the parties to make their own contract, each party determining what is valuable to him. However, there are certain exceptions.

(3) Exception—equitable relief.
Where the plaintiff seeks specific performance of the contract (*i.e.,* P asks for equitable relief), equity requires a showing of fairness before it will enforce the contract.

(a) Overreaching--

McKinnon v. Benedict, 157 N.W.2d 665 (Wis. 1968).

Facts. McKinnon (P) owned a large tract of land in a resort area and assisted Benedict (D) in purchasing a neighboring tract by providing $5,000 interest-free and promising to assist D in making the resort business a success. D was not to cut timber on a section of his property and was not to build any structure closer to P's property than those that existed when the property was purchased. The loan was repaid within seven months and P provided little assistance, so D bulldozed a portion of his property to allow its use as a tent and trailer camp. P sued for an injunction. D appeals from the injunction preventing further construction and use.

Issue. Where there is evidence of overreaching by one of the parties, may the court examine the adequacy of the consideration?

Held. Yes. Judgment reversed.

♦   D could not have purchased the property without P's assistance and was therefore unable to deal at arm's length with P. The law does not favor restrictions on the use of land, and in this case the restrictions impose a significant burden on D's property while potential damage to P's property is slight. The reasonable value of the $5,000 for seven months was slight in comparison with the restraints imposed on D's property.

(b) Services as consideration--

Tuckwiller v. Tuckwiller, 413 S.W.2d 274 (Mo. 1967).

Facts. Mrs. Tuckwiller (P) rented a farm half-owned by Mrs. Morrison. Mrs. Morrison contracted Parkinson's disease and returned to the farm. She asked P to care for her for the rest of her life and promised, in exchange, to will her the farm. Before Mrs. Morrison could change her will, which directed that the property be sold and the funds used for a student loan fund at Davidson College, she died. P brought suit for specific performance of the contract against the college and the decedent's executor (D). From a grant of relief for P, D appeals.

Issue. Is a contract to provide personal care in return for an inheritance sufficiently fair and equitable and supported by adequate consideration to permit specific performance?

Held. Yes. Judgment affirmed.

♦   P gave up her employment to undertake an obligation unknown and uncertain in duration involving duties which would have become increasingly onerous. Further, decedent insisted that the contract be witnessed prior to her hospitalization for her last illness. The court stated that the contract was fair, not unconscionable, and supported by adequate consideration.

♦   Although prior services cannot provide the consideration essential to a binding contract, such prior services and the past relation of the parties may properly be considered in connection with the fairness of the contract and the adequacy of the consideration. While the services provided by P were of a brief duration and therefore slight in value in comparison with the value of the farm, the obligation to care for Mrs. Morrison for the remainder of her life was fair and adequate consideration.

---

3)   "Excessive" consideration--

Black Industries, Inc. v. Bush, 110 F. Supp. 801 (D.N.J. 1953).

Facts. Black Industries, Inc. (P) agreed to supply certain items to third parties for ultimate delivery to the United States Government. P contracted with Bush (D) to manufacture these parts for such resale by P. The compensation to P was to be the difference between P's purchase price from D and its sale price to the third parties. D was to ship directly to the third parties, but P was to handle all paperwork and be responsible for differences between D's price and P's ultimate selling price to the third parties. P's profits ranged from 39.13% to 84.09% on the various items. When D failed to deliver the items, P sued D, alleging lost profits of $19,000. D defended on the basis that P's contracts were against public policy as the profits were excessive during the time of the Korean War and moved for summary judgment on this ground.

Issue. Is a contract void as against public policy if one party's profits are excessive?

Held. No. Motion for summary judgment denied.

♦   Neither P nor D had dealings with the United States Government by virtue of the contract between them, and the profits were therefore not received as a result of inducing governmental action or interfering with the system of competitive bidding. The contract is therefore not void as against public policy. The profits were legitimate. The relative values of the consideration in a contract where there is no fraud or deceit will not affect its validity.

Comment. If one party gets the best of the bargain, it is of no consequence unless there is fraud, collusion, or deceit. In general, courts should not look to the equality of the bargain, although such matter has become an issue when one party seeks specific performance as an equitable remedy.

B.   STANDARD FORM AND ADHESION CONTRACTS

1.   **Adhesion Contracts.** An adhesion contract is one where the parties occupy substantially unequal bargaining positions and the inferior party, in order to obtain some essential item or service, is forced to "adhere" to the terms dictated by the superior party. The distinguishing feature of an adhesion contract is this substantial disparity in the respective bargaining positions of the parties, which causes the party in the inferior position to accept the contract "as is" if she wants to make a deal, notwithstanding its unfairness or one-sided provisions favoring the superior party. Typically, loan agreements, residential leases, insurance policies, employment agency contracts, and shipment and bailment agreements fall into the adhesion contract category.

   a.   **Standard form contracts.** Because of their practical utility in controlling or excluding business risks and in minimizing negotiating time, preprinted standard form contracts have become commonplace in the business world. Often, however, such standard form contracts result in contracts of adhesion because of the substantially disproportionate economic or bargaining power of the parties (requiring the weaker party to adhere to the terms presented or reject the contract) or because the party offering the standard form contract has had the advantage of time and expert legal advice in preparation of the one-sided form, while the other party may be unfamiliar with its terms and/or unable to reasonably review or understand its contents. Users of standard form contracts also sometimes use cosmetic devices such as fine print, screening to minimize contrast between print and paper, convoluted clauses, etc., to further gain advantage over the parties to whom such contracts are offered.

b. **Tickets, passes, and stubs.** Printed tickets, passes, and stubs often include preprinted statements that attempt to limit the liability of the issuer for injury or loss to person or property. While courts have held both for and against issuers sued by issuees who suffered losses in excess of the liability limitation set forth on the stub, the question usually turns on whether the person receiving the stub understands, or as a reasonable person should understand, that it contains essential terms of the contract. For example, in *Klar v. H. & M. Parcel Room, Inc.*, 61 N.Y.S.2d 285 (1946), *aff'd,* 73 N.E.2d 912 (N.Y. 1947), the court stated that a person checking a parcel (valued at $1,000) for a fee of 10¢ was not chargeable with knowledge that the parcel checking stub contained in fine print a limitation of $25 for loss of the parcel unless the limitation was called to his attention and he assented thereto, or the limitation was made so conspicuous (as with large signs, etc., at the point of checking) that a reasonable person would have been aware of it. Note, however, that blanket limitations against liability, whether printed on ticket stubs and made conspicuous on signs or otherwise, *e.g.,* in ski areas, roller skating rinks, etc., are not effective to limit the liability of the issuer for its active negligence, when the issuee sustains personal injury as a result thereof.

c. **Incorporation by reference.** In some lines of business, the allocation of risks has become "standardized" through the development of standard terms and conditions by a trade association representing merchants who deal in a particular line of business (*e.g.,* textiles, building contractors). Instead of setting forth the full text of the standard terms and conditions in use in a particular line of business, merchants often will incorporate them by reference in their contracts. This technique reduces the volume of the working contract document (which sets forth the essential elements of the contract), but still makes available all of the detailed terms and conditions which have been developed for the particular line of business.

d. **Applications.**

1) **Exculpatory clause--**

O'Callaghan v. Waller & Beckwith Realty Co., 155 N.E.2d 545 (Ill. 1958).

Facts. O'Callaghan (P) was the lessee in Waller & Beckwith Realty Co.'s (D's) building. P was injured crossing the paved courtyard and sued D for damages based on negligence. The lease provided that D was not to be liable for personal injuries to lessee caused by D's negligence. Nonetheless, P sued and won, but an appellate court reversed the decision. P appeals.

Issue. Is a lease clause exculpating the landlord from negligence enforceable?

Held. Yes. Judgment affirmed.

♦ An exculpatory clause in a lease is enforceable unless against public policy. The landlord-tenant relationship is a matter of private concern.

Dissent. The shortage of housing means that tenants have no bargaining power. The exculpatory clause is not a matter of private concern in this situation, but a matter for public policy. Exculpatory clauses have been voided in other contexts and should be voided here as well.

Comment. Shortly after this case was decided, the state legislature passed a law that made clauses exculpating a party from negligence unenforceable. Most states now have statutes that follow this approach.

---

2)   Arbitration clause--

Graham v. Scissor-Tail, Inc., 171 Cal. Rptr. 604 (1990).

Facts. Graham (P), a concert promoter, entered four separate contracts with Scissor-Tail, Inc. (D), which represented musician Leon Russell. Each contract was an identical form known as an "American Federation of Musicians ("A.F. of M.") Form B contract. The contract included an arbitration clause that appointed the A.F. of M. International Executive Board as the arbitrator. The parties had used the same contract for 15 previous concerts, and P had been a party to thousands of such contracts during his career. After the Leon Russell concert tour, P wanted to apply losses from one concert against the profits from another. D objected, and the dispute went to arbitration. The board ruled in favor of D. P appealed, claiming that the contracts were unenforceable contracts of adhesion and that the arbitration clause was unconscionable.

Issue. May a contract of adhesion containing an arbitration clause be unenforceable for not falling within the reasonable expectations of the adhering party where that party has been a party to thousands of contracts using the same form?

Held. No. Judgment affirmed in part.

♦   The contract in this case fits within the traditional notion of an adhesion contract. Even though P was a prominent and successful concert promoter, he was required to adhere to the Form B contract because all concert artists and groups of any significance are members of the A.F. of M., and the members are not allowed to sign any form of contract other than that issued by the union.

♦   Just because a contract is one of adhesion does not mean it is unenforceable. Contracts of adhesion may be unenforceable where they contain provisions that either do not fall within the reasonable expectations of the adhering party, or are unduly oppressive or unconscionable.

♦   In this case, P was fully familiar with the arbitration clause because he had been a party to many prior contracts that used the form and actually had resorted to arbitration to resolve disputes in previous deals.

Comment. The court did conclude that the arbitration clause was unconscionable because the arbitrator would be presumptively biased in favor of the union member artist. This aspect of the case is discussed *infra*.

---

3)   Passenger tickets and forum-selection--

Carnival Cruise Lines, Inc. v. Shute, 499 U.S. 585 (1991).

Facts. The Shutes (Ps) purchased a ticket for a seven-day cruise on a ship operated by Carnival Cruise Lines, Inc. (D). Ps bought the ticket through a Washington state travel agent, who forwarded the payment to D's headquarters in Miami, Florida. D sent the tickets to Ps in Washington. Each ticket bore a legend that provided that all disputes arising under the contract would be litigated in Florida state court. Ps boarded the ship in Los Angeles, sailed to Mexico, and returned to Los Angeles. While in international waters, P slipped on a deck mat and was injured. Ps sued D in federal court in Washington, claiming negligence on the part of D and its employees. D moved for summary judgment, based on the forum-selection clause on the ticket. The district court granted the motion, but the court of appeals reversed on the ground that "but for" D's solicitation of business in Washington, Ps would not have taken the cruise and would not have been injured. The solicitation was sufficient contact with Washington to support the exercise of personal jurisdiction. The Supreme Court granted certiorari.

Issue. Is a forum-selection clause contained in a ticket for passage on a ship enforceable?

Held. Yes. Judgment reversed.

- Because this is a case in admiralty, federal law governs the enforceability of the forum-selection clause. Ps concede that they had sufficient notice of the forum clause. However, Ps claim that the clause was not negotiated like the clause in *The Bremen v. Zapata Off-Shore Co.*, 407 U.S. 1 (1972), was.

- In *The Bremen*, there was strong evidence that the forum clause was a vital part of the agreement, and that the parties conducted their negotiations with that clause in mind. The contract in that case involved companies from two different nations and the tow of a costly piece of equipment across the ocean, so the provision for forum selection was carefully negotiated. In this case, D's passage contract was routine and probably not subject to negotiations by Ps or other passengers. The ticket was a form contract.

- The court of appeals held that a non-negotiated forum-selection clause in a form ticket contract is never enforceable simply because it is not the subject of bargaining. But a cruise line such as D has a special interest in limiting the fora in which it potentially could be subject to suit, since it carries passengers from many locales. A forum-selection clause eliminates confusion about where suits arising from the contract must be litigated, and by reducing D's potential legal costs, the clause reduces fares for passengers such as Ps.

- Ps have not satisfied the heavy burden of proof required to set aside the clause on grounds of inconvenience. Florida is not a "remote alien forum," and the accident occurred off the coast of Mexico, not near Washington State. There is no evidence of fraud or overreaching by D in specifying Florida as a forum, since D is headquartered there.

- The forum-selection clause does not violate 46 U.S.C. App. section 183c, which prohibits ship owners from limiting their liability for negligence or from requiring arbitration. That statute does not prohibit forum-selection clauses.

Dissent (Stevens, Marshall, JJ.). The notice of forum selection on Ps' ticket is in fine print and found in the eighth of 25 paragraphs, so it is questionable that they actually had notice. More importantly, traditional principles of federal admiralty law render exculpatory clauses unenforceable, and forum-selection clauses are not enforceable if they were not freely bargained for, create additional expense for one party, or deny one party a remedy. The forum-selection clause would have been unenforceable prior to *The Bremen,* and nothing in that case changed the law as it applies to this case.

Comment. Congress overruled *Carnival Cruise Lines* to the extent it applies to tickets for passenger vehicles by prohibiting forum-selection clauses.

---

4)   **Dating services contract not complying with state law--**

Doe v. Great Expectations, 809 N.Y.S.2d 819 (N.Y. Civ. Ct. 2005).

Facts. Two plaintiffs (Ps) brought similar suits against Great Expectations (D), and their cases were consolidated. One plaintiff paid D $1,000 for Internet dating services, and the other paid $3,790. The New York Dating Services Law provided that a dating service could charge no more than $25 unless it assured a client that it would provide him with a specified number of social referrals per month. The law specified mandatory contract provisions, including a cancellation option, limits on revealing clients' personal information without written consent, and a client's unilateral right to place his membership on hold for up to one year. The law also required providers to give clients written notice of a mandatory "Dating Service Consumer Bill of Rights." Finally, the law provided that any person injured by violations of the law could recover actual damages or $50, whichever was greater. Ps are suing D for a full refund.

Issue. Is a consumer who signs a form contract that does not comply with statutory requirements entitled to a complete refund?

Held. Yes. Judgment for Ps.

◆ D was engaged in dating services, and its contracts were subject to the Dating Services Law. The Dating Services Law applies to services that make the matching of members available or supplies the means for matching the members, as well as those that actually match members. The statute also includes services that utilize the Internet.

◆ D's contracts violated every mandate of the Dating Services Law, except that the contracts did contain notice of a three-day "cooling off" right to cancel. D was prohibited from charging more than $25 unless it furnished Ps with a specified number of social referrals per month. Instead, D's form contracts stated that there would be no referrals. Also, D did not provide Ps with the Dating Service Consumer Bill of Rights.

◆ Under the statute, Ps are entitled to recover actual damages, which is the difference between the contract price and the $25 maximum fee permitted for these contracts. However, we find that Ps would not have signed the contracts if they had been given the Dating Service Consumer Bill of Rights and known of their rights. Thus, Ps are also entitled to the $25. The amount Ps paid reflects their actual damage. Ps are entitled to a full refund as restitutionary damages, with interest from the date of the contract payments.

◆ Finally, this court will exercise its judicial discretion to report D's unlawful conduct to the appropriate governmental authorities, which in this case would be the New York State Attorney General's Consumer Fraud Unit and the New York City Department of Consumer Affairs.

C. UNCONSCIONABILITY

1. **Introduction.** Unconscionability refers to terms so one-sided as to be unfair or even oppressive.

   a. **Common law.** At common law, unconscionability referred to contracts which were manifestly unfair or oppressive (*i.e.,* contracts which no one in her senses and not under a delusion would make).

   b. **U.C.C.** Several sections of the U.C.C. deal with unconscionability or related concepts in contracts for the sale of goods.

      1) **U.C.C. section 2-302.** Section 2-302 provides that if a court as a matter of law finds a contract or clause therein to have been unconscionable at the time the contract was made, it may:

         a) Refuse to enforce the contract;

         b) Enforce the remainder of the contract without the unconscionable clause; or

         c) Limit the application of the unconscionable clause so as to avoid any unconscionable result.

      2) **U.C.C. section 2-718.** Section 2-718 provides that any liquidated damages clause that fixes unreasonably large damages in the event of breach as a penalty is void.

      3) **U.C.C. section 2-719.** Section 2-719 provides that the parties by agreement may limit or exclude consequential damages unless such limitation or exclusion would be unconscionable. Further, the limitation of consequential damages for personal injury from consumer goods is prima facie unconscionable, though such a limitation with respect to commercial losses is not.

   c. **Procedural vs. substantive unconscionability.**

      1) **Procedural unconscionability.** Procedural unconscionability generally arises in connection with formation or execution of the contract, *e.g.,* when one party either lacks knowledge or understanding of the terms of the agreement or there is a lack of voluntary assent, as in adhesion contract situations.

      2) **Substantive unconscionability.** Substantive unconscionability arises from the oppressive character of the substantive terms of the agreement, such as excessive price, lack of remedy for breach, unreasonable forfeiture provisions, unreasonable warranty disclaimers, etc.

d. **Burden of proof.** Under U.C.C. section 2-302, unconscionability is a question of law to be determined by the court. While the court may raise the unconscionability question on its own motion, if it is raised as an affirmative defense to enforcement of a contract, the party asserting unconscionability bears the burden of pleading and establishing it.

e. **Discretionary remedy.** When a court determines as a matter of law that a contract or clause is unconscionable, it has broad discretion and can enforce in total, enforce in part, or rewrite the offending contract or clause.

f. **Rationale.** The basic rationale for not enforcing unconscionable contract provisions is public policy; *i.e.,* there ought to be some limit to the power of parties in superior bargaining positions to dictate unfair terms. Note that in reaching decisions based on this doctrine the courts often allude to duress and fraud as well.

g. **Repossession--**

Williams v. Walker-Thomas Furniture Co., 350 F.2d 445 (D.C. Cir. 1965).

Facts. Walker-Thomas Furniture Co. (P) adopted a standard form contract for credit sales which provided (i) that all credit transactions of a buyer were to be lumped into one account and each installment payment made was to be spread pro rata over all items being purchased (even when purchased at different times) until all items were paid off, and (ii) that if the purchaser defaulted, P could repossess all items. Williams (D) purchased several items on credit; she failed to make payments sufficient to cover the most recent item (a stereo). D was on welfare, separated from her husband, and caring for seven children. P brought an action to repossess all items D was purchasing on credit. Judgment for P. D appeals.

Issue. Is P's contract provision on repossession unconscionable?

Held. Yes. Judgment reversed.

♦ The common law rule of caveat emptor is modified by U.C.C. section 2-302. D is in a poor economic class where the inequality of bargaining position makes it easy for P to exploit D by contract provisions such as the one here, which is unconscionable.

Dissent. This case presents questions of public policy that are best addressed by the legislature.

Comment. What are the policy considerations favoring P's position, given the risks of lending to welfare recipients?

h. Excessive price--

Jones v. Star Credit Corp., 298 N.Y.S.2d 264 (N.Y. Sup. Ct. 1969).

Facts. Jones (P), on welfare, purchased a freezer worth $300 (retail) for $900 ($1,235 when all charges were included). P had already paid $620 and sued to reform the contract on the basis that it was unconscionable.

Issue. Will a court refuse to enforce a contract as unconscionable on the basis that the price is excessive compared to actual value?

Held. Yes. Judgment for P.

♦ U.C.C. section 2-302 permits a court to reform a contract on the basis of excessive price. Factors to be considered are price to value ratio, the financial resources of the buyer, the knowledge of the seller concerning the buyer's situation (*i.e.,* did the seller take advantage of the buyer), and the relative bargaining position of the parties. Here the contract is reformed by making the full price the amount already paid.

Comment. Note that the idea of having a court substitute its judgment on price for that of the parties is a potentially dangerous doctrine and needs to be very carefully rationalized.

---

i. Mandatory arbitration in employment agreement--

Armendariz v. Foundation Health Psychcare Services, Inc., 6 P.3d 669 (Cal. 2000).

Facts. Foundation Health Psychcare Services, Inc. (D) hired Armendariz and another woman (Ps) after Ps filled out and signed an employment application form. The form included an arbitration clause pertaining to any future claim of wrongful termination. Ps later signed employment arbitration agreements. A year later, Ps were terminated when their positions were eliminated. Ps sued, claiming that during their year of employment, they had been sexually harassed and that they had been terminated because of their heterosexual orientation. D sought to compel arbitration. The trial court held that the arbitration clause was unconscionable so the entire agreement was unconscionable. The court of appeal held that the damages provision was unconscionable but the rest of the arbitration agreement should be enforced. D appeals.

Issue. If an employment contract requires arbitration of the employee's claims but not of the employer's, is it unconscionable?

Held. Yes. Judgment reversed regarding severability.

♦ The principle that a court can refuse to enforce an unconscionable provision in a contract has been codified in California. Unconscionability has both a procedural (focusing on oppression or surprise due to unequal bargaining power) and a substantive (focusing on overly harsh or one-sided results) element. Both elements must be present to justify nonenforcement of a contract due to unconscionability, but the greater the procedural unconscionability, the less substantively oppressive the contract need be, and vice versa.

♦ It is clear that the contract in this case is adhesive because Ps had to sign it as a condition of employment. Few employees are in a position to refuse a job because of an arbitration requirement. Studies have shown that arbitration is advantageous to employers because arbitration awards are lower than judicial awards.

♦ Ps note that the lack of mutuality is unconscionable. Ps have to arbitrate their claims against D, but D does not have to arbitrate its claims against P. In *Stirlen v. Supercuts, Inc.*, 60 Cal. Rptr. 2d 138 (1997), the court held that such a lack of mutuality may make an arbitration agreement substantively unconscionable. This is a correct approach, because the lack of mutuality gives the employer substantial advantages in asserting its own claims. An adhesive contract that includes an arbitration clause requiring the adhering party, but not the other, to arbitrate all claims arising out of the same transaction simply lacks basic fairness and mutuality.

♦ The contract also contained a clause that limited damages to the amount of back pay lost up until the time of arbitration, thereby excluding damages for prospective future earnings. This compounds the unconscionable one-sidedness of the agreement.

Comment. In *Circuit City Stores, Inc. v. Adams*, 532 U.S. 105 (2001), the United States Supreme Court has held that mandatory arbitration agreements in employment agreements are generally enforceable under the Federal Arbitration Act. Many employers are making such provisions a condition of employment. Also, note that in the *Scissor-Tail* case, *supra*, the court held that the provision requiring arbitrations to be heard by the A.F. of M. was unconscionable, regardless of the fairness of the procedures, because it failed to meet minimum levels of integrity. The state's strong public policy in favor of arbitration led the court to sever the provision appointing A.F. of M. as the arbitrator, substituting a requirement that the parties would select an arbitrator.

---

j. **Waiver of class actions unconscionable--**

Scott v. Cingular Wireless, 160 Wash. 2d 843 (Wash. 2007).

Facts. Scott and other consumers (Ps) bought cellular telephones and calling plans from Cingular Wireless (D). The form contracts contained a mandatory arbitration clause that prohibited consolidation of cases, class actions, and class arbitration. D later unilaterally revised the agreement to provide that D would pay the filing, administrator, and arbitration fees unless the plaintiff's claim was found to be frivolous, and D would reimburse plaintiffs for attorney fees and expenses incurred for arbitration as long as the plaintiffs recovered at least the demand amount. Ps filed a class action suit against D when they determined that they had been overcharged up to about $45 a month because of improper billing practices. D moved to compel individual arbitration. The trial court granted D's motion on the ground that D's contract was neither procedurally nor substantively unconscionable. The Washington Supreme Court granted review.

Issue. Is the class action waiver in the arbitration clause unconscionable?

Held. Yes. Judgment reversed and case remanded.

- ◆ Washington law authorizes class actions and favors aggregation of small claims to promote efficiency, deterrence, and access to justice. Agreements that tend to be against the public good violate public policy and may be void and unenforceable. When consumer claims are small but numerous, a class action is the only effective way to vindicate the public's rights by resolving the claims of the individual class members and deterring future similar wrongful conduct.

- ◆ The legislature created a private right of action to enforce the Consumer Protection Act ("CPA"). Class actions are a critical tool for private enforcement of the CPA because, without the class action, individual claims may be too small to justify bringing individual lawsuits. A waiver of the right to file a class action is substantively unconscionable to the extent that it prevents CPA cases.

- ◆ Exculpation from potential liability for unfair or deceptive acts or practices in commerce violates public policy. D's class action waiver here effectively exculpates D from liability for a large class of wrongful conduct because the cost of pursuing a claim is greater than the potential recovery. Ps' ability to file a class action transforms what would otherwise be a theoretically possible remedy into a real remedy.

- ◆ D claims that it has cured concerns about access by promising to pay the cost of arbitration if a claim is not frivolous and by promising to pay attorney fees when a plaintiff recovers the amount of his demand. While commendable, these provisions are inadequate because a plaintiff could recover most of his claim and still not receive attorney fees. And attorneys are generally unwilling to take on individual arbitrations to recover trivial amounts of money.

- ◆ The class action waiver provides that if it is found unenforceable, then the entire arbitration clause is void. Therefore, on remand the court may not compel arbitration.

Dissent (Madsen, J.). The legislature, not the courts, should decide whether there should be a state policy forbidding class action waivers in consumer agreements. The result of this opinion is to disfavor arbitration, contrary to the Federal Arbitration Act. The waiver in this case is not unconscionable in light of D's promise to pay the costs of arbitration, including attorney fees.

D. PERFORMING IN GOOD FAITH

1. **Introduction.** Every contract includes an obligation to act in good faith. Some courts characterize this as an implied covenant of good faith and fair dealing. The courts require good faith as a means of making sure the parties are treated fairly, and they often fashion remedies accordingly.

2. **Implied Good Faith Requirement--**

Dalton v. Educational Testing Service, 663 N.E.2d 289 (N.Y. 1995).

Facts. Dalton (P) took an SAT test provided by Educational Testing Service (D), for a second time. P's scores increased by 410 points, which led D to investigate the test documents. D concluded that the documents were completed by separate individuals and refused to release P's second SAT scores. The test registration materials provided that if D believed there was reason to question the validity of a score, D would notify the test-taker and offer five options, including the opportunity to retake the test or to provide additional information. D notified P of its decision to cancel his scores based on the handwriting disparity and higher score. P provided additional information, including a medical record from the time of the first test, test results from a preparatory course he took before the second test, and statements from witnesses that he had taken the second test. D continued to question the test results. P sued, claiming a breach of contract, and sought specific performance and money damages. The trial court found for P and ordered D to release the scores. The court of appeals held that P was entitled to have D consider, in good faith, the material submitted by P that showed he had taken the test, but not that P was entitled to the release of his test scores. P appeals.

Issue. Where a testing institution breaches a contract by failing to consider evidence provided by a test-taker regarding his having actually taken the test, may the institution be required to release the test score as a remedy for the breach?

Held. No. Judgment affirmed as modified.

♦ The parties had a contract that allowed D to cancel a test score if D found reason to question the validity of the score after offering the test-taker the five options to respond to D's concerns. D did not have a duty to initiate an external investigation into a questioned score, but it did have a duty to consider any relevant material that P supplied.

♦ The trial court concluded that D did not consider P's evidence based on testimony from D's board of review members that they thought P's evidence was irrelevant. This conclusion is supported by the evidence. D's failure to consider the evidence was a breach of its contract with P.

♦ D's breach is similar to the breach by a university of its contract with a student. The courts cannot compel an educational institution to issue a diploma because the diploma certifies that the student has certain skills. Other remedies for such a breach must be found. In this case, the courts cannot compel D to release the test scores for a similar reason.

♦ P is entitled to specific enforcement of D's promise to consider P's evidence in good faith. P can still resort to some of his other options as well.

---

3. Failure to Object--

Eastern Air Lines, Inc. v. Gulf Oil Corp., 415 F. Supp. 429 (S.D. Fla. 1975).

Facts. The facts are set forth *supra.* This portion of the opinion deals with D's allegation that P breached the contract through fuel freighting, a practice whereby airlines would buy more fuel for its aircraft than it needed for a particular flight at cheaper stations to avoid the more expensive stations.

Issue. Does an established course of performance and dealing between the parties, which is also an established usage of the trade, become part of the terms of the contract when not objected to?

Held. Yes.

♦ D claims that P's practice of fuel freighting is a breach of contract. However, the evidence indicates that this practice is established in the industry. Oil companies take this practice into consideration in making fuel contracts.

♦ D never objected over the years until the price problem arose under the current contract. The practical interpretation D gave to the contract during performance before the dispute arose is the best indication of the intent of the parties. P's fuel freighting does not constitute a breach of contract.

---

4. Duty to Remind Other Party of Contract Term--

Market Street Associates v. Frey, 941 F.2d 588 (7th Cir. 1991).

Facts. Market Street Associates (P) was the successor under a lease that allowed it to buy the leased property in the event Frey (D), representing the pension fund lessor, failed to provide financing for improvements to the property. P desired to buy the property and formally requested financing from D, without mentioning the lease paragraph giving P the purchase option. D declined to provide the requested financing, which was below D's deal threshold. P notified D it was exercising its option to buy. D refused to sell, and P sued for specific performance. The trial court granted summary judgment for D on the theory that P had not acted in good faith. P appeals.

Issue. Does the requirement of good faith require a party to alert the other party to a contract to any terms of the contract that might be unfavorable to the other party?

Held. No. Judgment reversed.

♦ The trial court found that P did not want financing from D and merely wanted to buy the property. To act in good faith, the court held that P should have reminded D about the option.

♦ The duty of good faith does not require complete candor. A party to a contract may take advantage of another based on his superior knowledge of the market. A party is not required to relax the terms of a bargain when the other party has trouble performing. So P was not required to alert D to the existence of the option, unless P was taking deliberate advantage of D's oversight. P's state of mind must be examined on remand.

Comment. After a trial, the court still found that P breached the duty of good faith because he knew D was not aware of the option and failed to bring it to D's attention.

---

5. "Best Efforts" Clause--

Bloor v. Falstaff Brewing Corp., 601 F.2d 609 (2d Cir. 1979).

Facts. Falstaff Brewing Corp. (D) acquired trademarks, labels, and other assets, except the physical facilities, from a family-owned brewery named Ballentine, which had experienced increased sales but significant losses. The sales agreement required D to "use its best efforts to promote and maintain a high volume of sales"; D was to pay a 50¢ per barrel royalty for the use of the Ballentine name. A separate provision specified liquidated damages if D substantially discontinued distribution of Ballentine beer.

D continued Ballentine's advertising and distribution practices for three years and lost $22 million on the brand. A new, experienced brewer took control of D, reduced advertising, changed distribution from retail to wholesale, and generally pursued profit over volume. Ballentine sales plummeted but D became profitable overall. Bloor (P), the reorganization trustee of the Ballentine brewery, sued D for breach of the best efforts clause and for liquidated damages. The trial court granted an award on the first claim but dismissed the second, and both parties appeal.

Issue. In a suit for breach of a "best efforts" clause, must the performing party show that there was nothing significant it could have done to perform that would not have been financially disastrous?

Held. Yes. Judgment affirmed.

♦ D's policy of pursuing profits regardless of volume did not fulfill its contract obligation to promote a high volume of sales of Ballentine beer. D at least had to explore whether steps not involving substantial losses could have been taken to stop or at least lessen the rate of decline of sales. Instead, D acted in total disregard to Ballentine's volume of sales.

♦ D says it was only obligated to treat Ballentine as well as it treated its own brands, but under the contract it was required to promote Ballentine volume even if it reduced volume in its other brands in order to maximize profits.

♦ P need not show what D should have done. Once P shows that D did not care about Ballentine's volume and let it fall, D has the burden to show that it could have done nothing that would not have been financially disastrous.

♦ Damages awarded by comparison to the performance of other brands similar to Ballentine are a reasonable estimate. P cannot recover liquidated damages, however, because D did not substantially discontinue distribution even though it changed the type of distribution.

Comment. In *Parev Products Co. v. I. Rokeach & Sons*, 124 F.2d 147 (2d Cir. 1941), the court held that in the absence of an express agreement, no promise not to sell a competing product should be implied to prevent a licensee from so doing.

---

6.   **Reasonable Time for Exclusivity Agreement--**

Lockewill, Inc. v. United States Shoe Corp., 547 F.2d 1024 (8th Cir. 1976).

Facts. In 1965, Lockewill, Inc. (P) acquired the exclusive right (through an oral agreement) to sell Pappagallo products in the St. Louis area. P spent $100,000 and consider-

Facts. Bovard (P) agreed to sell American Horse Enterprises, Inc. (D) to Ralph. Ralph failed to pay on the promissory notes, and P sued. D was in the business of manufacturing jewelry and drug paraphernalia used to smoke marijuana and tobacco. The trial court held that there was a public policy against the manufacture of drug paraphernalia, even if it was not illegal at the time the parties entered the contract. The court held that the consideration in the contract was contrary to public policy, so the contract was illegal and void. P appeals.

Issue. Is a contract for the sale of a business that is engaged in legal activity but whose products are used primarily for illegal purposes contrary to public policy and therefore unenforceable?

Held. Yes. Judgment affirmed.

♦ Whenever a court discovers that a contract is illegal, it has a duty to refrain from enforcing it. A court must apply subjective judgment in determining whether a contract violates public policy and should be cautious in making such a determination.

♦ The factors a court should consider include: (i) the nature of the conduct; (ii) the extent of public harm that may be involved; and (iii) the moral quality of the conduct of the parties in light of the prevailing standards of the community. The Restatement (Second) section 178 also provides guidance.

♦ In this case, the interest in enforcing the contract is very tenuous. Neither party could reasonably expect the government to permit D to continue producing drug paraphernalia. In fact, the manufacture of drug paraphernalia was made illegal in California five years after the parties entered the contract. Any forfeiture suffered by P would be limited to the loss of assets relating to the paraphernalia manufacturing, since he did recover the machinery used to manufacture jewelry. There is no special public interest in enforcing this contract apart from the general interest in preventing D from avoiding a debt.

♦ There are strong public policy reasons against enforcing the contract arising from the public policy against facilitating the illegal use of marijuana. Refusing to enforce this contract will notify other paraphernalia manufacturers that they do not have access to the legal system to protect their business interests. Even though paraphernalia manufacturing was not illegal when the parties entered the contract, they knew D's products would be used for illegal purposes.

Comment. The court distinguished *Moran v. Harris*, 182 Cal. Rptr. 519 (1982), which involved two lawyers who disputed a fee splitting agreement. Such agreements were not precluded by a rule of professional conduct when they made the agreement, but they were precluded when the case was settled and the fee generated. During the pendency of the litigation, the rule was changed to allow fee splitting agreements. The court enforced the agreement on the ground that public policy at the time of the litigation permitted the agreement.

d. Antitrust violation as a defense--

X.L.O. Concrete Corp. v. Rivergate Corp., 634 N.E.2d 158 (N.Y. 1994).

Facts. X.L.O. Concrete Corp. (P) entered a construction contract as a subcontractor to Rivergate Corp. (D). P fully performed and sought payment of the balance of $844,000. D refused to pay on the ground that the contract was part of an extortion and labor bribery operation known as the "Club," which was run by a group of organized crime family bosses known as the Commission of La Cosa Nostra ("Commission"). The Commission decided which concrete companies would be allowed to work on construction jobs worth more than $2 million. The successful contractors would pay the Commission 2% of the contract price for guaranteed "labor peace." The Commission rigged the bidding so the designated company would submit the lowest bid. P was a member of the Club. D negotiated the contract with P knowing all about the Club and its rules. When D refused to pay, P sued. The trial court dismissed the complaint, but the appellate court reinstated it. Both parties appeal.

Issue. May a plaintiff have recourse to the courts for nonpayment of a contract that was awarded in violation of antitrust law?

Held. Yes. Judgment affirmed.

♦ Antitrust defenses in contract cases are not favored because they are too likely to enrich parties who benefit from the contract. Courts allow antitrust defenses where necessary to avoid enforcement of the precise conduct that is made illegal by antitrust laws, but a contract that is legal on its face and does not require unlawful conduct in its performance is not voidable simply because it resulted from an antitrust conspiracy.

♦ In the current posture of this case, it is not clear whether the contract was so integrally related to the illegal combination that its enforcement would result in compelling performance of the precise conduct made unlawful by the antitrust laws. For example, evidence that the contract price is excessive due to an unlawful restraint of competition is not available. The equities of the parties must be examined to assure that P would not suffer a forfeiture while D is enriched. The illegality defense might make the contract completely void, or it could lead to recovery on a quantum meruit basis. These and other related issues must be examined at trial.

Comment. Antitrust law allows entities that are injured by illegal combinations to sue for treble damages. In addition, the state can seek remedies and criminal sanctions.

2. **Public Policy.** There are several types of agreements that may violate public policy by their very nature. Inducing official action through lobbying is con-

sistent with public policy so long as it is limited to addressing the reason of legislators. Contracts for bribing public officials, however, are obviously unenforceable. Commercial bribery agreements are also unenforceable. For example, in *Sirkin v. Fourteenth St. Store*, 108 N.Y.S. 830 (1908), the vendor had agreed to pay the buyer's purchasing agent a percentage of the purchase price of all the orders he made. When the store found out, it refused to pay the vendor for the goods. The court held that the bribe was illegal so the store did not need to pay under the contract, even though it kept the goods.

a.   Rule of reason approach to covenants not to compete--

Hopper v. All Pet Animal Clinic, 861 P.2d 531 (Wyo. 1993).

Facts. Hopper (D) worked as a veterinarian for the All Pet Animal Clinic (P) pursuant to a written employment contract that allowed termination by either party on 30 days' notice, and provided that, upon termination, D would not work as a small animal veterinarian in the area for three years. D was new to the area and had access to P's clients, pricing policies, and practice development techniques. D was terminated after P's president heard she was considering buying another practice. D did in fact purchase the other practice and obtained 187 of P's clients. P sued for an injunction and for damages. The court granted P an injunction but denied any award for damages, which it deemed too speculative. Both parties appeal.

Issue. Is a covenant not to compete enforceable as long as it does not create an unreasonable restraint of trade?

Held. Yes. Judgment affirmed in part.

♦   The common law did not enforce contracts in restraint of trade, and covenants not to compete are construed against the party seeking enforcement. The employer has the burden of proving that the covenant is reasonable and both has a fair relation to, and is necessary for, the business interests for which protection is sought.

♦   As a general rule, an employer may be protected against improper and unfair competition of a former employee, but not against ordinary competition. Under the rule of reason approach, a covenant not to compete can be enforced only if it is (i) in writing; (ii) part of a contract of employment; (iii) based on reasonable consideration; (iv) reasonable in duration and geographical limitation; and (v) not against public policy.

♦   In this case, the contract was in writing, it was part of D's employment contract, and D received a raise in connection with signing the contract. The evidence showed that D obtained access to P's clients through her employment, and because she took 187 of them, P suffered actual harm from unfair competition.

- The covenant not to compete was limited to small animal practice, so D could have practiced as a large animal veterinarian without relocating. This is a reasonable restriction that avoids undue hardship to D while protecting P's special interests, and the public would not suffer harm from its enforcement. The geographical limit of a five-mile radius from city limits is also reasonable.

- The three-year limitation is not reasonable, however. A one-year limit would secure P's interests in proprietary information, since its pricing policies were changed annually, and practice development information becomes dated within a year. The injunction should be modified to last for one year from the date of termination.

Dissent. The court should at least start the injunction from the date the trial court enters its modified judgment. Otherwise, the covenant not to compete is truly not worth the paper it is written on, as D told P before being terminated.

Comment. The case did not go to trial until over two years after D was discharged, and P did not seek a temporary injunction, so the denial of damages meant that P effectively had no remedy.

---

b.   Public policy limitations on at-will employment--

Sheets v. Teddy's Frosted Foods, 427 A.2d 385 (Conn. 1980).

Facts. Sheets (P) was employed as quality control director and then as operations manager for Teddy's Frosted Foods (D). P discovered that some of the food D packaged was not in compliance with state regulations, and that possible criminal violations existed because of false labeling. P brought the problem to the attention of D and was discharged in retaliation. P brought suit for wrongful discharge, but D sought to dismiss the complaint. The trial court ruled for D. P appeals.

Issue. May an employee be discharged for calling the employer's attention to possible criminal violations by the employer?

Held. No. Judgment reversed.

- Generally, contracts of permanent employment are terminable at will. P does not claim that D could terminate him only for just cause, but that D could not terminate him for a demonstrably improper reason in violation of public policy. Public policy does place some limits on an employer's right to terminate an at-will employee.

- The difficulty in wrongful discharge cases is determining which claims genuinely involve public policy and which involve ordinary disputes. Here, P was possibly subject to criminal liability because of his position within D. P had the responsibility of seeing that the labeling laws were complied with. Therefore, he had to choose between criminal sanctions and jeopardizing his continued employment. In such a situation, a retaliatory discharge is actionable.

Dissent. P could have resolved the problem by going to the appropriate public official, without risking his employment. The majority here has lowered the threshold for suits based on wrongful discharge. The legislature has declined to go so far. This cause of action should extend only to cases in which a retaliatory discharge would be within a specific statutory prohibition.

Comment. In *Daley v. Aetna Life & Cas. Co.*, 734 A.2d 112 (Conn. 1999), the court held that an employer's compliance with express statutory obligations is all that is required, so that the public policy exception to the at-will doctrine is a narrow exception.

---

c.   **Retaliatory discharge of in-house counsel--**

Balla v. Gambro, Inc., 584 N.E.2d 104 (Ill. 1991).

Facts. Balla (P) was in-house counsel for Gambro, Inc. (D), a distributor of kidney dialysis equipment. P was responsible for regulatory affairs as well as legal matters. P told D's president to reject a shipment of dialyzers because they did not comply with FDA regulations, but D accepted them anyway. P told D's president that he would stop the resale of the dialyzers. D fired P. P reported the shipment to the FDA. The FDA seized the shipment. P sued for retaliatory discharge. The trial court granted D summary judgment on the ground that D had the right to discharge its attorney. The appellate court remanded to give P a right to a trial. D appeals.

Issue. Does an in-house counsel have a right to sue for the tort of retaliatory discharge when he is fired after reporting his client's illegal conduct?

Held. No. Judgment reversed.

♦   In-house counsel normally do not have a right to claim the tort of retaliatory discharge, which is a narrow exception to the general rule of at-will employment. P had a duty under the Rules of Professional Conduct to report D's intention to sell the illegal dialyzers because of the risk that use of these dialyzers would cause death or serious bodily injury.

♦   P claims that he had a choice of complying with D's plans or refusing to comply with D and risk losing his job. Actually, P did not have a choice because as a lawyer, he was obligated to comply with the Rules of Professional Conduct and he had to report D's intention to sell the dialyzers.

- A client may discharge his attorney at any time, with or without cause, and this rule applies equally to in-house counsel. If in-house counsel had the right to sue employers for retaliatory discharge, employers would be inhibited from disclosing facts to get advice about potentially questionable corporate conduct. It is better to avoid such a chilling effect by not extending the tort of retaliatory discharge.

- D as the employer/client should not bear the economic costs of P's duty to comply with the Rules of Professional Conduct. Lawyers may at times be required to forgo economic gains to protect the integrity of the legal profession.

- The fact that P also acted as manager of regulatory affairs is not relevant because his discharge resulted from conduct that he performed as general counsel.

Comment. California and Massachusetts have rejected this approach. In *General Dynamics Corp. v. Superior Court*, 876 P.2d 487 (Cal. 1994), the court held that attorneys should have a retaliatory discharge remedy when their ethical duties collide with illegitimate demands of their employer. That approach advances public policies by encouraging employees, including lawyers, to comply with them.

---

d.   Prenuptial agreements--

Simeone v. Simeone, 581 A.2d 162 (Pa. 1990).

Facts. Simeone (P), a 23-year-old unemployed nurse, was presented with a prenuptial agreement the night before her wedding to Simeone (D), a 39-year-old neurosurgeon. The agreement provided that in the event of separation or divorce, D would not have to pay P more than $25,000. P signed the agreement, and the parties were married the next day. They separated seven years later and started divorce proceedings two years after that. P sought alimony, but D objected on the ground that he had paid P $25,000 during the time they were separated. The lower courts upheld the agreement. P appeals.

Issue. Does public policy require that, to be enforceable, a prenuptial agreement must make reasonable provision for the spouse?

Held. No. Judgment affirmed.

- In *Estate of Geyer*, 533 A.2d 423 (1987), the court held that a prenuptial agreement must either make a reasonable provision for the spouse or be entered after a full and fair disclosure of the parties' financial positions and the statutory rights being relinquished. *Geyer* was based on the presumption that spouses are of unequal status and that women do not understand the nature of contracts they enter. These stereotypes are no longer viable. Men and women have equal status in modern society.

♦   The *Geyer* rules also departed from traditional contract law. Prenuptial agreements should be treated as any other type of contract. Traditional contract law provides adequate remedies for fraud, misrepresentation, and duress. P must be bound by her agreement, which she signed voluntarily.

♦   To avoid assertions of material misrepresentation, however, the parties to a prenuptial agreement must provide each other a full and fair disclosure of their respective financial positions. The parties do not stand at arm's length but have a relation of mutual confidence and trust that requires such disclosure.

♦   The evidence in this case supports the findings that P voluntarily entered this agreement and that there was no misrepresentation involved.

---

e.   **Surrogate parenting--**

In the Matter of Baby M, 537 A.2d 1227 (N.J. 1988).

Facts. William Stern (P) and Mary Beth Whitehead (D) negotiated an agreement whereby D would be artificially inseminated with P's sperm, D would bear the child, and upon its birth she would give the child to P and P would pay D $10,000. D also agreed that she would give up her parental rights so P's wife could adopt the child. However, once the child was born, D did not want to part with it. P sued for enforcement of the surrogacy contract. The trial court held that the contract was valid and ordered that D's parental rights be terminated. D appeals.

Issue. Is the contract for surrogate motherhood enforceable?

Held. No. Judgment reversed and case remanded.

♦   The surrogacy contract violates New Jersey statutes, which: (i) prohibit paying or accepting money in connection with any placement of a child for adoption, except for fees paid to an approved agency; (ii) require proof of parental unfitness or abandonment before termination of parental rights is ordered or an adoption is granted; and (iii) make surrender of custody and consent to adoption revocable in private placement adoptions. Violation of the laws prohibiting the use of money in connection with adoption is a misdemeanor that carries a penalty of three to five years' imprisonment.

♦   There are many evils inherent in baby-bartering. The baby is sold without regard for whether the purchasers will be suitable parents. The highest bidders likely become the adoptive parents. The natural mother does not receive the benefit of counseling to help her make her decision, and she must surrender custody of the child without any right of revocation. Depending on her financial circumstances, the monetary incentive to sell her child may make her decision less voluntary.

♦ The surrogacy contract conflicts with New Jersey's public policy. It disregards the best interests of the child and prevents D from ever making an informed decision, since any decision made before a baby's birth is uninformed. D's consent is irrelevant; our society recognizes that there are some things money cannot buy. Just as minimum wage laws prevent employers and employees from agreeing to certain wage amounts, public policy prohibits a woman from selling her child before it is born.

♦ There is no legal prohibition against surrogacy if the surrogate mother volunteers, without payment, and is given the right to change her mind and assert her parental rights. However, this surrogacy contract is void, and the case is remanded for a determination of custodial rights based on the best interests of the child.

━━━━━━━━━━━━━━━━━

VII. REMEDIES FOR BREACH

A. INTRODUCTION

1. **Compulsion or Relief.** Under Anglo-American principles of jurisprudence, remedies for breach of contract are designed to provide relief to the aggrieved party, rather than to compel a party to perform instead of breach when the bargain ceases to be advantageous to him or her. The relief provided to aggrieved promisees is generally compensatory damages, though rarely punitive damages may be awarded. Breach of contract is nowhere a crime.

2. **Nature of Relief.** Generally, relief for breach of contract is either specific, as when it secures to the promisee that which was promised, or substitutional, as when it gives something as a substitute for that which was promised.

   a. **Specific relief.** Specific relief or specific performance developed in the common law system through the courts of equity but such a remedy was considered extraordinary and available to an injured party only if the remedy available in the courts of law (*i.e.,* money compensation) was inadequate.

   b. **Substitutional relief: expectation, reliance, or restitution.** Because a contract is generally a bargain, relief for breach is generally the "benefit of the bargain" or what the promisee *expected* to receive, measured in money compensation, had the promisor performed. However, where claims are based upon something other than the bargain element, recovery may be more limited. For example, in *Hoffman v. Red Owl Stores, supra*, reliance was the basis of the transaction and recovery was limited to Hoffman's out-of-pocket expenditures plus actual losses sustained on the sales of his businesses measured by the difference between the sales price and the fair market value. Also, in *Callano v. Oakwood Park Homes Corp., supra*, where a remedy was sought on the basis of quasi-contract for restitution of the benefit conferred, recovery was limited to the reasonable value of the shrubbery planted.

3. **Election of Remedies.**

   a. **Introduction.** The remedies stated above (specific performance or substitutional performance, *i.e.,* money damages based on expectation, reliance, or restitution) may often be inconsistent in their legal effects. For example, rescission seeks to cancel the contract, whereas an action for damages seeks to affirm the contract and to collect damages for a breach thereof. Where remedies are inconsistent, the plaintiff must elect which remedy she will seek to pursue.

b. **Time of election.**

    1) **Filing legal action.** Even a mere filing of a legal action based on one remedy can amount to an election of remedies, at least where the defendant changes her position in reliance thereon. For example, if the plaintiff seeks rescission of a land sales contract and defendant-seller relies and sells the land to another party, filing an action for rescission will amount to an "election."

    2) **Modern pleading.** Normally, however, pleadings may be amended and an election occurs only when the plaintiff has pursued one remedy to a final judgment.

4. **Material vs. Minor Breach.**

    a. **Introduction.** It makes a difference in legal effect whether the breach of contract is a "major" (or "material" breach) or a "minor" breach. The question of the "materiality" of the breach is a question of fact that must be determined in each case. The Restatement (First) section 275 indicates six factors that are considered in making this factual determination:

        1) The extent to which the breaching party has already performed (the greater the performance, the more likely it is a minor breach).

        2) Whether the breach was willful, negligent, or the result of innocent behavior (if willful, it is more likely to be a material breach).

        3) The degree of certainty that the party who has breached will perform the remainder of the contract (the more certain, the more likely it is a minor breach).

        4) The extent to which the nonbreaching party will obtain or has obtained the substantial benefit she bargained for (if the nonbreaching party has obtained substantial benefit, it is likely to be a minor breach).

        5) The extent to which the nonbreaching party can be adequately compensated for the defective or incomplete performance through her right to damages.

        6) The degree of hardship imposed on the breaching party by holding the breach to be material and terminating all of his rights under the contract (the more hardship, the less likely it is to be a major breach).

    b. **The effect of a material breach.**

1) **Excuses counterperformance.** A material breach by A excuses B from any duty of performance owed under the contract.

2) **Remedies.** B (the nonbreaching party) would also be entitled to a remedy for breach of the entire contract (and not just for some minor provision of the contract).

c. **The effect of a minor breach.** If the breach is only a "minor" one (such as an insignificant delay in performance), then:

1) **Remedies.** The aggrieved party gets damages (or some other remedy) limited to those caused by the breach, rather than damages or other remedies based on the entire contract. This means that the remaining provisions of the contract would be enforced.

2) **Delay in counterperformance.** Thus, the duty to perform by the nonbreaching party is not totally excused; it is simply suspended temporarily until the breach is cured or damages are given for the minor breach.

3) **Example.** A promises to pay B $1,000 if B paints his house by June 1. B begins and is 90% finished on June 1. The job is completed on June 2. The breach is probably minor and A must pay the $1,000. But A may collect damages for B's failure (breach) to complete the job on June 1.

5. **Specific Performance.** In some instances where damages will not be adequate to give plaintiff the benefit of the bargain, the court may authorize specific performance (requiring the defaulting party to perform its obligations under the contract). However, the general rule is that executory contracts for the sale of personal property will not be specifically enforced by the courts.

6. **Types of Damages.** Generally, money damages recoverable in breach of contract actions are either compensatory, punitive, or nominal.

a. **Compensatory damages.** Every breach of a contract allows the aggrieved party to sue for damages. The objective of damages is to compensate in money for the loss sustained by the plaintiff. Thus, there may be two parts to compensatory damages.

1) **The standard measure.** These are the damages that a reasonable person would expect to flow from a breach of contract.

2) **Individualized measure.** In addition, the plaintiff may be able to recover for special damages which are a consequence of the breach in the particular case (for example: A promises to repair machin-

ery for B. A delays her performance unduly. B cannot run his plant and loses profits he otherwise would have made). (*See* D.2, *infra*)

    b.   Punitive damages. Punitive damages (*i.e.,* damages to punish the breaching party) are recoverable in a contract action only if expressly required and authorized by law (*e.g.,* antitrust statutes).

    c.   Nominal damages. Every breach of contract, no matter how slight, entitles the aggrieved party to at least nominal damages, even if no actual loss can be shown. Normally such damages amount to $1. However, a few states leave it to the discretion of the trial judge as to whether to award nominal damages.

7.   Sale of Goods Under the U.C.C. The principal source of the law of sales is the U.C.C., enacted in all states except Louisiana. Article 2 of the U.C.C. applies to "transactions in goods," which the Code defines as "all tangible chattels which are removable at the time of identification to the contract of sale." [*See* U.C.C. §2-105(1)]

    a.   Organization of Article 2. Article 2 is organized into seven parts which parallel the sequence of events in a sales transaction:

        1)   Part 1. Short title, general construction and subject matter.

        2)   Part 2. Form, formation, and readjustment of contract.

        3)   Part 3. General obligation and construction of the contract.

        4)   Part 4. Title, creditors, and good faith purchasers.

        5)   Part 5. Performance.

        6)   Part 6. Breach, repudiation, and excuse.

        7)   Part 7. Remedies.

    b.   Remedies of seller and buyer under sales contracts.

        1)   Seller's pre-litigation remedies.

            a)   Right to withhold delivery or demand cash payment. When the seller has not been paid for goods she has in possession, she may withhold delivery if the buyer (i) wrongfully rejects, (ii) rescinds (*i.e.,* revokes acceptance), (iii) fails to make a payment when due, or (iv) anticipatorily breaches the contract. [U.C.C. §2-703(a)] If the buyer becomes insolvent and the seller learns of it, she may demand payment in cash, both as to past deliveries and future deliveries. [U.C.C. §2-702(1)]

b) **Right to reclaim goods.** If the seller who has delivered goods on credit discovers after such delivery that the buyer is insolvent, she may reclaim the goods by demanding them back within 10 days after the buyer received them. [U.C.C. §2-702(2)] If any such reclamation is successful, it excludes all other remedies (*i.e.,* the seller cannot thereafter sue for loss of profits on the sale). [U.C.C. §2-702(3)]

c) **Right to stop goods in transit.** Where the goods are still in transit and the seller discovers that the buyer is or has become insolvent, she may stop the goods in transit. [U.C.C. §2-705(1)]

d) **Right to resell goods.** When the seller is in possession of goods which the buyer has refused to accept, she may resell them and then sue the buyer for any loss sustained by such resale. The Code provides that the seller can recover in such instance as damages, the difference between the resale and the contract price, less any expenses saved in consequence of the buyer's breach. [U.C.C. §2-706(1)]

e) **Cancellation.** The seller may cancel the contract for the buyer's breach [U.C.C. §2-703(f)], retaining any remedy for breach of the whole contract or any unperformed balance [U.C.C. §2-106(4)].

2) **Buyer's pre-litigation remedies.**

a) **Revocation of acceptance.** Where goods delivered fail to conform to the contract, the buyer may reject them [U.C.C. §2-601], though when the buyer accepts nonconforming goods, he must pay for them at the contract price. However, if the defects are substantial, the buyer may revoke his prior acceptance. [U.C.C. §2-608(1)]

b) **Sale of nonconforming goods.** The buyer may sell nonconforming goods to recover prepayments. The Code gives the buyer a security interest in the goods for his prepayment and provides that if the buyer offers to restore the seller's goods and demands repayment of the price paid, and the seller refuses, the buyer may sell the goods. [U.C.C. §2-711(3)]

c) **Cover.** The buyer has the right to go into the market and purchase substitute goods (*i.e.,* "cover") if the seller delivers nonconforming goods or fails to deliver. The buyer may then (after covering) sue the seller for any excess of the cover price over the contract price, even if the cover price is more than the market. [U.C.C. §2-712(1)]

d) **Setoff.** The buyer has the right to deduct from his payments any damages incurred as a result of the seller delivering non-conforming goods. [U.C.C. §2-717]

e) **Capture.** If the buyer has paid for goods and the seller is or has become insolvent, the buyer may "capture" the goods for which he has paid (in a manner similar to the seller's "reclaim" remedy). [U.C.C. §2-502] Also, where the seller is solvent but repudiates the contract, the buyer may, by tendering the full price of goods "identified" to the contract, demand that the seller turn them over to him. [U.C.C. §2-711(2)(a)] This is similar to replevin and specific performance; if the seller refuses to turn over the goods, the buyer obviously will have to resort to litigation.

3) **Seller's litigation remedies.**

a) **Action for full purchase price.** If the seller has delivered possession of the goods and the buyer has failed to pay, the seller may sue for the full purchase price. If the seller has possession and the buyer breaches, the seller is generally limited to her action for damages; *i.e.,* she must resell the goods and then sue the buyer for any loss on the resale. [U.C.C. §2-709(1)(a)]

b) **Damages for nonacceptance.** When the seller resells goods which the buyer refused to accept, she may recover either the difference between the resale price and the contract price [U.C.C. §2-706(1)] or the difference between the contract price and the market price at the time and place the goods were tendered [U.C.C. §2-708(1)]. Where the goods are standard items, both measures will generally be the same; a large disparity between the two methods of measuring damages (*i.e.,* if the resale is made at lower than market) may indicate that the seller has not acted reasonably in reselling the goods and she may be precluded from recovering anything beyond the difference between the contract and the market price. Where the damages determined under either of the above methods are inadequate to place the seller in as good a position as she would have been if the buyer had performed, then the seller may also recover lost profits and incidental damages. [U.C.C. §§2-706(1), 2-708(1), 2-708(2)] However, the seller must always deduct from her damages any expenses saved in consequence of the buyer's breach.

4) **Buyer's litigation remedies.**

a) **Replevin and specific performance.** Where the goods are identified to the contract and the buyer has been unable to cover after reasonable effort, he may seek replevin. [U.C.C. §2-716(3)] Where the goods are unique or the circumstances otherwise proper, the buyer may seek specific performance. [U.C.C. §2-716(1)]

b) **Action for damages for nondelivery.** When the seller fails to deliver the goods contracted for, the buyer who has covered may recover the difference between the cover price and the contract price [U.C.C. §2-712(2)] or the buyer, as an alternative, may recover the difference between the contract price and the market price at the time and place the buyer learned of the breach [U.C.C. §2-713(1)]. In addition, the buyer may recover incidental and consequential damages. [U.C.C. §2-715]

c) **Damages for breach of warranty.** Where the seller breaches the warranty applicable to the goods, the buyer may recover for the loss in value of the goods because of the breach, plus incidental and consequential damages.

d) **Limitation of remedies.** The U.C.C. provides that the parties may by agreement alter or limit the remedies otherwise provided in the Code. Typical of such provisions are liquidated damages clauses (*see* discussion *supra*), clauses limiting or excluding incidental and consequential damages, and clauses disclaiming or limiting express and implied warranties. [U.C.C. §§2-718, 2-719] Such clauses are subject to strict construction by the courts and, if they prove unconscionable or cause the contract to fail of its essential purpose, will be held of no effect, restoring to the aggrieved party under the contract all the remedies which otherwise would have been available under the U.C.C. without the objectionable clauses.

B. SPECIFIC PERFORMANCE

1. **Introduction.** Where damages are shown not to be an adequate and just remedy, equity may allow specific enforcement of the contract. The classic example is a contract for the sale of real property; since each parcel of land is unique, the buyer can only get the benefit of his bargain by actually getting the particular parcel contracted for; *i.e.,* damages will not let him realize the benefit of his bargain.

2. **Specific Performance for Special Goods--**

Campbell Soup Co. v. Wentz, 172 F.2d 80 (3d Cir. 1948).

Facts. Campbell Soup Co. (P) contracted with George and Harry Wentz (Ds) to buy all of the Chantenay red cored carrots to be grown on Ds' farm. The price depended on the time of delivery, but was set at $30 per ton for delivery in January. After Ds harvested 100 tons of carrots, they told P they would not deliver the carrots at the contract price. The market price in January was $90 per ton. Ds sold 62 tons of the carrots to another farmer, who sold most of them on the open market. P bought some of these and, suspecting they were the contract carrots, sued Ds to enjoin the sale of the carrots to others and to compel specific performance of the contract. The trial court concluded that P had failed to establish that the carrots were unique goods. P appeals.

Issue. Is specific performance an appropriate remedy when special goods are not otherwise available on the market?

Held. Yes. Judgment affirmed on other grounds.

♦ Specific performance is available if the legal remedy is inadequate. In this case, the legal remedy is inadequate because there were no Chantenay carrots available on the open market other than Ds'. P prefers this variety because its shape makes it easier to process, it has a brighter color, and its appearance is uniform.

♦ When a good is unique or special, such as the carrots in this case, and is unavailable on the open market, specific performance is an appropriate remedy.

Comment. The court still denied specific performance because it found that some of the contract provisions were unconscionable.

---

3. No Specific Performance Where Money Damages Are Adequate--

Klein v. PepsiCo, 845 F.2d 76 (4th Cir. 1988).

Facts. Klein (P) wanted to buy a used corporate jet, model G-II. P contacted Janas, the President of Universal Jet Sales, who told P about a suitable jet owned by PepsiCo (D). P's employees inspected D's jet in New York, and D flew the jet to Arkansas for P to personally inspect. P paid Janas $200,000 as a deposit and told him to offer $4.4 million. D counteroffered to Janas with $4.7 million, then lowered its offer to $4.6 million, which Janas accepted with the intent to sell the jet to P for $4.75 million. Within a week, D's chairman used the jet and asked that it be withdrawn from the market. D refused to tender the aircraft or negotiate further. P sued, seeking specific performance. The court ordered specific performance. D appeals.

Issue. May specific performance be awarded where there are substitute goods that can be purchased to satisfy the original contract?

Held. No. Judgment reversed.

♦ Although the final written contract between the parties was never executed, the confirming telex from Janas to D, combined with D's actions in compliance with the provisions of the written contract, support the trial court's findings that the parties did have a binding contract.

♦ Under U.C.C. section 2-716, a nonbreaching buyer of goods may seek specific performance of the contract if the goods sought are unique. The trial court found that D's jet was unique and that P could not cover by purchasing a comparable jet. However, specific performance is inappropriate where money damages are recoverable and adequate. The evidence in this case showed that three other comparable G-II jets were available for purchase, and that P wanted the plane to resell it for a profit anyway. Money damages would have been adequate, so specific performance should not have been ordered.

---

4. **Peculiar and Unique Personal Value--**

Morris v. Sparrow, 287 S.W.2d 583 (Ark. 1956).

Facts. Morris (D) owned a cattle ranch and participated in rodeos. Sparrow (P) was a cowboy who trained horses. P agreed with D to work at D's ranch while D went out of town. P was to receive $400 and an untamed horse named Keno. During his spare time, P trained Keno. D paid P the $400 but refused to give Keno to him because he claimed that P did not do satisfactory work at the ranch. P sued. The trial court ordered D to deliver Keno to P. D appeals.

Issue. Is specific performance an appropriate remedy for breach of a contract to sell a chattel if the chattel has a peculiar and unique value?

Held. Yes. Judgment affirmed.

♦ As a general rule, equity does not ordinarily enforce a contract to sell chattels by ordering specific performance. The exception is where special and peculiar reasons exist that make a legal remedy of damages inadequate.

♦ In this case, where P trained Keno to be a roping horse, the horse had peculiar and unique value to him. Therefore, P should receive the horse instead of its market value.

---

5. Practical Approach--

Laclede Gas Co. v. Amoco Oil Co., 522 F.2d 33 (8th Cir. 1975).

Facts. Laclede Gas Co. (P) and Amoco Oil Co. (D) agreed to an arrangement to provide central propane gas distribution systems to certain residential areas until natural gas mains were extended. D, as supplier, was to provide the necessary supply facilities. P, as distributor, was to provide and operate all distribution facilities from the outlet of D's piping. P promised to pay D four cents per gallon above a particular posed price. P could terminate the agreement on 30 days' notice at the end of any year or when natural gas mains were extended. D had no right of termination. After a price dispute, D terminated the agreement, claiming it lacked mutuality. P sought an injunction against the continuing breach, but the trial court agreed with D. P appeals.

Issue. Is specific performance an appropriate remedy for breach of a contract involving personal property?

Held. Yes. Judgment reversed.

♦ The law does not require that both parties be mutually entitled to specific performance for one of them to receive that remedy. All that is required is inadequacy of a remedy at law.

♦ D also argues that specific performance would be difficult for the court to enforce, but the court itself has discretion to take this factor into account, and the public interest outweighs the potential burden on the court. D contends that the contract is indefinite and uncertain, but any uncertainties are resolvable.

♦ D claims that P has an adequate remedy at law, so specific performance is inappropriate, especially since personalty, not realty, is involved. However, applying a practical approach to the adequacy of a legal remedy, we conclude that P could not with certainty find an alternative long-term supplier. While P has alternative propane suppliers, these provide only backup for peak shortages, not full-time residential supply.

♦ Although specific performance is a discretionary remedy, when certain equitable rules have been met and the contract is fair and plain, specific performance is available as a matter of right.

Comment. In *Eastern Rolling Mill Co. v. Michlovitz*, 145 A. 378 (Md. 1929), the court ordered specific enforcement of a long-term supply contract, partly because the damages were not ascertainable. Any award to the plaintiff could not constitute adequate compensation.

6. **Specific Performance of Construction Contracts.** Courts have ordered specific performance of construction contracts where the construction was part of a conveyance or lease of the underlying property. However, courts are unlikely to order specific performance where supervision of the performance would be impractical. For example, in *Northern Delaware Industrial Development Corp. v. E.W. Bliss Co.*, 245 A.2d 431 (Del. Ch. 1968), the court declined to award specific performance of a contract that would have required the hiring of 300 workers to complete a second shift on a $27 million plant modernization contract. The court considered such an order impractical to effectively enforce, and ruled that money damages for any losses caused by a delay could be determined at the appropriate time.

7. **Economic Considerations--**

Walgreen Co. v. Sara Creek Property Co., 966 F.2d 273 (7th Cir. 1992).

Facts. Sara Creek Property Co. (D) leased space in a shopping mall to Walgreen Co. (P), which operated a pharmacy. D promised not to lease space in the mall to any other pharmacies. However, D later informed P that it intended to lease space to Phar-Mor, which would operate a pharmacy and was a "deep discount" chain, unlike P, which was just a "discount" chain. P sought an injunction against D to enjoin D from leasing the property to Phar-Mor. The trial court entered a permanent injunction against D until P's lease expired. D appeals, claiming that P's damages could be readily estimated.

Issue. Is it appropriate for a judge to issue an injunction once he determines that the costs and benefits of injunctive relief outweigh the costs and benefits of determining monetary damages?

Held. Yes. Judgment affirmed.

♦ D asserts that damages are typical in breach of contract cases and that breaches are "efficient" in that they allow resources to be allocated to a more valuable use. In this case, D claims having Phar-Mor in the mall exceeds the cost to P of the increased competition, and D is willing to pay P damages for the breach.

♦ There are benefits to substituting an injunction for damages. First, an injunction shifts to the parties the burden of determining the cost of the breach; *i.e.*, the parties can settle the dispute and dissolve the injunction. This is preferable to costly litigation. Second, the market can determine prices and costs better than the courts, which must rely on a battle of experts.

♦ On the other hand, the cost of issuing injunctions includes the requirement of continuing judicial supervision and potential costs imposed on third parties. In economic terms, an injunction may create a bilateral monopoly. Here, P could "sell" its injunctive right only to D, and D could "buy" P's surrender of its right to enjoin the leasing of the space to Phar-Mor only from P. Both P and D would have an incentive to spend substantial resources of time and money on the negotiation process.

♦ There are also costs and benefits with the damages remedy. It avoids the cost of continuing supervision, the cost of a bilateral monopoly, and the effects on third parties. However, it imposes costs—less accuracy in the determination of value, the cost of preparing and presenting evidence of damages, and the time of the court in evaluating the evidence.

♦ A judge asked to enter a permanent injunction should weigh these costs and benefits. If the balance between the two remedies is even, the court should not enter the injunction. The trial court in this case could reasonably have concluded that determining P's damages would be costly and inaccurate, since 10 years remained on the lease. Thus, an injunction was appropriate.

C. MEASURING EXPECTATION

1. **Measure of Damages.** Where claims are based on the bargain element (as distinguished from the reliance or restitutionary elements), the objective of damages is to give the injured party the benefit of the bargain. However, the benefit of the bargain can be measured in several ways. For example, the damages could be measured by the cost to give the injured party that performance which was bargained for (*i.e.,* the cost to complete); or it could be measured by the loss of advantage incurred by the injured party (*i.e.,* the diminution in value). Two general formulations for determining damages are given by the following equations:

   a. **Damages = (loss in value) - (costs avoided) + (other losses).** For example, if P expected to be paid $100 for a job which would have cost her $80 to perform and P had to pay $10 to return the materials she purchased to do the job, her damages on D's breach would be calculated as follows:

   Damages = $100 - $80 + 10, or

   Damages = $30

      1) **Part performance.** The above formulation applies in the case of breach of an executory contract or a partially executed contract. For example, if P had expected to be paid $100, expected costs of $80, had spent $10, and had to pay $10 to return materials already purchased, her damages would be $40, *i.e.,* $100 - ($80 - $10) + $10 = $40.

b.   Damages = (cost of reliance) + (profit) + (other losses). For example, where P did not commence work in the example in a. above, her reliance cost was $0, her expected profit was the contract price of $100 less her expected costs of $80, or $20, and her other losses were $10, resulting in damages of $30.

       1)   Part performance. In the example in a.1) above, P's cost of reliance is $10 (the amount she spent); her expected profit is $20 (contract price less expected cost), and other losses are $10 (cost to return already purchased materials), resulting in damages of $40, *i.e.,* $10 + $20 + $10.

2.   Overhead--

Vitex Manufacturing Corp. v. Caribtex Corp., 377 F.2d 795 (3d Cir. 1967).

Facts. Vitex Manufacturing Corp. (P) and Caribtex Corp. (D) entered into a contract obligating P to reopen a wool processing plant in the Virgin Islands to process imported wool. Wool processed in the Virgin Islands was given an import duty exemption, and D failed to deliver the wool to P because of questions about the availability of the exemption. P sued for breach of contract and recovered the gross profits under the contract less costs saved by not having to perform the contract. D appeals the computation of the costs saved.

Issue. Is overhead properly chargeable as a cost saved in computing an award for breach of contract?

Held. No. Judgment affirmed.

♦   Overhead remains constant whether the contract is performed or not, so P should be allowed to recover the contribution to overhead expected from performance of the contract. D's breach reduces the profitability of other contracts if overhead is not an allowed item of recovery, since a higher amount of overhead will have to be allocated to other contracts. U.C.C. section 2-708 allows the recovery of reasonable overhead, and while it is not applicable here, it is persuasive authority.

---

3.   "Cover" in Contracts for the Sale of Goods--

Laredo Hides Co. v. H & H Meat Products Co., 513 S.W.2d 210 (Tex. Ct. App. 1974).

Facts. Laredo Hides Co. (P) contracted to purchase all of the hides produced by H & H Meat Products Co. (D) from March through December. D made two deliveries in March, but P's payment for the second delivery was delayed in the mail. D demanded payment within a few hours, but P failed to do so. D canceled the contract, and P purchased hides from other suppliers in order to meet its commitments. P spent $142,254.48 more to buy these hides than it would have cost to buy them from D. P also spent an extra $3,448.95 in transportation and handling charges. P sued to recover these amounts from D, but the trial court found for D. P appeals.

Issue. May a buyer recover the extra expense of buying goods elsewhere when the original contract seller cancels the contract to sell goods?

Held. Yes. Judgment reversed.

♦   D's cancellation of the contract was not justified by the temporary delay of P's payment. Therefore, D is liable for the damages P suffered.

♦   When D breached the contract by canceling it, P could buy the goods else-where (cover) and recover the difference between the contract price and the cover price, or P could recover the difference between the contract price and the market price at the date of breach. P chose the former alternative and should recover $152,960.04 plus interest. P acted reasonably and did nothing to increase its damages beyond what was necessary to meet its needs.

---

4.   **Lost Profits--**

R.E. Davis Chemical Corp. v. Diasonics, Inc., 826 F.2d 678 (7th Cir. 1987).

Facts. R.E. Davis Chemical Corp. (P) contracted to purchase medical diagnostic equipment from Diasonics, Inc. (D), which P was going to put into a medical facility building for Dobbin and Valvassori. The latter breached their contract with P, and P breached its contract with D, refusing to take delivery of the equipment. D sold the equipment to a third party for the same price. P had paid D a $300,000 deposit on the equipment, which it asked that D return. D refused, and P sued for restitution. D counterclaimed on the ground that as a lost volume seller, it lost the profit on the sale to P. The trial court granted summary judgment for P and awarded P the $300,000 plus interest, less D's incidental damages, on the ground that D was only entitled to the difference between the resale price and the contract price under U.C.C. section 2-706(1). D appeals.

Issue. Are a lost volume seller's damages limited to the market price/contract price differential provided under U.C.C. section 2-706(1)?

Held. No. Judgment reversed.

♦ Although Illinois has never before addressed this issue, other states have unanimously held that a lost volume seller may recover lost profits under section 2-708(2). This is the better approach and would be followed in Illinois.

♦ P is entitled to recover its down payment, less $500, under section 2-718(2)(b). Under section 2-718(3)(a), however, this right of restitution is subject to D's right to recover damages. A seller has four measures of general damages under the U.C.C.: (i) section 2-706, contract price less resale price; (ii) section 2-708(1), contract price less market price; (iii) section 2-708(2), profit; and (iv) section 2-709, price.

♦ The trial court's approach to these remedies was to refer to section 2-708 only if neither section 2-706 nor section 2-709 applies. Because D resold, section 2-706 was the only remedy. However, the seller's remedies under the U.C.C. are cumulative, and a plaintiff is not compelled to use any particular remedy unless the U.C.C. specifically so provides.

♦ The accepted rule for lost volume sellers applies section 2-708 instead of section 2-706. The lost profit measure under section 2-708(2) may be used only if the contract price less market price measure under section 2-708(1) is inadequate to put the seller in as good a position as performance would have done. The lost profit measure is appropriate when the seller can show that it could have profitably produced the units that were rejected in addition to its actual volume produced. D has the burden of proof.

♦ U.C.C. section 2-708(2) requires that the profit be figured with due credit for proceeds of resale. This provision has been interpreted to apply only to proceeds realized from the resale of uncompleted goods for scrap. Otherwise, this measure would eliminate the profit measure.

———————

5. **Alternatives to Expectation.** When the breaching party commits a total breach of the contract, the injured party may elect to sue for restitution of the benefits conferred if this amount would exceed the amount determined by the benefit of the bargain rule. For example, if P contracted to perform a job for D for $100 and D refused to pay on completion of the job, which is now worth $200, P may elect to sue D for the value of the benefit conferred (*i.e.,* $200) rather than the contract price that D agreed to pay (*i.e.,* $100). Also, if P pays D $100 in advance for a job and D fails to perform, but the cost of doing the job decreases to $60, P can still sue D to recover the benefit conferred (*i.e.,* $100) rather than the value of the substitute performance (*i.e.,* $60).

6. Recovery of Restitution Damages--

United States v. Algernon Blair, Inc., 479 F.2d 638 (4th Cir. 1973).

Facts. Coastal Steel Erector, Inc., a subcontractor, suing in the name of the United States (P), had contracted with Algernon Blair, Inc. (D) to supply certain equipment and perform steel erection as part of D's construction of a United States naval hospital. P performed about 28% of the subcontract before it terminated its performance, citing D's refusal to pay for crane rental. P sued to recover for labor and equipment furnished. The trial court held that P's termination was justified, but that while P was entitled to $37,000 in restitution, it would have lost a like amount had it completed performance and should therefore receive nothing. P appeals.

Issue. May a plaintiff recover in restitution even if he would have recovered nothing in a suit on the contract?

Held. Yes. Judgment reversed.

♦ An accepted principle of contract law is that the promisee, upon breach, has the option to forgo any suit on the contract and claim only the reasonable value of his performance. This is true even where the complaint joins a quantum meruit claim with a claim for damages from breach of contract.

♦ D has retained benefits, conferred at P's own expense, without having fully paid for them. This entitles P to restitution in quantum meruit. Such relief is appropriate regardless of whether P would have lost money on the contract and been unable to recover in a suit on the contract. P should recover the reasonable value of its performance, undiminished by any loss it would have suffered by fully performing.

D. LIMITATIONS ON DAMAGES

1. Duty to Mitigate.

a. **Introduction.** The nonbreaching party is not permitted to recover damages which he could have avoided by reasonable efforts. That is, he is under an affirmative duty to exercise reasonable efforts to avoid the consequences of the other party's breach. This is the so-called duty to "mitigate the damages."

b. **Reasonable conduct.** The nonbreaching party is held to a standard of reasonable conduct in responding to the other party's breach of contract. He must neither increase the loss by affirmative action, nor by inaction fail to minimize the loss where ordinary prudent conduct would have had that effect.

c.   **Refusal to avoid loss--**

Rockingham County v. Luten Bridge Co., 35 F.2d 301 (4th Cir. 1929).

Facts. Luten Bridge Co. (P) contracted to build a bridge for Rockingham County (D). After P spent $1,900 on labor and material, D, in response to adverse public opinion, unjustifiably canceled the contract. P refused to accept the cancellation and continued to build; upon completion, P sued for $18,301.37. From a judgment for P, D appeals.

Issue. Must the nonbreaching party attempt to mitigate the damages caused by the breach?

Held. Yes. Judgment reversed.

♦   Although D breached the contract by attempting to cancel it without the right to do so, P, on notice of D's cancellation (which amounted to a breach), had the duty to attempt to mitigate damages resulting from the breach.

♦   Here, P did nothing to mitigate the damages and in fact increased them, if recovery for all work done is allowed. Therefore, D is only liable for P's expenditures at the time of the breach plus the profit P would have realized if P had totally performed.

---

d.   **Market price damages for nondelivery--**

Tongish v. Thomas, 840 P.2d 471 (Kan. 1992).

Facts. Tongish (D) contracted to deliver sunflower seeds for a fixed price. Prior to the delivery date, the market price of the seeds doubled and D declined to deliver as agreed. Instead, D sold the seeds to another party for $5,153 more than the contract price. The buyer, Coop, sued D and recovered $455, which represented the profit Coop would have made for handling the seeds. The court of appeals reversed, holding that the proper measure of damages was U.C.C. section 2-713 (market price differential). D appeals.

Issue. Is the proper remedy for breach of a contract to deliver goods the difference between the contract price and the market price?

Held. Yes. Judgment affirmed.

◆ The market-price contract-price formula specified by U.C.C. section 2-713 does not normally represent the buyer's actual loss. Some courts consider this provision to be a statutory Liquidated Damages Clause. In this sense, section 2-713 conflicts with section 1-106, which provides that the injured party should recover the actual loss. The jurisdictions are split as to which measure of damages is appropriate, but the majority view awards market damages even though they are greater than the buyer's actual loss.

◆ The rationale of the majority approach is that market damages discourage the breach of delivery contracts and encourage a more efficient market. This is the better approach.

◆ Cases that limit the buyer's recovery to actual loss typically involve sellers who do not breach in bad faith, such as where the seller's crop is destroyed. In this case, there was no valid reason for D's breach. In addition, Coop was obligated to purchase the seeds at the contract price, even if the market price dropped by delivery time. It is only fair to hold D responsible for the market value of the seeds he refused to deliver.

---

e.   **Personal service contract--**

Parker v. Twentieth Century-Fox Film Corp., 474 P.2d 689 (Cal. 1970).

Facts. Parker (P) was a well-known actress who had a contract to appear in a certain movie production for a minimum compensation of $750,000. Twentieth Century-Fox Film Corp. (D) was the producer of the film and decided not to produce the film. D notified P of its intent not to produce the film and offered P a starring role in a different movie. P let the offer lapse and sued for breach of contract. The trial court awarded P summary judgment, and D appeals.

Issue. Does a wrongfully discharged employee have a duty to accept any available employment to mitigate damages under a contract of employment?

Held. No. Judgment affirmed.

◆ A wrongfully discharged employee has no duty to accept employment of a different kind which is inferior simply to mitigate damages. Here, the first movie was a musical and the second a western, so that the talents required by P in each would be substantially different. The contracts were different in that P had more control over the choice of a director in the first than in the second.

Dissent. The two contracts were substantially equivalent in that both called for the same kind of work to be performed by P.

---

f. **Cost to remedy--**

Jacob & Youngs v. Kent, 129 N.E. 889 (N.Y. 1921).

Facts. Jacob & Youngs (P) built Kent (D) a house. One of the specifications for the plumbing work was the use of "Reading" pipe. Nine months after D occupied the house, D learned that some of the pipes were from factories other than Reading. D's architect directed P to replace those pipes, but this would have required the demolition of parts of the house at great expense. P asked for the final payment, but D's architect refused to give the required certificate. P sued for the payment. At trial, P was not allowed to show the identical quality, appearance, and cost of the installed pipe. Verdict was directed for D. The appellate court reversed and a new trial was granted.

Issue. If a discrepancy in performance would be very expensive to remedy but does not affect the value of the final product, is the buyer entitled to recover the cost to remedy?

Held. No. Judgment affirmed.

- ◆ Normally, the measure of damages for defective performance is the cost of replacement. But when the cost is grossly and unfairly out of proportion to the good to be gained, the correct measure is the difference in value.

- ◆ P substantially performed and is entitled to the contract price, less any diminution in value attributable to the use of the wrong brand of pipe.

---

g. **Cost to complete--**

Groves v. John Wunder Co., 286 N.W.235 (Minn. 1939).

Facts. Groves (P) leased his land to John Wunder Co. (D) for $105,000 for seven years under an agreement which provided that D could remove sand and gravel from the property during the term of the lease and that D would restore the land to a uniform grade at the end of the term. When D failed to restore the land to its existing grade, but instead turned the land over to P in a rugged and uneven condition, P sued and was awarded slightly more than $15,000 based on evidence that the land in its restored condition would be worth only $12,160. P appealed, claiming that the damages should have been measured by the cost to restore the land, or $60,000.

Issue. Is cost to complete rather than diminution in value the proper measure of damages?

Held. Yes. Judgment reversed for D.

♦ In a construction contract, the law attempts to give the injured promisee as far as money will do it, what he was promised; and the cost of remedying the defect is the amount awarded as compensation for failure to render the promised performance.

♦ Here, D's breach was willful and without good faith; where a breach is willful, the breaching party may not sue on the contract nor invoke the benefit of the doctrine of substantial performance to limit damages to the diminution in value.

Dissent. The diminished value rule should apply unless the completed product is to satisfy the personal taste of the promisee.

---

h. **Measure of damages where cost of performance greatly exceeds diminution in value caused by breach--**

Peevyhouse v. Garland Coal & Mining Co., 382 P.2d 109 (Okla. 1963).

Facts. The Peevyhouses (Ps) leased their farm for five years to Garland Coal & Mining Co. (D) for coal mining purposes. One of the covenants in the lease provided that D would perform certain restorative work at the end of the lease period. D did not perform the work, which would have cost about $29,000. Ps sued for $25,000. The jury awarded Ps $5,000. The farm would have been worth $300 more if the work had been done. Both parties appeal.

Issue. Is the correct measure of damages the cost of doing the work rather than the diminution in value caused by the breach?

Held. No. Judgment modified to $300 and affirmed.

♦ Ps rely on *Groves v. John Wunder Co., supra.* In *Groves*, the court applied the "cost of performance" rule to award $60,000 in damages, even though the property would have been worth only $12,160 if the contracted work had been done. However, *Groves* is the only case that we know of in which the cost of performance rule has been followed where the cost of performance greatly exceeded the diminution in value caused by the breach of contract.

♦ In the present case, the primary purpose of the lease contract was to accomplish the economical recovery and marketing of coal from the land, to the profit of Ps and D. The provisions of the lease contract pertaining to remedial work were incidental to the main object.

♦ Although the analogy of building and construction contracts is not strictly applicable to this case, it has been held in some cases involving such contracts, such as *Jacob & Youngs v. Kent, supra,* that if the defect can be repaired without undue expense, the cost of performance is the proper measure of damages. But if the defect cannot be remedied without an expenditure that is disproportionate to the end to be attained, the value rule should be followed.

♦ We hold that where there is a coal mining lease in which the lessee agrees to perform remedial work on the property at the end of the lease period, and the contract is fully performed by both parties except that the lessee defaults on the remedial work, the measure of the lessor's damages for breach of contract is ordinarily the reasonable cost of performance of the work. But if the contract provision breached was merely incidental to the main purpose, and if the economic benefit that would result to the lessor by full performance of the work is grossly disproportionate to the cost of performance, the damages that the lessor may recover are limited to the decrease in value resulting to the premises because of the nonperformance.

Dissent. D knew that Ps would not agree to the lease unless the provisions regarding restorative work were included. Ps were entitled to specific performance of the contract, and D failed to perform. Thus, the proper measure of damages is the cost of performance. Otherwise, the restorative provisions mean nothing, D receives benefits without a resulting obligation, and a new contract is made.

───────────

2. **Foreseeability.**

   a. **Introduction.** In some cases, the standard measure of damages does not provide full compensation for the loss of the benefit of the bargain. In many cases there are special circumstances which may aggravate the economic loss to one party if the other party fails to perform. Where such special circumstances were known to both parties at the time the contract was made, the breaching party will be deemed to have assumed the liability for such additional damages in the event of breach. [Restatement (First) §330; U.C.C. §2-710]

   b. **Awareness of special circumstances.** The assumption is that the breaching party was aware at the time she contracted of the losses likely to result in the event of her breach. Thus, it must be shown that defendant had (or a reasonable person should have had) a clear understanding of the "special circumstances" facing the other party.

   c. **Lost profits: established business--**

Hadley v. Baxendale, 156 Eng. Rep. 145 (Ex. 1854).

Facts. Ps stopped operation of their mill when a crankshaft broke. They contracted with D to have it shipped for repairs, delivery to the manufacturer to be made within a "reasonable time." D was negligent in not completing delivery within a reasonable time, and for five days P lost profits and wages paid (amounting to £300). Contrary to the excerpt from the lower court, D was not informed that the mill would not operate until the shaft was repaired. The jury awarded P £50 damages. D appeals.

Issue. Does the proper measure of damages for "special situations" include actual damages where actual damages are greater than the natural consequences of breach?

Held. No. New trial granted; damages given by the jury to P were improper.

♦ Normally, damages are those which arise naturally from a breach of the contract (*i.e.,* those which would be expected by both parties to probably flow from a breach). In addition, where there are damages because of special circumstances (here lost profits due to the mill shutdown), they will be assessed against the defendant only where they were reasonably within the contemplation of both of the parties as being the probable consequence of a breach.

♦ Here, D did not know that the mill was shut down and would be until the new shaft arrived. The jury should not have considered P's loss of profits.

Comment. Damages arising from special situations may be awarded where plaintiff informs defendant of special circumstances or where these damages are reasonably foreseeable by the defendant at the time that the contract is formed.

---

d. Buyer's damages for unfilled orders--

Delchi Carrier SpA v. Rotorex Corp., 71 F.3d 1024 (2d Cir. 1995).

Facts. Rotorex Corp. (D) agreed to sell compressors to Delchi Carrier SpA (P) in three shipments. D provided a sample with specifications before the parties executed the contract. While the second shipment was en route at sea, P discovered that the first lot of compressors did not conform to the sample and the specifications. P was unable to cure the defects and asked D to supply new conforming compressors. D refused. P cancelled the contract and sued for breach of contract. The court awarded P damages of $1,248,331, which included consequential damages for lost profits from lost sales, but it denied P's claims for shipping expenses on D's two shipments and other incidental expenses. Both parties appeal.

Issue. Are lost profits on unfilled orders sufficiently foreseeable to be recovered as damages for breach?

Held. Yes. Judgment affirmed in part, reversed in part, and case remanded.

♦ This case is governed by the United Nations Convention on Contracts for the International Sale of Goods ("CISG"), although the courts may take guidance from U.C.C. case law interpreting analogous provisions.

♦ The CISG provides that damages consist of the loss suffered as a consequence of the breach, subject to the foreseeability principle of *Hadley v. Baxendale* (*supra*). In this case, it was foreseeable that P would take orders for sales based on the number of compressors it had ordered from D. The court properly awarded damages for D's lost sales.

♦ The court should also have awarded incidental damages pertaining to D's defective compressors, including the shipping costs and special materials and tooling purchased for use only with those compressors. The award of the incidental and consequential damages does not duplicate lost profit damages. These expenses were foreseeable to D because they were necessary for P to be able to receive and use D's compressors.

---

e. **Loss of anticipated appreciation in real estate--**

Kenford Co. v. County of Erie, 537 N.E.2d 176 (N.Y. 1989).

Facts. The County of Erie (D) authorized itself to construct a domed sports stadium to be financed by a $50 million bond. Kenford Co. (P) offered to donate the land in exchange for hiring Dome Stadium, Inc. ("DSI") to manage the stadium. D accepted P's offer. While the parties were negotiating, P exercised options to purchase land in the vicinity. D, P and DSI entered a contract whereby P would donate 178 acres of land and D would commence construction within 12 months. D was required to negotiate a 40-year lease with DSI for operation of the facility, or agree to a predetermined 20-year lease. Among the payments to D were increased real property taxes from the increased assessments on P's other land in the vicinity. When D found out that the project would cost $72 million, it terminated the contract. P sued for breach of contract. The jury awarded P $18 million for the lost appreciation on its peripheral property, plus $6 million in out-of-pocket expenses. DSI received $25.6 million in lost profits on the management contract. The appellate court reversed the award to DSI and ordered a new trial on P's claim for loss of anticipated appreciation. On retrial, the jury awarded P $6.5 million for lost appreciation. D appeals.

Issue. Is a developer entitled to recover the loss of anticipated appreciation in the value of its real estate located in proximity to a planned sports stadium when the government decides not to build the stadium?

Held. No. Judgment reversed.

♦ In determining what damages are foreseeable and within the reasonable contemplation of the parties, the nature, purpose and particular circumstances of the contract known by the parties should be considered. The court should also determine what liability D fairly should have assumed consciously, or what P reasonably should have supposed that D assumed, when the contract was made.

♦ The parties here clearly expected and anticipated that construction and operation of the sports stadium would increase land values and property taxes from property in the vicinity of the stadium. However, nothing in the contract provides a remedy based on this anticipated appreciation.

♦ Where the contract does not provide a remedy for default, the court should consider what the parties would have concluded had they considered the subject. D was aware that P had purchased peripheral lands, but there was no contractual requirement for P to do so. D's awareness of P's ownership of the peripheral property is insufficient as a matter of law to impose liability on D for the loss of anticipated appreciation in that property.

♦ P purchased the peripheral property with the hope of realizing the anticipated appreciation, but, in so doing, he assumed the risk that the property would not appreciate in value if the stadium was not built. Without evidence that D specifically assumed this risk, it is illogical to infer that D would do so. There is no indication that D reasonably contemplated that it would assume liability for P's unrealized appreciation in land values. P's damages must be limited to those that were reasonably foreseen or contemplated by the parties when the contract was executed.

---

3. **Certainty.**

   a. **Introduction.** One overall limitation on the plaintiff's right to recover damages is that the amount of his loss must be reasonably certain of computation. That is, damages which are too "uncertain" (*i.e.,* speculative) are not allowed, since any award in excess of the plaintiff's actual loss would in effect be a penalty, and punitive damages are not allowed in contract actions (*see supra*) unless required and authorized by statute (*e.g.,* antitrust laws).

   b. **Lost profits: new business.**

      1) **Damages uncertain.** Often "lost profits" are found to be too uncertain for their recovery as part of damages. For example, in a new business, where the parties have bargained for a share of the profits to be made, a breach that occurs before any profits are realized may be noncompensable, since the profits are too uncertain.

However, some courts will not deny recovery on grounds of uncertainty if there is a reasonable probability that damages did arise.

2) Sufficiency of evidence--

Fera v. Village Plaza, Inc., 242 N.W.2d 372 (Mich. 1976).

Facts. Fera (P) leased a book and bottle shop in a shopping center planned by Village Plaza, Inc. (D). The lease was to last 10 years with a minimum rent plus a percentage of sales. D defaulted, and the bank assumed management. When the center opened, P discovered that his space had been leased to other tenants because his lease had been misplaced. The alternative space offered to P was unsuitable, and P sued for lost profits. At trial, P testified that he would have probably made $270,000 in profits. D's witnesses testified that P could not obtain a liquor license and that the proof of possible profits was too speculative. The jury awarded P $200,000, but the court of appeals reversed on the ground that lost profits was an incorrect measure of damages. P appeals.

Issue. May lost profits be awarded to a new business which is prevented from starting due to breach of contract?

Held. Yes. Judgment reversed.

♦ Traditionally, the measure of damages for the lessee when the lessor does not deliver possession has been the difference between the actual rental value and the contract rent. This measure was the sole recovery if the business was new because there was no basis for estimating profits. Interruption of a business, by contrast, would result in damages for proven lost profits. While this is the general rule, it applies because prospective profits for a new business are usually too speculative.

♦ When proof of prospective profits is available, however, they may be recovered, even by a new business. The jury may not speculate or guess, but if the evidence is sufficient, a new business can recover damages for lost profits.

♦ In this case, the evidence before the jury was sufficient to support its verdict; even though an appellate court might disagree with the jury, it cannot say that as a matter of law P's evidence was legally insufficient.

Dissent. The evidence in this case did not prove with a reasonable degree of certainty P's anticipated profits. A new trial should be awarded unless P agrees to a remittitur to $60,000, representing the anticipated profits from the bookstore and none for the liquor store.

---

3) Strict approach. *Evergreen Amusement Corp. v. Milstead*, 112 A.2d 901 (Md. 1955), involved an action for the breach of a contract that caused a delay in the opening of a drive-in theater. The court held that lost profits from a business that had not gone into operation are too speculative and uncertain to consider when awarding damages.

E. LIQUIDATED DAMAGES AND PENALTIES

1. **Introduction.** The parties may include in the contract specific provisions limiting or fixing the amount of damages that can be recovered in the event of a breach (a liquidated damages clause).

2. **Provisions Excluding or Limiting the Amount of Damages.** The contract may provide that no damages at all may be recovered for certain types of breach (so-called "exculpatory" clauses); or that any damages recoverable be limited to a maximum sum. Courts tend to construe such provisions narrowly and will strike down provisions that are unconscionable or unreasonable.

3. **Stipulated Damages Provisions.**

   a. **Introduction.** The contract may include a provision stipulating a fixed, definite sum to be paid in the event of breach (*i.e.,* "damages shall be $1,000, in the event of any breach"). The enforceability of such a provision depends on whether the court finds it to be a valid liquidated damages clause or an attempted "penalty."

   b. **Penalty provisions unenforceable.** If the court determines that the damages provision would operate as a "penalty," it is unenforceable. A provision may be held to be a penalty where it was intended as a pecuniary threat to prevent breach, or to provide a kind of security to insure the other party's performance, etc.

   c. **Where enforced.** If the court determines that such a damages clause was made in good faith as an effort by the parties to estimate the actual damages that would probably ensue from a breach, it may be enforced. There are, therefore, two requirements for a valid stipulated damages clause:

      (i) Damages must be difficult to estimate at the time of contract.

      (ii) The amount agreed upon must be a reasonable forecast of actual damages, *i.e.,* a reasonable forecast of fair compensation for the harm that would occur on breach.

1) **Comment.** Note that these tests are really contradictory (if damages are difficult to estimate, how can they also be assured of being a reasonable forecast of actual damages?).

2) **U.C.C. section 2-718.** U.C.C. section 2-718 permits liquidated damages agreements if the tests above are met and if it is inconvenient or infeasible to otherwise obtain an adequate remedy; unreasonably large liquidated damages provisions are declared void as penalties.

4. **Disproportionate Liquidated Damages--**

Wasserman's Inc. v. Township of Middletown, 645 A.2d 100 (N.J. 1994).

Facts. The Township of Middletown (D) owned commercial property which it leased to Wasserman's Inc. (P) for use as a store. The lease contained a cancellation clause that required D to pay P 25% of P's average annual gross receipts, based on a three-year average, if D canceled the lease. D canceled the lease 16 years later. P and its sublessee sued for damages under the lease. P's sublessee had an average annual gross of over $1 million, but an average net profit of only around $1,000. D sought a declaration that the cancellation clause was invalid. The court granted P partial summary judgment regarding the clause and awarded P damages of $290,000 for the 25% of annual receipts. D appeals.

Issue. May a liquidated damages clause be enforced if it awards the nonbreaching party nearly $300,000 when that party's actual loss is only around $1,000?

Held. No. Judgment reversed.

♦   Penalty clauses in contract cases have been disapproved since early common law. Such clauses are intended to punish the breach of a contract instead of estimating probable actual damages, which a liquidated damages clause attempts to do. The latter is enforceable, but the former is not.

♦   To qualify as a liquidated damages clause, the clause must constitute a reasonable forecast of the provable injury resulting from breach. One element of assessing the reasonableness of a liquidated damages clause is the uncertainty or difficulty of estimating actual damages; *i.e.,* the more difficult it is to estimate damages, the more likely the stipulated damages will be deemed reasonable.

♦   Some courts determine the enforceability of a liquidated damages clause as of the time of the making of the contract, but the modern trend looks at the clause both at the time of contracting and at the time of breach. Actual damages may be a guide to the reasonableness of the parties' prediction. Liquidated damages clauses are presumptively reasonable, and the party challenging the clause has the burden of proving its unreasonableness.

♦ The clause in this case was likely to result in unreasonable damages because gross receipts do not reflect actual losses incurred because of cancellation. This measure of damages is inherently speculative and uncertain, and can result in a windfall. In this case, it appears that the liquidated damages were so far in excess of actual losses that the clause might be an unenforceable penalty. On remand, the court should consider the reasonableness of using gross receipts as the measure of damages and all other factors relevant to the enforceability of this clause.

5. **No Provable Actual Damages--**

Dave Gustafson & Co. v. State, 156 N.W.2d 185 (S.D. 1968).

Facts. Dave Gustafson & Co. (P) performed highway construction work for the state (D). The contract provided for liquidated damages of $210 per day of delay (an amount based on the size of the contract). The work was delayed 67 days, and D withheld $14,070 from the total contract price of $530,724. P sued for the difference. The trial court found for D. P appeals.

Issue. May a liquidated damages clause be enforced where there is no way to measure actual damages?

Held. Yes. Judgment affirmed.

♦ Liquidated damages clauses should be enforced when they are fair and reasonable attempts to fix just compensation for anticipated loss caused by breach of contract. Such clauses are especially useful when damages are uncertain in nature or amount or are unmeasurable.

♦ There is no way to measure actual damages for the delay in construction of a new highway. As long as the amount specified by the liquidated damages clause was intended as fair compensation for the loss, inconvenience, added costs, or deprivation of use caused by the delay, it may be deemed reasonable. As such, this clause is enforceable.

Comment. Many government contracts involve projects such as the one in this case, where delay does not cause any measurable loss, but does cause inconvenience to the public generally. An important factor for the court was that the daily rate was based on the size of the contract, suggesting that the larger the project, the larger the loss. Using a daily rate roughly reflects the incremental inconvenience.

VIII. PERFORMANCE AND BREACH

A. CONDITIONS

1. Conditions and Covenants Distinguished.

a. **Breach of contract depends on failure to perform an absolute duty.** In order for a breach of contract to occur, a party must fail to perform some absolute duty. Thus, the contract must be analyzed to determine whether the promisor is under such an absolute duty, since sometimes the duty to perform is conditioned on some event (and thus the promisor is under no duty to perform until the contingency first occurs).

b. **Covenants.** A covenant is an absolute, unconditional promise to perform (or refrain from performing) some act. That is, it is a contractual promise to which no conditions are attached.

　1) A failure to perform a covenant is always a breach of contract.

　2) For example, if A promises to pay B $1,000 if B paints A's house by June 1st, the painting of the house by June 1st is a condition precedent to A having to pay the $1,000; but once B has performed, then A has an absolute promise (covenant) to pay the $1,000.

c. **Conditions.** A condition is a fact or event, the happening or non-happening of which creates or extinguishes a duty to perform on the part of the promisor. Failure of a condition to occur is not a breach of contract.

2. Interpretation of Doubtful Provisions.
It is important whether a condition or a covenant is intended, since failure to perform a covenant results in breach of contract and failure of a condition to occur does not (since contractual duties may never become absolute duties or may be excused).

a. **The intent of the parties.** The general rule is that the intent of the parties is to determine whether a particular provision is a covenant or a condition. However, in many instances it is not clear from the contract itself as to whether the parties intended a covenant (absolute promise) or a condition (qualification of a promise). Each case must be decided on its own facts.

b. **Factors considered.**

　1) **Words used.** Words such as "provided," "if," "when," etc., usually indicate that a condition is involved. Words such as "promise," "agreed," etc., generally indicate a covenant.

2) **Custom.** Common usage or understanding may be determinative.

3) **Protection of expectancies of the parties.** This is the most important factor, since it relates to the intention of the parties.

    a) Thus, doubtful provisions will normally be construed as covenants rather than conditions. [Restatement §261]

    b) The rationale is that this operates to uphold and make enforceable the contract and allow damages for nonperformance.

3. Express Conditions.

    a. **Introduction.** Note that conditions may be classified as to whether they are express or implied. An express condition is one explicitly stated by the parties in the contract. An implied condition (discussed *infra*) is one that the parties would probably have agreed to if they had thought about the subject. The courts will imply whatever conditions are inherent in the promises given as necessary to the performance of the contract (conditions such as "good faith performance," etc.).

    b. **Legal effect of conditions.** Where a promise to perform is conditional, there can be no breach of the promise until the duty to perform becomes absolute (*i.e.,* until the occurrence of the conditions attached to the duty). Thus, conditions create or extinguish the absolute duty to perform, depending upon the time of the occurrence of the condition.

        1) **Conditions precedent.** A condition precedent is one which must occur in order to create an absolute duty to perform; that is, there is no duty owed until the conditional fact or event first occurs.

            a) **Example.** If A promises to pay B $1,000 if B paints A's house by June 1st, painting the house by June 1st is a condition precedent of A's absolute duty to pay B $1,000. When B completes the painting by June 1st, then A's promise to pay becomes absolute and unconditional. However, if B does not complete the painting, there is no breach of contract by anyone.

            b) **Comment.** A condition may also be a covenant. That is, in the above example, A may promise to pay B $1,000 and B may promise A to paint the house by June 1st. Thus, the promise to paint the house by June 1st is now both a promise and also a condition precedent to A's duty to pay B $1,000. Now if B fails to paint the house by June 1st, she has breached the contract (and A may collect damages) and there is also a failure of a condition precedent to A's duty to pay; thus, A's duty to pay never arises.

c) Strict compliance--

Luttinger v. Rosen, 316 A.2d 757 (Conn. 1972).

Facts. Rosen (P) contracted to purchase a house from Luttinger (D) for $85,000, subject to and conditioned upon P obtaining a first mortgage of $45,000 for not less than 20 years and at no more than 8½% interest. P paid a 10% deposit. P's attorney, who was fully informed as to the mortgage lending market, applied for a mortgage at the only institution which would lend $45,000 for a house. This institution would not agree to a rate less than 8¾%, so P sought a return of the deposit, but D refused, instead offering to fund the difference. P sued and won; D appeals.

Issue. Does one party's offer to compensate for the failure of a condition precedent prevent the operation of the condition?

Held. No. Judgment affirmed.

♦ D first claims that P should have applied elsewhere for a loan, but offers no proof to negate P's attorney's information. The law does not require the performance of a futile act.

♦ Obtaining a mortgage with the maximum interest rate was a clear condition precedent to performance of the contract. D's claim that it would have made up the difference between that maximum rate and the actual rate is entirely irrelevant. P was not required to accept D's compensation for the failure of the condition.

d) Failure by buyer to provide delivery instructions--

Internatio-Rotterdam, Inc. v. River Brand Rice Mills, Inc., 259 F.2d 137 (2d Cir. 1958), *cert. denied,* 358 U.S. 946 (1959).

Facts. Internatio-Rotterdam, Inc. (P) was an exporter and River Brand Rice Mills, Inc. (D) was a wholesaler and processor of rice. P contracted in July to purchase rice from D for delivery in December. P was to provide shipping instructions no later than two weeks prior to delivery. P delivered the shipping instructions for half of the contract amount which was going to one port, but by December 17 had not given instructions regarding the balance of the shipment. On December 18, D canceled the contract for the balance of the shipment but continued deliveries to the port for which instructions had been given. P sued for damages for nondelivery. The trial court dismissed P's complaint. P appeals.

Issue. When a sales contract specifies a delivery time and requires the buyer to provide delivery instructions, is the buyer obligated to provide timely delivery instructions as a condition precedent to receiving the goods?

Held. Yes. Judgment affirmed.

♦ The contract clearly called for a December delivery date, and P was obligated to notify D of the delivery instructions in sufficient time to allow D two weeks to complete the delivery. This means that P should have notified D by December 17. Notification was a condition precedent to D's duty to ship.

♦ Because D's facilities were working at full capacity in December and its storage capacity was limited, the requirement for December shipment went to the essence of the contract. Once P failed to satisfy the condition precedent, D could rescind the contract or treat its contractual obligation as discharged.

♦ The contract was severable as to the two ports, so D's continued shipments to one port did not constitute an election to proceed with the entire contract.

---

2) **Conditions subsequent.** A condition subsequent is one in which the occurrence of the condition extinguishes a previously absolute duty to perform.

   a) **The effect.** Occurrence of a condition subsequent extinguishes the previously absolute duty to perform.

   b) **Example.** For example, if A agrees to work for B for one year, unless he is drafted into the military service, then A is under an absolute duty to perform, unless during the term he is called into the service (which occurrence extinguishes the duty of A to perform).

   c) **Interpretation.** Conditions subsequent are rare. Courts do not favor interpreting contracts in this manner. Thus, many provisions that appear to be conditions subsequent are interpreted as conditions precedent. For example, if an insurance policy provides that a claim will be paid only if submitted within 90 days of the accident, this appears to be a condition subsequent, but courts hold that it is a condition precedent (insurer has no duty to pay unless the condition of submitting the claim within 90 days is first complied with).

3) **Conditions concurrent.** Conditions concurrent are mutually dependent performances which are capable of nearly simultaneous performance by the parties. These occur when the parties to the

contract are bound to render performance at the same time. For example, in a contract for the sale of goods, A covenants to deliver widgets on June 1st and B promises to pay for them. Each promise (by A and B) is also a condition of the other's performance, and since they are mutually dependent and capable of simultaneous performance, they are conditions concurrent.

c.   Conditions of satisfaction.

1)   Introduction. A specific type of condition is examined in this section, that of performing something to the "satisfaction" of another party.

a)   For example, if A promises to paint B's house and B promises to pay A $1,000 if "I am satisfied with the work," B's being satisfied is a condition precedent to having to pay the $1,000.

b)   The issue is always one of how "satisfaction" is to be measured.

2)   Where the parties specify subjective "satisfaction." In some contracts the contract specifically mentions that satisfaction is "my personal satisfaction" (*i.e.*, subjective satisfaction of one of the parties). Normally courts read the word "satisfied" literally and the party is under no obligation to pay unless she is personally satisfied.

3)   Where the standard of satisfaction is not specified. Other contracts use the term "satisfaction" without specifically indicating that it is the personal satisfaction of one of the parties; *e.g.*, if the work is performed "satisfactorily." In this situation, the basis for determining satisfactory performance depends on the context of the contract.

a)   **Where the subject matter of the contract is not personal.** In contracts where the subject matter is not "personal," satisfaction tends to be read as a performance that would satisfy a "reasonable person," *e.g.*, construction contracts and contracts for the sale of fungible goods.

b)   **Where the subject matter is personal.** In these situations, the courts hold that personal satisfaction is required even though it is not expressly stated, *e.g.*, a contract to do a portrait painting.

4)   Performance to the satisfaction of some third party. Most courts hold that where the contract provides that work must be performed to the satisfaction of some third party, this means the personal satisfaction of this party.

4. Interpretation Problems.

    a. Introduction. A party who wants to make sure the other party to the contract performs may have the obligee simply undertake a duty to perform or make the obligee's performance a condition of the obligor's duty. Deciding whether a provision is a condition or duty can be difficult. The courts generally prefer an interpretation that avoids a condition because of the harsh results that can arise from nonoccurrence of a condition.

    b. Judicial interpretation--

Peacock Construction Co. v. Modern Air Conditioning, Inc., 353 So. 2d 840 (Fla. 1977).

Facts. Peacock Construction Co. (D) was the general contractor on a condominium project. Modern Air Conditioning, Inc. (P) was a subcontractor. D contracted to make final payment to P "within 30 days after completion . . . and full payment therefore by the Owner." D failed to pay within the 30 days because it had not been paid by the owner. P sued for payment; D claimed the provision was a condition precedent, and the trial court granted D summary judgment. D lost on appeal and applied for certiorari, on grounds that an earlier case, *Edward J. Gerrits, Inc. v. Astor Electric Service, Inc.* 328 So. 2d 522 (Fla. 3d DCA 1976), held that such contractual provisions present a factual question as to the parties' intent.

Issue. May the courts determine the intention of the parties from the written contract, as a matter of law, when the nature of the transaction lends itself to judicial interpretation?

Held. Yes. Judgment affirmed.

♦   The contract provision may be interpreted as setting a condition precedent or as fixing a reasonable time for payment. The *Gerrits* case held that a fact finder should interpret the provision. We disagree and overrule *Gerrits*. These contract provisions may be interpreted as a matter of law.

♦   The relationship between generals and subs is common and their intent will not differ from transaction to transaction. That intent is that such provisions do not create conditions precedent because subs will not ordinarily assume the risk of the owner's failure to pay. The parties may shift this risk to the sub, but only by clear, unambiguous language.

---

c.   Personal satisfaction--

Gibson v. Cranage, 39 Mich. 49 (1878).

Facts. Gibson (P) agreed to make a portrait of the deceased daughter of Cranage (D) based on a small picture. When P presented the picture, D refused to accept it, claiming he had agreed to accept the picture from P only if it was "perfectly satisfactory" to him. P was unable to find out from D what his objections were. D wrote P a letter stating that the picture was unsatisfactory and that he declined to take it or any similar picture. P sued for the purchase price. The court found for D. P appeals.

Issue. Can contractual liability be conditioned on subjective personal satisfaction?

Held. Yes. Judgment affirmed.

♦   P agreed that the picture when finished must be satisfactory to D. Where the parties deliberately enter into an agreement which violates no rule of public policy, and which is free from all taint of fraud or mistake, there is no hardship whatever in holding them bound by it.

♦   It makes no difference that third parties might think the picture is excellent. It must be satisfactory to D.

---

5.   **Mitigating Doctrines.** The nonoccurrence of a condition can lead to a harsh effect for a party to a contract. The courts have adopted several doctrines to mitigate what would otherwise be unfair harm.

   a.   **Prevention.** The obligation of good faith normally requires that a party do nothing to prevent the occurrence of a condition, so that a party who does prevent the occurrence of a condition may not assert the nonoccurrence of that condition.

   b.   **Waiver, estoppel, and election.** The parties may always waive a condition. A party who does waive a condition is actually excusing the nonoccurrence of a condition or duty. A waiver may be retracted before the time for occurrence, but if the other party has relied on the waiver, the waiving party may be estopped from retracting. If a party waives a condition after the time for occurrence, the waiver cannot be retracted, regardless of whether the other party has relied on the waiver. After the time for occurrence has passed, the party must elect to enforce the condition or to waive it.

c.   **Implied waiver.** In *McKenna v. Vernon*, 101 A. 919 (Pa. 1917), McKenna was building a theatre for Vernon. The contract required an architect's certificate prior to each installment payment, but Vernon made six of seven progress payments without receiving a certificate. McKenna requested the final payment without a certificate. Vernon refused, and McKenna sued. At trial, the architect testified that McKenna had complied with the specifications. The court granted McKenna judgment because Vernon had waived the condition repeatedly during the progress of the work. This case illustrates the dilemma of lenience. A party may choose not to enforce contract requirements in the interest of efficiency and thereby lose the benefit of the condition when the relationship deteriorates.

d.   **Parol condition precedent--**

Hicks v. Bush, 180 N.E.2d 425 (N.Y. 1962).

Facts. Hicks (P) brought an action for specific performance of a written agreement pursuant to which Bush (D) and P and others had intended to merge into a stock holding company. The written agreement, however, made no mention of the condition (orally agreed to) that the sum of $672,500 had to be raised in order for the written document to take effect. P claims that Ds breached the agreement by not transferring their stock to the holding company, in that the written document embodies the entire agreement between the parties. The trial court allowed the introduction of testimony which related to the oral agreement that was allegedly binding on the written agreement in question. P appeals the introduction of such evidence.

Issue. May parol evidence be introduced to prove a parol condition precedent to a written contract?

Held. Yes. Judgment affirmed.

♦   Parol evidence is admissible to prove a condition precedent to the legal effectiveness of a written agreement. One of the conditions under which the holding company was formed was that the $672,500 would be raised for working capital. This condition was not fulfilled; therefore, there was no binding contract.

♦   This parol condition is not contradictory or inconsistent with the written agreement. It is merely an additional condition.

Comment. The parol evidence rule says that an oral agreement cannot be used as evidence to change a subsequent written agreement. However, if an oral agreement is for a condition precedent to the effectiveness of the contract, then such evidence may be introduced.

B. CONSTRUCTIVE CONDITIONS

1. **Introduction.** A party may fail to render an agreed performance, but the contract may not specify that such a failure excuses performance by the other party. The effect of this failure depends on what the parties intended. While the implied covenant of good faith and fair dealing is a means of insuring that the parties' expectations are met, the doctrine of constructive conditions, or implied conditions, is used to supply conditions in the interest of fairness and justice.

   a. **Early common law approach.** At early common law, courts did not recognize constructive conditions. Parties to a bilateral contract were deemed to have bargained for the promise by the other party, rather than the performance itself. Each party got what he bargained for—the other's promise. The fact that the other party had not yet performed was immaterial to each party's duty to perform his own side of the bargain. The promises were deemed independent.

   b. **Development of dependent covenants--**

Kingston v. Preston, 99 Eng. Rep. 437 (K.B. 1773).

Facts. Kingston (P) agreed to work for Preston (D) for one and one-quarter years as a servant, and then D, upon P's presenting good security, would transfer his business and stock in trade to P at a "fair valuation." When the time arrived, D refused to perform the transfer. P sued for nonperformance, claiming that he had begun performance and was willing to continue to perform but that D refused to perform. D claimed that P did not offer sufficient security.

Issue. Must a party fully perform before the other may be forced to perform?

Held. Yes. Judgment for D.

♦ Before receiving the business from D, P was required to show good security for the payment of the money. Because P failed to give good security, D had no obligation to perform.

Comments. The court delineated three types of covenants:

♦ **Mutual and independent.** Either party may recover damages from the other in the event of breach by the other, and an alleged breach by one party is not an excuse for the other party.

♦ **Conditional and dependent.** Performance of one party depends on the prior performance of the other and, until the prior condition is performed, the other party will not be held to performance of his covenant. This is the rule applied in *Kingston*.

◆ **Simultaneous.** If one party tenders and the other party refuses to perform, the first party has an action for default against the refusing party.

---

c. **Modern approach.** Under modern law, each party's performance, or tender of performance, is deemed a constructive, or implied-in-law, condition to the other's obligation to perform. Thus, neither party's duty to perform arises until the other has performed or tendered performance. The legal and procedural effects of constructive conditions are ordinarily the same as if the conditions had been expressly set forth in the contract.

2. **Progress Payments May Not Be Inferred--**

Stewart v. Newbury, 115 N.E. 984 (N.Y. 1917).

Facts. Stewart (P) contracted to do some construction work for Newbury (D). The time for payment was not mentioned in the written contract, but P argued that there was an oral understanding that payment would be made according to custom, which was to pay 85% of work completed each month. After three months, P submitted a bill. D refused to pay. P discontinued work and sued for the amount due. P won at trial, and the appellate court affirmed. D appeals.

Issue. Is a contractor entitled to part payment if the contract makes no provision for it?

Held. No. Judgment reversed.

◆ The jury was instructed that if the contract did not provide for payments, P would be entitled to part payments at reasonable times, and if such payments were refused, he could terminate performance. This is incorrect.

◆ Where a construction contract makes no provision for installment payments, then the work must be substantially performed before payment can be demanded.

C. MITIGATING DOCTRINES

1. **The Doctrine of Substantial Performance.** Normally this doctrine is applied in construction contracts where hardship is created if the owner is allowed to retain the value of the building without payment just because the builder made some small mistakes. In other situations (such as the sale of

goods under U.C.C. section 2-601), the courts have been less willing to protect a party whose performance of a condition has been defective.

a.   **The elements of substantial performance.**

   1)   **Minor breach.** Normally the breach of the condition must be minor. (*See* the six factors used to make this determination under the Restatement (First) section 275, *supra*.)

   2)   **Nonwillful.** Most courts hold that a willful breach, even though minor, will preclude to the breaching party the benefits of the doctrine of substantial performance.

b.   **Measure of damages.** Where A substantially performs a condition in his contract with B, A may enforce the contract (the condition of his complete performance being excused). B may, however, collect damages for the minor defective performance of A. Damages are generally measured by the diminution in value of A's performance rather than the cost to complete or cure the defects.

c.   **Excuse of conditions by substantial performance.** Where complete performance by one party is a condition precedent or concurrent to the other party's duty of counter-performance, that condition may be excused if the party has rendered "substantial" performance. The other party's duty of counter-performance then becomes absolute, although he can deduct any damages suffered by the first party's incomplete performance.

d.   **Unsubstantial omissions in performance--**

Jacob & Youngs v. Kent, 129 N.E. 889 (N.Y. 1921).

Facts. The facts are set forth *supra*.

Issue. Should the doctrine of substantial performance be applied in this case to avoid the oppression of a forfeiture?

Held. Yes. Judgment affirmed.

♦   P's conduct was neither fraudulent nor willful, but was the result of P's subcontractor's oversight and inattention. The trial court excluded P's evidence that the substituted brand of pipe was the same as the specified brand, except manufactured in a different place. This evidence suggests that the defect was insignificant in the context of the overall project.

♦   A trivial and innocent omission in the performance of a contract does not always constitute a breach of a condition to be followed by a forfeiture. Legal rules should be applied in a practical manner, adapted to attain a just result. The certainty and consistency of a stricter standard are important but must be balanced against equity and fairness.

♦ Defective performance that frustrates the purpose of the contract cannot be tolerated. However, if the defect is unintentional and trivial, the transgressor may be allowed to atone for it by an allowance to the owner of the resulting damage, rather than by a forfeiture.

Dissent (McLaughlin, J.). P did not perform its contract, either intentionally or as the result of gross negligence. P did not explain why it failed to install the correct brand of pipe. D had a right to receive what he contracted for. The rule of substantial performance, with damages for unsubstantial omissions, should not apply in this case.

---

e. Defects in construction--

Plante v. Jacobs, 103 N.W.2d 296 (Wis. 1960).

Facts. Plante (P) contracted to build the Jacobses (Ds) a house for $26,750; Ds paid $20,000 and refused to pay more, on the basis that there was faulty construction (a living room wall was misplaced one foot, etc.). P refused to complete the job and sued for breach of the entire contract; Ds defended on the basis that P had not substantially performed the contract. There had not been any detailed plans for the construction. P sued and won. Ds appeal.

Issue. Has P substantially performed on the contract?

Held. Yes. Judgment affirmed.

♦ There were no detailed plans for construction. Thus, since P performed to the substantial purpose of the contract, P rendered substantial performance and is due the contract price. However, D should receive damages for P's failure to perform in finishing the home. Each element of damages should be separately assessed (minor items on the basis of cost of completion, major items on the basis of loss in value). The misplaced living room wall did not diminish the value of the home and so does not amount to a material breach.

---

2. Divisibility.

  a. **Introduction.** A party to a contract ordinarily has no right to refuse performance due to a breach by the other party of a separate contract between them. Even a single contract may consist of divisible portions. A contract will be construed as severable if the part to be performed by one party consists of several distinct items and the price to be paid by the other (i) is apportioned to each item to be performed, or (ii) is left to be implied by law.

b.   Consideration apportioned--

Gill v. Johnstown Lumber Co., 25 A. 120 (Pa. 1892).

Facts. Gill (P) agreed to drive four million feet of logs on a river for Johnstown Lumber Co. (D) at the rate of $1 per thousand feet of oak, $0.75 per thousand feet of all others, $0.03 for ties driven to Bethel, and $0.05 for ties driven to all points below Bethel. A flood caused a number of logs to be swept past D's boom at the point of extraction, and D refused to pay for those delivered. The trial court gave judgment for D on the basis that the contract was entire and P's failure to deliver all the logs barred recovery for those delivered. P appeals.

Issue. Is the contract severable so that P may recover for those logs actually delivered?

Held. Yes. Judgment reversed.

♦   The consideration to be paid was not an entire lump sum, but was apportioned among several items at various rates. The contract is therefore severable, and P is entitled to compensation at the specified rate for all logs delivered.

♦   However, with respect to those logs swept past the delivery point, the contract was like a contract of common carriage, *i.e.,* if the carrier fails to deliver the goods, he may not recover pro tanto for that part of the route over which he has carried the goods.

Comment. An assignment for the benefit of creditors acts as a breach of the contract because it makes performance impossible for the insolvent party. Such an assignment prevented recovery where the debtor had fulfilled all the preparation phases of a contract that was not divisible. [*See* Pennsylvania Exchange Bank v. United States, 170 F. Supp. 629 (Ct. Cl. 1959).

---

c.   Divisible contracts: exceptions to the general rule. Divisible contracts are exceptions to the general rule that there will be no recovery until the contract is fully performed. By finding divisibility, the courts allow recovery through implying a condition on the contract rather than resorting to restitution, which probably would be on a different basis than that set up in the contract (*i.e.,* restitution is generally awarded on an unjust enrichment basis and is based on reasonable value, whereas compensation on a divisible contract is awarded at the contract rate).

3. **Restitution.**

    a. **Majority rule.** Where a breaching party has rendered only part performance under a contract (and such performance does not fall within the doctrine of substantial performance—*see supra*), no recovery for such part performance will be allowed.

    b. **Minority rule.** Where a breaching party has rendered part performance under a contract (and the doctrine of substantial performance does not apply), recovery will be allowed to the extent of the reasonable value of the benefits conferred less any damages arising out of the breach.

    c. **Employment contract--**

Britton v. Turner, 6 N.H. 481 (1834).

Facts. Britton (P) worked for Turner (D) under a contract to work for one year. P only worked for 9½ months and then left without cause. D refused to pay P anything for his work, and P sued in quantum meruit to recover the value of his services. D did not prove any damages from P's early departure, and the jury awarded P $95. (The contract called for payment of $120 for one year's work.) D appeals.

Issue. May an employee who voluntarily leaves the employ of an employer before the termination of an employment contract recover the net benefit received by his employer but not exceeding the contract amount?

Held. Yes. Judgment affirmed.

♦   The employee may recover the benefit to the employer less damages the employer suffers by reason of the early termination, with the contract providing a limit on the amount of recovery. To deny recovery would place the party committing the earlier breach in a better position than one who substantially completes the contract, thus defeating the policy of encouraging the fulfillment of contracts. The employer should not be allowed to receive a windfall at the expense of the employee.

    d. **Construction contract--**

Kirkland v. Archbold, 113 N.E.2d 496 (Ohio Ct. App. 1953).

Facts. Kirkland (P) contracted to make alterations and repairs on Archbold's (D's) dwelling. Payment was to be received after each 10 days of satisfactory work. The contract called for lining the outside walls with rock lathe and rock wool, but P lined the walls with wood lathe and plaster. D refused to allow P to continue with the work after she had paid $800. P sued to recover the value of the work done, which he asserted was $2,985. The trial court found P in breach but held that D's payment of $800 was admission that the first installment was due and awarded P $200. P appeals.

Issue. May a party who has not willfully abandoned performance or broken his contract recover the benefit conferred on the other party less damages caused by inadequate performance?

Held. Yes. Reversed and case remanded for retrial.

♦   A negligent breach should not be treated the same as a willful breach where forfeiture of the value of the work completed is a punishment. P should be awarded the reasonable value of the work done less the damages suffered by D through the improper and incomplete work performed by P.

D. SUSPENDING PERFORMANCE AND TERMINATING THE CONTRACT

1.   **Introduction.** Where a party fails to perform a contract promise, the injured party's remaining duties may be discharged and there may be a claim for damages for total breach. Also, if one party to a contract acts so as to prevent the other party from performing, that conduct is an excuse for nonperformance. The issue usually raised is whether performance was really prevented or merely made more difficult.

2.   **Materiality of Breach--**

Walker & Co. v. Harrison, 81 N.W.2d 352 (Mich. 1957).

Facts. Harrison (D) "rented" an electric sign from Walker & Co. (P). The contract provided that D would own the sign at the end of the term. Shortly after installation, the sign was hit with a tomato and otherwise became dirty. D refused to make further payments until P cleaned the sign. P sued for breach and won. D appeals.

Issue. Must a party's breach be material before it can justify the other party's repudiation of the contract?

Held. Yes. Judgment affirmed.

- Repudiation is a permissible response to a material breach, but the injured party's determination that there has been a material breach is fraught with peril. A court may not view the breach as material, thus rendering the repudiator himself guilty of a material breach.

- P's delay in cleaning the sign was irritating but not so material as to justify repudiation. Most of the dirt and tomato was washed off by rain, although some stain remained. But this did not justify D's repudiation.

- The trial court's award of damages, which was the cash price of the sign plus whatever services were rendered by P, was proper.

―――――――――

3. Failure of Performance by One Party as an Excuse for Nonperformance by the Other--

K & G Construction Co. v. Harris, 164 A.2d 451 (Md. 1960).

Facts. Harris (D), a subcontractor, performed excavation work for K & G Construction Co. (P). P was required to pay D by the 10th of each month for work done per requisitions submitted by D by the 25th of each preceding month. D did work in July and submitted a timely requisition. On August 9, one of D's men negligently damaged P's house to the extent of $3,400, and P refused to make the August 10 payment of $1,484. D quit working in September, despite P's request that D continue work, because of P's refusal to pay. P hired another contractor to finish D's work at $450 above the contract price. P sued for the damages to the house and for the $450. D counterclaimed for the $1,484 and lost profits of $1,340. P recovered the $3,400, but D recovered the $2,824. P appeals.

Issue. Is an owner's promise to pay dependent on the contractor's performing in a workmanlike manner?

Held. Yes. Judgment reversed.

- The basic question is whether the promises are independent or mutually dependent. The modern rule is that mutual promises in a contract are presumed dependent. Still, the intent of the parties governs.

- These promises are clearly dependent, and by the terms of the contract, D's promise to perform is precedent to P's promise to make monthly payments. It would be unreasonable to require P to make the monthly payments regardless of whether D performed in a workmanlike manner.

◆ D breached by not performing in a workmanlike manner when it damaged P's house. Thus, P was justified in refusing payment and did not breach. P treated D's breach as partial. D again breached by refusing to perform, so P should recover the $450 and is not liable to D for the other amounts.

---

4. Performance Made Difficult--

Iron Trade Products Co. v. Wilkoff Co., 116 A. 150 (Pa. 1922).

Facts. Wilkoff Co. (P) contracted to buy rails from Iron Trade Products Co. (D), but D failed to perform due to an increase in the market price of rails. P sued for the added amount which it had to pay to buy the rails elsewhere. D claimed that the increase in price was due to P buying additional rails from D's supplier, which reduced the available supply so much that the price became exorbitant. D also showed that P had contracted to sell the rails to a third party who had agreed to let P out of the contract without paying damages. The trial court found for P. D appeals.

Issue. Is a seller's performance excused if the buyer makes the goods more expensive by making additional purchases from the seller's supplier?

Held. No. Judgment affirmed.

◆ A party who prevents the other party from performing may excuse the other party's performance. But something more must be alleged than that P began buying rails in the market, making D's performance more difficult.

◆ D did not show that P had knowledge that the supply was limited and that P intended to prevent or interfere with D's performance or cause D to default. There was no express understanding that P would not buy elsewhere as well as from D. And it makes no difference what P intended to do with the rails.

---

5. Notice of Breach--

New England Structures, Inc. v. Loranger, 234 N.E.2d 888 (Mass. 1968).

Facts. Loranger (P) hired New England Structures, Inc. (D) to do roofing work on a school that P was building. The contract called for D to provide sufficient skilled workers and spelled out the specifications for the work. The contract also allowed P certain termination rights if D failed to perform the work properly or provide sufficient workers. After D had completed most of the work, P complained about the way it was done and also about a shortage of workers. P exercised its option under the contract and sent a telegram terminating the contract for failure to provide sufficient workers. D responded that delays were occasioned by P's failure to provide approved plans and by unauthorized changes. P refused to allow D to continue work during the five-day notice period preceding termination. P hired another contractor to finish the work at a price in excess of the contract price and sued D for the difference. D counterclaimed for breach of contract and recovered. P appeals.

Issue. When notification of a ground for termination is sent to a party deemed to be in breach, is the notifier limited to that ground in defending his action in terminating?

Held. No. Judgment reversed.

♦   The real issue is the justification for terminating the contract where there is no opportunity for cure. If D could show detrimental reliance on the ground asserted, P would be restricted to that ground; otherwise, P may assert any defense available.

♦   The five-day notification period was not intended to give an opportunity for cure, but was intended to give D time to protect itself from injury by removing its equipment and releasing its employees.

E. PROSPECTIVE NONPERFORMANCE

1. Anticipatory Breach (Repudiation).

    a. Introduction. If either party to an executory bilateral contract, in advance of the time set for performance, repudiates the contract by words manifesting his apparent intent not to perform as he has promised, the other party may treat such anticipatory repudiation as a present, material breach of contract and bring an immediate action for the entire value of the promised performance. [Restatement (Second) §250, comment b]

    b. Rationale. The purpose of this rule is to avoid forcing the innocent party to hold herself in readiness and to tender performance on the date set in the contract. The other party's repudiation excuses the condition requiring the innocent party to tender performance and renders the repudiator's duty immediately due.

        1) Note that this rationale does not apply to unilateral contracts, since in these contracts party A has already performed, and therefore a

repudiation by B does not force A to remain in readiness to perform. [Restatement (Second) §§243(3), 253]

2) Thus, if B promises to pay A a year-end bonus if A can increase company sales by 25% by July 1st, and A performs but B repudiates her promise, A must wait until year-end to bring an action against B. Thus, B at any time before year-end can retract her repudiation.

c. **Requirement of an unequivocal repudiation.** The words used by the repudiator must be unequivocal concerning her refusal to perform. Ambiguous expressions may create doubt as to whether the party will perform; in these situations U.C.C. section 2-609 provides that the aggrieved party may request an assurance that the other party will perform and, until such assurances are given, the first party has the right to suspend any performance due by her. Furthermore, any unjustified refusal to comply with a demand for assurances for a period exceeding 30 days constitutes a repudiation of the contract.

d. **Good faith.** The majority of the courts hold that the repudiator's good faith makes no difference; that is, even though refusal is based on a good faith belief that there is no valid contract or that some condition precedent has not occurred, if the repudiator is wrong, it still constitutes a repudiation.

e. **The legal effect of a repudiation.**

1) **Excuses duty of counter-performance.** If A repudiates his duties under a contract with B, the repudiation excuses B's duty of performance or tender of performance. [Restatement (Second) §253(2)] However, the repudiator may retract his repudiation by notifying the other party that he will perform. This will revive the other party's duty of performance unless the other party has already accepted the repudiation or has changed his position in detrimental reliance on the repudiation. [U.C.C. §2-611; Restatement (Second) §256]

2) **Cause of action for damages.** Also, the aggrieved party that accepts a repudiation may sue immediately for damages for breach (whether this should be the case is much disputed by the commentators). Note also that the aggrieved party need not sue immediately but may wait until after the date set for performance. [U.C.C. §2-610]

f. **Early case--**

Hochster v. De La Tour, 118 Eng. Rep. 922 (Q.B. 1853).

Facts. Hochster (P) was hired by De La Tour (D) to accompany him on a tour to begin June 1. On May 11 D wrote to P repudiating the agreement. P sued for breach on May 22. P was hired for another job between May 22 and June 1. D appealed a judgment for P.

Issue. May the promisee bring an immediate action for damages when the promisor repudiates the contract before the date set for performance?

Held. Yes. Judgment affirmed.

♦   P may either wait until the date set for performance or sue immediately.

Comment. The court reasoned that P was caught in a conflict (he had either to remain idle waiting for the date of performance and then sue, or obtain another job and thus lose his right of action against D, presumably since he would then not be ready and willing to perform, a condition of the performance by D). But the alternative would be simply to hold that the repudiation is an excuse of the constructive condition that P be ready, willing, and able to perform on June 1 and the cause of action against D is not destroyed. In the meantime, until June 1 P would have the duty to mitigate the damages by looking for other work.

---

g.   **Duty to mitigate damages.** Where the promisee elects to not bring an action for damages until the promisor's performance date, most courts hold that the promisee must mitigate the damages arising from repudiation. So, for example, if the promisee is to receive a performance from the promisor and the promisor repudiates the contract, the promisee after a reasonable time must look for performance elsewhere.

h.   **Measure of damages.** U.C.C. section 2-713 provides that a buyer's damages are to be computed by the difference between the market price at the time when the buyer learned of the breach and the contract price (*i.e.,* the buyer may not delay unreasonably after learning of the repudiation). Note that prior to adoption of the U.C.C., damages for anticipatory repudiation were measured by the difference between the contract price and the market price on the date delivery was due.

i.   **Prospective buyer's ability to perform--**

Kanavos v. Hancock Bank & Trust Co., 479 N.E.2d 168 (Mass. 1985).

Facts. Kanavos (P) had an option to purchase the stock of a corporation that owned an apartment building. Hancock Bank & Trust Co. (D) agreed to pay P $40,000 to surrender this option, in addition to a 60-day right of first refusal on the stock should D decide to sell it. The building was worth $4 million and the balance on the mortgage was $2.5 million. D later sold the stock for $760,000 to a third person without giving P notice and an opportunity to buy it first. P sued for breach of contract. The trial court awarded P the promised $40,000, plus the difference between the sale price and the equity in the building, which totaled $740,000. D appeals on the ground that the judge failed to instruct the jury that P could not recover unless he proved that he was ready, willing, and able to buy the stock for $760,000.

Issue. To recover for breach of contract, must the owner of a right of first refusal prove that, had he been notified of the impending sale, he would have been ready, willing, and able to exercise his right?

Held. Yes. Judgment remanded.

♦   In a bilateral contract containing simultaneous obligations, one party's repudiation does not relieve the other from proving that he could perform his obligation. One party cannot put another in default unless he is ready, willing, and able to perform.

♦   D had an obligation to give P the right to match the offer D received. Had D done so, P could have tendered the purchase price and D would have had to deliver the stock to P. P's financial ability is a material issue in his suit for damages for D's breach of agreement to sell.

♦   P has the burden of proof as to his financial ability because that ability must be shown to make D liable. P also is better suited than D to produce evidence of his financial ability.

♦   There was evidence sufficient to support a finding that P was financially able to exercise his right of first refusal, had that issue been given to the jury. Even though P had financial difficulty, he presumably could have acquired funds because he would have obtained an equity interest worth $1.5 million for only $760,000, and D owed him another $40,000. This issue must be retried.

2.   **Prospective Inability to Perform.**

a.   **Introduction.** One of the parties by her conduct may indicate that she will not be able to perform when the time for her duty to perform arises. For example, A may contract to sell property to B on June 1 but convey the property to C on May 1. By her conduct A has made it appear that she will be unable to perform her promise to B, and since A's performance is a constructive condition concurrent to B's duty to pay A on June 1, the prospective failure of the condition excuses B's duty immediately—B need no longer hold herself ready to perform or make an actual tender of payment on June 1 in order to put A in breach of contract. [Restatement (Second) §251]

b. Compared with anticipatory breach of contract. The distinction between prospective inability to perform and anticipatory breach is merely one of degree, since an anticipatory breach involves an express repudiation of the contract, whereas voluntary disablement is merely ***conduct*** by the promisor which manifests his intention not to perform. Because of this close similarity, the Restatement and some courts actually merge these concepts.

c. Conduct constituting voluntary disablement. Any conduct by a party to the contract, prior to the time his performance is due, which makes it appear that he will be unable to perform, is sufficient to show voluntary disablement. The conduct must be such that a reasonable person would conclude that the promisor probably will not perform. [Restatement (Second) §251]

d. The legal effect of voluntary disablement.

    1) The duty of counter-performance is excused. Voluntary disablement is a prospective failure of condition which excuses the duty of counter-performance by the other party. Some courts hold that this duty of counter-performance is permanently excused. Other courts (and the Restatement) hold that the voluntary disablement may be cured by notice to the other party (before detrimental reliance) prior to performance that the formerly disabled party will be able to perform.

    2) Cause of action for breach of contract. Most conduct which amounts to voluntary disablement also constitutes a breach of contract, giving the innocent party an immediate cause of action for damages.

e. Equivocal prospective ability to perform--

McCloskey & Co. v. Minweld Steel Co., 220 F.2d 101 (3d Cir. 1955).

Facts. McCloskey & Co. (P) contracted with Minweld Steel Co. (D) to have D supply and erect structural steel for a hospital. The contract allowed P to set up schedules for delivery and erection of the steel. P sent the specifications and plans to D and asked for a delivery estimate. D's schedule was not quick enough for P so P requested assurance that the work would be completed within 30 days. D replied that it would like to meet that deadline but required P's assistance in acquiring the steel, since steel was in short supply. P terminated the contract and hired another contractor to do the work. P obtained the steel for the new contractor without difficulty. P sued D for anticipatory

breach. D moved for dismissal after P's proof and P appeals from the granting of the dismissal.

Issue. To show an anticipatory breach, must the party breaching express an absolute and unequivocal refusal to perform?

Held. Yes. Judgment affirmed.

♦   D expressed a desire to comply with the requested delivery date and only sought P's assistance in obtaining the materials in a timely fashion. P was not entitled to an assurance that the work would be completed by the scheduled date under the terms of the contract.

♦   Failure to make timely preparations to perform is not an expression of anticipatory breach. P must wait until the time for performance to ascertain whether D is in breach absent absolute and unequivocable refusal to perform.

Comment. A party that asserts a particular interpretation of contract language does not thereby breach or repudiate the contract. The other party is free to rely on its own interpretation, accept the other party's interpretation, or seek a declaratory judgment. [*See* Bill's Coal Co. v. Board of Public Utilities, 682 F.2d 883 (10th Cir. 1982)]

---

f.   Stopping performance to secure written agreement--

C.L. Maddox, Inc. v. Coalfield Services, Inc., 51 F.3d 76 (7th Cir. 1995).

Facts. C.L. Maddox, Inc. (P) had a contract to replace a loading facility in a mine. P arranged to subcontract the preliminary demolition work to Coalfield Services, Inc., for $230,000. The work was to be done within three weeks, and P was to make bi-weekly progress payments. P never signed D's proposal, but D began working anyway. After nearly three weeks, when P had still failed to sign D's proposal, D stopped work and told P it would not proceed until P signed the proposal and paid $103,500, representing work D had done to that point. P told D that he would accept D's proposal, but added a one-week extension and a liquidated damages clause of $1,000 per day beyond that. D estimated that completion would take another five weeks. D rejected P's proposal and never resumed work when P refused to meet D's terms. P sued for damages, and D counterclaimed for the $103,500. The trial court found for D. P appeals.

Issue. May one party cease performance under an oral contract where the other party refuses to sign a written contract?

Held. Yes. Judgment affirmed.

♦ The parties had an oral contract, although it was missing many terms, and D breached when it stopped work, unless it had a legitimate right to stop in light of a breach or anticipatory repudiation by P.

♦ When P refused to sign D's proposal or even to communicate with D about it, P gave D substantial ground to interrupt its work in order to avoid incurring additional costs without assurance of payment. D's decision to stop working was vindicated when P insisted on a liquidated damages clause, which was unlikely to be accepted. This suggests that P was seeking excuses for not paying D anything.

♦ The request for a liquidated damages clause was not by itself a breach of contract, and D was not obligated to accept P's request, but combined with the other circumstances, it justified D's work stoppage.

3. **Damages.**

   a. **Basic rule.** The buyer may recover against the seller the difference between the contract price and the market price at the time and place the buyer learned of the breach. [U.C.C. §2-713(1)] If the seller refuses to deliver, the relevant place is where the buyer should have tendered the goods; if he makes a nonconforming tender, the place is the place of arrival.

   b. **Anticipatory repudiation and the timing of the price differential--**

Cosden Oil v. Karl O. Helm Aktiengesellschaft, 736 F.2d 1064 (5th Cir. 1984).

Facts. Karl O. Helm Aktiengesellschaft (P) sued Cosden Oil (D) for anticipatory repudiation. The district court found for P and awarded damages based on the market price at a commercially reasonable point after D informed P that it was canceling the orders. Both parties appeal.

Issue. When a seller anticipatorily repudiates a contract, should the buyer's damages be based on the market price at a commercially reasonable point after the seller notifies the buyer of the repudiation?

Held. Yes. Judgment affirmed.

♦ D claims damages should be measured by the market price at the time P learned of the repudiation; P claims the market price on the last day of delivery should govern. The issue is not clearly settled by the U.C.C.

U.C.C. section 2-609, not on any contractual language. Thus, P would only have a right to demand assurances if it had reasonable grounds for insecurity.

♦ When P agreed to the contract, it was willing to wait 30 days after completion for payment. D's failure to obtain the loan was not reasonable grounds for insecurity because the money was not needed for several months. There was simply no change of condition affecting D's ability to pay. P's action constituted anticipatory repudiation of the contract.

Concurrence. There need not be a fundamental change in the buyer's financial position before the seller can invoke the protection of section 2-609. Still, P's demands in this case were more than is permitted by section 2-609 because it sought to redraft the contract rather than simply obtain adequate assurance of due performance.

---

c.   **Non-U.C.C. application--**

Norcon Power Partners v. Niagara Mohawk Power Corp., 705 N.E.2d 656 (N.Y. 1998).

Facts. The Niagara Mohawk Power Corp. (D), a public utility provider, entered a 25-year electricity supply contract with Norcon Power Partners (P). The contract provided for three pricing periods. In the first period, D would pay six cents per kilowatt-hour. In the second, D would pay its "avoided cost," or the cost it would pay to purchase power from a third party or to produce power itself. This price was subject to a floor and a ceiling, but the price differential between the avoided cost and the floor or ceiling would be accrued as a credit or liability for D. During the third pricing period, D would pay its avoided cost without a floor or ceiling, and would recoup any credits or pay any liabilities over the pricing period. After five years, D determined that it would accumulate a credit of $610 million during the second pricing period. Concerned that P would be unable to pay this credit during the third period, D demanded that P provide adequate assurance to D that P would perform its future repayment obligations. P sued for a declaration that D had no contractual right to demand adequate assurance and for an injunction to stop D from anticipatorily repudiating the contract. The district court granted P summary judgment on the ground that New York common law only allowed a demand for adequate assurance when the promisor becomes insolvent, or under the U.C.C. The second circuit certified the question to the New York Court of Appeals.

Issue. Does a party have the right to demand adequate assurance of future performance when reasonable grounds arise to lead that party to believe that the other party will commit a breach by nonperformance of a contract governed by New York law, where the other party is solvent and the contract is not governed by the U.C.C.?

Held. Yes.

♦ A demand for adequate assurance is an effective means of addressing the dilemma faced by a promisee concerned about the other party's ability to perform. The promisee may regard an apparent repudiation as an anticipatory repudiation and terminate his or her own performance, but then risk a judicial determination that the other party did not anticipatorily repudiate. Alternatively, the promisee may continue to perform despite the uncertainty and risk losing post-repudiation expenditures if it is determined that in fact the other party did anticipatorily repudiate.

♦ The U.C.C. doctrine of demanding assurance of future performance under U.C.C. section 2-609 resolves the uncertainty by deeming the repudiation as confirmed if the adequate assurance is not provided. Some states have adopted U.C.C. section 2-609 as part of its common law, and it has been adopted in the Restatement (Second) as section 251.

♦ So far, New York has not adopted the doctrine as part of its common law despite its advantages. D proposes that this court adopt the U.C.C. section 2-609 and Restatement rule as a general principle of contract law. That approach is unnecessary, however. Instead, the rule should be evaluated on a case-by-case basis.

♦ In this case, the power supply contract is analogous to a contract for the sale of goods. If the contract were identical except for goods instead of electricity, D would be entitled to demand adequate assurance of performance under U.C.C. section 2-609. Therefore, it makes sense to adopt U.C.C. section 2-609 as part of the common law of contracts where there is a long-term commercial contract between corporate entities which is complex and not reasonably susceptible of all security features being anticipated, bargained for, and incorporated in the original contract.

———————

IX. BASIC ASSUMPTIONS: MISTAKE, IMPRACTICABILITY, AND FRUSTRATION

A. INTRODUCTION

This section discusses several ways in which contractual duties can be discharged other than by actual performance or tender of performance. Note also that these same ways serve to discharge conditions as well as actual promises.

B. MUTUAL MISTAKE

1. **Introduction.** Obstacles to performance that exist at the time the contract was entered into but are not known by the parties at that time are referred to as mutual mistakes. Generally, where a mutual mistake exists that is material to the contract, the party who is adversely affected may obtain rescission, unless that party assumed the risk of the mistake.

2. **Unknown Land Conditions--**

Stees v. Leonard, 20 Minn. 494 (1874).

Facts. Leonard (D) contracted with Stees (P) to construct a building on P's property. D attempted to perform the contract but the unfinished building collapsed twice due to wet soil conditions. D then quit work, alleging that construction was impossible because P had not drained the land and that without drainage, a building to P's specifications could not be built. They also alleged that after the contract was signed, P had orally agreed to drain the land. The court found for P. D appeals.

Issue. If a contractor contracts to build a building which collapses through no fault of his own, must the contractor complete the building?

Held. Yes. Judgment affirmed.

♦ Where a party creates a duty by contract, he is bound to perform unless there is an absolute impossibility of performance. The building could be built on this land, if the land was drained, so performance was not impossible. D contracted to do everything necessary to complete the building, and thereby assumed the risk of poor soil conditions.

♦ Parole evidence regarding which party was responsible to drain the land cannot be used to vary the terms of the written contract. Also, because there was no consideration alleged for P's oral promise, there can be no modification of the contract.

Comment. Note that the court also indicated that although impossibility would excuse performance, its definition of impossibility was rather narrow. It excluded fire, flood, lightning, earthquake, etc. The court indicated that a party must guard against these contingencies by contract or insurance.

---

3. No Consequential Damages upon Rescission--

Renner v. Kehl, 722 P.2d 262 (Ariz. 1986).

Facts. Renner (P) contracted to lease about 2,000 acres from Kehl (D) for $100 per acre. The parties understood that P intended to cultivate jojoba on the land and required adequate water, and both parties believed there was sufficient underground water to support the crop. P made a down payment and drilled five test wells, which showed that there was not sufficient quantity or quality of water present. P sought rescission. The court ordered D to repay P the deposit of $80,200, plus another $229,000 to reimburse P for the cost of drilling the test wells. The court of appeals affirmed, and D appeals.

Issue. Is a party who rescinds a contract for mutual mistake of fact entitled to consequential damages?

Held. No. Judgment reversed.

♦ Mutual mistake of fact is an accepted basis for rescission where it is an essential part and condition of the contract. Here, the sole purpose of the contract was for P to grow jojoba on the land. There would have been no sale if the parties had not believed it was possible to grow jojoba on the leased land.

♦ The existence of adequate water supplies was a basic assumption on which both parties made the contract. When it turned out they were mistaken about the water, the contract was voidable.

♦ When a party rescinds a contract for mutual mistake, he is entitled to restitution for any benefit conferred on the other party. The objective is not compensation but the avoidance of unjust enrichment of the other party. The rescinding party is not entitled to consequential damages.

♦ In a rescission, the rescinding party must return, conditional on restitution, any interest in property he received in the bargain. This includes reimbursement for the fair market value of the use of the property. P was required to return the land and the leases to D in return for P's down payment and the fair rental value of the land during P's occupancy.

♦ To avoid unjust enrichment, D must also pay P for any enhancement of the property due to P's efforts. D is not required to pay P's development costs, however.

Comment. Resolution of a mistake case can depend on how far along the parties are. In *Wood v. Boynton*, 25 N.W. 42 (Wis. 1885), Wood found a stone that she showed to Boynton, a jeweler. Boynton told Wood it might be a topaz and that he would buy it for $1. Wood decided to keep it, but returned two or three months later and accepted the $1. It turned out that the stone was a rough diamond worth $700. Wood sought rescission and offered Boynton $1.10 (with interest), but Boynton refused to return it. The appellate court affirmed the dismissal of Wood's suit. In *Sherwood v. Walker*, 33 N.W. 919 (Mich. 1887), Walker agreed to sell a cow to Sherwood, who was a banker, for $80. Both parties believed the cow was sterile. Before delivering the cow, Walker discovered she was pregnant and had a value of $750 to $1,000. Walker then refused to deliver the cow. The appellate court held for Walker on the ground that the cow was not the same kind of animal the parties contemplated when they entered into the contract.

C. IMPRACTICABILITY OF PERFORMANCE

Performance of a contract will normally be excused if the performance has been made impracticable by the occurrence of an event whose nonoccurrence was a basic assumption on which the contract was made, unless the adversely affected party has explicitly or implicitly assumed the risk that the contingency might occur.

1. Performance Impractical Due to Cost--

Mineral Park Land Co. v. Howard, 156 P. 458 (Cal. 1916).

Facts. The defendant (D) contracted to haul gravel and earth from land owned by the plaintiff (P) for work on a bridge. D agreed to take all of its requirements from P's land, estimated at 114,000 cubic yards. D took 50,131 yards but obtained the rest of its requirements elsewhere. P sued for the contract price on the amounts D used but did not take from P's property. D claimed that it took all of the gravel and earth from P's land that was available. The trial court found that D took all of the gravel and dirt from P's land that was above the water level and that it would cost 10 to 12 times as much as the usual cost per yard to take the rest. The court found for P. D appeals.

Issue. May performance be excused as impractical when the performance would be much more expensive than anticipated?

Held. Yes. Judgment affirmed as modified.

- The trial court awarded P the balance owed on the 50,131 yards that D took but did not completely pay for, and that part of the judgment is affirmed.

- The main issue relates to D's failure to take all of its requirements from P's land. D did take all of the gravel and earth that was available on P's land in the sense of being capable of being taken advantageously from a financial standpoint.

- As a general rule, a party who agrees without qualification to perform an act that is not impossible to perform may not be excused just because performance is difficult. However, if performance depends on the existence of something that is assumed as the basis of the agreement, performance is excused to the extent that the thing ceases to exist or turns out to be nonexistent.

- In this case, both P and D assumed that P's land contained enough gravel and earth to satisfy D's needs for the project. We must view the conditions in a practical and reasonable way to determine how much earth and gravel were "available."

- D could not take more than it did by ordinary means and without a prohibitive cost. When something can only be done at an excessive and unreasonable cost, it is impracticable and, thus, legally impossible. This has the same legal effect as the total absence of earth and gravel beyond what D took. Therefore, P cannot recover the value of the gravel and earth D obtained elsewhere.

---

2. Performance Requiring Continued Existence of Person or Thing--

Taylor v. Caldwell, 122 Eng. Rep. 309 (K.B. 1863).

Facts. Taylor (P) contracted with Caldwell (D) for a music hall for four days in order to give concerts. The contract provided that the existence of the hall in a state fit for a concert was essential. Before the concerts were to be given, the hall was destroyed by fire. Neither party was responsible for the fire. P sued for damages for breach of contract.

Issue. Will D be excused from performance by the accidental destruction of the hall which made his performance of the contract impossible?

Held. Yes. Judgment for D.

- Both parties to the contract are excused. In a contract where the performance depends on the continued existence of a person or thing, a condition is implied that the impossibility of performance arising from the perishing of the person or thing shall excuse the performance of the contract.

Comments.

♦ Note that the court distinguished this case from a lease contract since there was authority that covered the situation of a lease holding that a lease must be performed despite unforeseen hardship on one of the parties. There is not, however, a satisfactory distinction for the lease cases.

♦ U.C.C. section 2-613 states that where a specified thing is destroyed, the contract is voided, or if the thing is goods which have deteriorated so as to no longer conform to the requirements set forth by the contract, then the contract can be avoided or the goods can be accepted with an allowance for their lesser value.

---

3. **Objective vs. Subjective Impossibility.** "Objective impossibility" means that the performance cannot be done by anyone. "Subjective impossibility" means that the performance cannot be done by the promisor, although someone could perform. Most courts hold that only objective impossibility will excuse the promisor's performance. The modern trend of authority takes the position that impossibility includes commercial impracticability because of extreme and unreasonable difficulty or expense. [*See* Restatement (First) §454; U.C.C. §2-615]

4. **Performance More Costly--**

Transatlantic Financing Corp. v. United States, 363 F.2d 312 (D.C. Cir. 1966).

Facts. United States (D) chartered a vessel operated by Transatlantic Financing Corp. (P) to carry a cargo of wheat from the United States to Iran. The charter did not specify a route. Six days after the vessel left port, the Egyptian government closed the Suez Canal, through which P's vessel intended to sail, and the vessel made the extended voyage around the Cape of Good Hope to reach its destination. P sought to recover additional compensation for its increased expenses but its action was dismissed. P appeals.

Issue. When a performance is rendered more difficult or expensive by unforeseen events, may the injured party proceed with performance, recover the contract price, and then, in addition, recover for its extra costs?

Held. No. Judgment affirmed.

- Legal impossibility really is commercial impracticability. When alleged, the court is asked to construct a condition of performance based on the changed circumstances, which involved three steps:

- First, a contingency must have occurred. The closing of the Suez is clearly an unexpected barrier to the expected method of performance.

- Second, the risk of the unexpected occurrence must not have been allocated either by agreement or by custom. There is no indication of any express allocation of risk, although P, by failing to include any terms regarding the occurrence of such a contingency, may have assumed abnormal risks.

- Third, the occurrence of the contingency must have rendered performance commercially impracticable. There is no indication that the extended voyage was physically impractical. Impracticability is urged on the basis of added expense alone (an additional $44,000 over the contract price of $305,000). This variation between expected and actual cost of performance cannot be construed as involving commercial impracticability. Therefore, P cannot recover.

- Even if P had proved commercial impracticability, the result would be to nullify the contract. Thus, P's theory of relief should have been quantum meruit for the entire trip, not only for the extra expense.

---

5. Supplier's Bankruptcy--

Selland Pontiac-GMC, Inc. v. King, 384 N.W.2d 490 (Minn. Ct. App. 1986).

Facts. King (D) had contracted to supply four buses to Selland Pontiac-GMC, Inc. (P). The contract provided that the bus bodies would be manufactured by Superior. P purchased the four bus chassis and had them delivered to Superior. Superior subsequently went out of business, and the buses were never manufactured. P sold the chassis at a loss and sued D. The trial court found for D. P appeals.

Issue. May a vendor's performance be deemed impractical when its supplier, who was specifically identified in the contract, goes out of business?

Held. Yes. Judgment affirmed.

- The trial court found for D because the contract specifically identified Superior as the supplier. Supply of Superior bus bodies was a basic assumption on which the contract was made. Superior's bankruptcy made D's obligation impracticable.

◆ This case is unlike *Barbarossa & Sons v. Iten Chevrolet, Inc.*, 265 N.W.2d 655 (Minn. 1978), where the seller's supplier, which cancelled the order but did not go out of business, was not mentioned by name in the contract. A partial failure of a seller's supplier is normally a foreseeable contingency for which the seller assumes the risk.

◆ In this case, neither P nor D knew of Superior's financial situation and D did not assume the risk of Superior going out of business.

---

6. **Force Majeure Clauses.** While section 2-615 may excuse delays or nonperformance due to impracticability, parties frequently prefer to include contractual provisions that more specifically allocate risk. A clause that simply excuses delays "due to causes beyond its control and not occasioned by its fault or negligence" would normally not preclude liability for any delay, regardless of its foreseeability, that is due to causes beyond its control. Such clauses are construed to excuse only unforeseen events. A typical force majeure clause lists specific events that will excuse performance, as well as a catch-all provision to include other similar but unlisted events. The promisor usually will want as inclusive a provision as possible, while the promisee will want the narrowest provision possible.

7. **Foreseeable Risk Not an Excuse--**

Canadian Industrial Alcohol Co. v. Dunbar Molasses Co., 179 N.E. 383 (N.Y. 1932).

Facts. The Dunbar Molasses Co. (D) agreed to sell to the Canadian Industrial Alcohol Co. (P) 1.5 million gallons of molasses "of the usual run from National Sugar Refinery." D shipped only 344,083 gallons because the total output of the refinery that year was only 485,000 gallons, much below the plant's capacity. P sued for damages. D claimed that the contract contained an implied term that delivery was conditioned on the refinery producing enough molasses, so that D's duty was discharged when the output was reduced. The lower courts held for P. D appeals.

Issue. May a seller be discharged from performance merely because its usual supplier reduced its production below what the seller had anticipated?

Held. No. Judgment affirmed.

◆ D failed to make any effort to secure the required quantity from the refinery. D relied on the mere chance that the refinery would produce enough. Business dealings require more certainty than this. D is properly liable to P.

Comment. The impossibility doctrine really exists to allocate risk between the parties. Thus, where a court believes that the risk was foreseeable and under the control of one of the parties (here, D could have foreseen the risk and gotten a contract with the refinery), then the court will not relieve performance due to impossibility (the theory being that the party with control has contributed to the impossibility). The court also stated that had the refinery been destroyed without D's fault (as by an act of God), then D would have been excused, since it would not have been a risk assumed by D.

---

8. Commercial Impracticability--

Eastern Air Lines, Inc. v. Gulf Oil Corp., 415 F. Supp. 429 (S.D. Fla. 1975).

Facts. The facts are set forth *supra*. This part of the opinion deals with D's claim that performance was commercially impracticable. D claims that the escalation indicator in the contract cannot work as intended because of government price controls, and that when crude oil prices increased dramatically without an increase in the escalation indicator, performance became commercially impracticable.

Issue. May a party to a contract avoid performance due to commercial impracticability when its costs are largely due to intracompany transfers?

Held. No.

- The common law doctrines of frustration of purpose and impossibility have been codified as U.C.C. section 2-615. A mere showing of unprofitability is not enough.

- The contract provisions on price escalation are clear and unambiguous. The parties intended to be bound by the published reference prices in *Platt's Oilgram Crude Oil Supplement*. *Platt's* still lists prices. Although it only lists prices of "old" oil, not imported oil, the production D relied on for this contract was old oil.

- D failed to prove how much it costs to make fuel for P, or whether it loses money on its sales to P. Even though D's costs allegedly increased, these costs included intracompany profits, including profits earned on foreign crude oil it imported. D cannot use intracompany profits to add to its costs and then claim commercial impracticability. D failed to prove sufficient hardship.

- Even if D had proved hardship, the energy crisis was foreseeable and thus outside the scope of section 2-615. Government price regulation was also foreseeable.

Comment. In *Eastern Air Lines, Inc. v. McDonnell Douglas Corp.*, 532 F.2d 957 (5th Cir. 1976), Eastern sued when McDonnell Douglas was late delivering new jet airplanes. The delay was attributable to the demands of military production. The court noted that an exculpatory clause phrased in general terms excuses only unforeseen events which make performance impracticable. However, in this case the contract excused McDonnell Douglas for delays not within its control, including governmental acts. This was sufficiently specific to protect McDonnell Douglas.

D. FRUSTRATION OF PURPOSE

1. **Introduction.** Closely related to impossibility of performance is frustration of purpose. Where the bargained-for performance is still possible, but the purpose or value of the contract has been totally destroyed by some supervening event, such frustration of purpose will discharge the contract. [Restatement (First) §288]

2. **Requisite Elements.** The following four elements must always appear in order to find frustration of purpose sufficient to discharge a contract:

   a. Some supervening act or event;

   b. The supervening act or event was not reasonably foreseeable at the time the contract was entered into;

   c. The avowed purpose or object of the contract was known and recognized by both parties at the time they contracted; and

   d. The supervening act or event totally or nearly totally destroys the purpose or object of the contract.

3. **Unforeseeable Supervening Event--**

Krell v. Henry, 2 K.B. 740 (1903).

Facts. Henry (D) contracted to hire Krell's (P's) apartment for two days. Both knew that the purpose was for D to see the King's coronation parade which would have been visible from the window; this purpose was not stated in the contract. The parade was postponed when the King became sick. P sued for the balance due on the contract. D counterclaimed for the money he put on deposit. Judgment to D. P appealed.

Issue. Will frustration of purpose excuse performance of a contract?

Held. Yes. Judgment affirmed.

◆   Where the purpose of the contract is frustrated by an unforeseeable supervening event, and the purpose was within the contemplation of both parties when the contract was made, then performance is excused. The purpose of the contract may be implied from extrinsic sources. It was clear, for example, in this case that the purpose of the high rent for the room was to view the parade.

Dissent. Where possible, the parties to a contract should be left where their bargaining puts them. The room could still be rented to D. Thus, the contract was not impossible to perform. Judgment should be for P.

Comment. Note that the attainment of the purpose of the contract becomes an implied condition precedent to performance.

---

4.   Notice of Refusal to Accept Performance Excuses Performance--

Swift Canadian Co. v. Banet, 224 F.2d 36 (3d Cir. 1955).

Facts. Swift (P) contracted to sell lamb pelts to Banet (D), f.o.b. P's plant in Toronto. After making the first delivery, a change in government import regulations occurred and D refused to accept any further deliveries, claiming that the change in regulations frustrated the contract. P then sold the pelts to other buyers for lower than the contract price. P sued D, and both parties moved for summary judgment; D's motion was granted, and P appeals.

Issue. In a contract where the risk of loss transfers from the seller to the buyer at the seller's plant, will a change of import regulations in the buyer's country which adversely affects the buyer's ability to resell the goods operate as a frustration of the purpose of the contract?

Held. No. Judgment reversed.

◆   The seller's obligation under the contract was to deliver the pelts at the f.o.b. point in Toronto, and such delivery would have fully completed its performance. When D notified P of its refusal to accept delivery, such refusal relieved P from its obligation to make the delivery.

◆   However, because P performed or was ready, able, and willing to perform, and because the risk of loss and possibility of profit were on the buyer before and after the goods were delivered at the f.o.b. point, P was entitled to the value of his bargain notwithstanding the change in import regulations in the United States.

---

5. Government Intervention--

Chase Precast Corp. v. John J. Paonessa Co., 566 N.E.2d 603 (Mass. 1991).

Facts. John J. Paonessa Co. (D) obtained two contracts from the Department of Public Works to resurface and improve a highway, including replacing a grass median strip with concrete median barriers. D hired Chase Precast Corp. (P) to supply the barriers. After the project began, the Department received public protests about the removal of the grass. Anticipating that the Department would modify the work, D notified P to stop producing the barriers. P promptly did so, but by then it had produced about one-half of the barriers required in the contracts. Subsequently, the Department deleted the barriers from the contracts with D. D paid P at the contract price for the barriers P had produced. P sought to recover its anticipated profits on the balance of the barriers, but D refused to pay. P sued. The court held for D on the basis of impossibility of performance. The appellate court affirmed. P appeals.

Issue. If a government entity eliminates certain requirements of a construction contract, is the private contractor excused from paying its subcontractor who was to supply those requirements?

Held. Yes. Judgment affirmed.

♦ The doctrine of frustration of purpose means that when an event neither anticipated nor caused by either party, the risk of which was not allocated by the contract, destroys the object or purpose of the contract and thereby the value of performance, the parties are excused from further performance. This is comparable to the U.C.C. defense of commercial impracticability.

♦ D was not responsible for the Department's elimination of the median barriers from the projects. Its contracts with the Department contain a standard provision that allows the Department to eliminate work found unnecessary. D's contract with P does not contain a similar provision, but this does not mean that D assumed the risk of reduction in the quantity of barriers. P knew that the Department had the power to change quantities of contract items.

♦ The court could reasonably have concluded that P and D did not contemplate the cancellation of the barriers and did not allocate the risk of such cancellation. Therefore, the cancellation constituted a frustration of purpose, and D is not liable to P.

---

6. Changes in Market Price Insufficient--

Northern Indiana Public Service Co. v. Carbon County Coal Co., 799 F.2d 265 (7th Cir. 1986).

Facts. The Northern Indiana Public Service Co. (P) was an electric utility which in 1978 contracted to purchase 1.5 million tons of coal each year for 20 years from Carbon County Coal Co. (D). The price started at $24 per ton, with escalation provisions which by 1985 produced a price of $44 per ton. The Indiana Public Service Commission ("PSC") regulated P's rates. Although the PSC granted P's request for higher rates, it directed P to seek to purchase electricity from other utilities that could provide it cheaper than P could generate it. The PSC also issued economy purchase orders that criticized the type of contract P entered with D which provided a guaranteed price and quantity. When P discovered that it could buy the electricity cheaper than it could produce it, and that the PSC would not allow P to recover the costs of buying coal from D, P stopped accepting coal from D and sought declaratory relief from its contractual obligation, on the ground that the PSC's economy purchase orders frustrated the purpose of the contract. D counterclaimed for breach of contract and sought a preliminary injunction requiring P to take delivery. The district court granted D's motion. Shortly thereafter, the trial began and resulted in a verdict for D for $181 million, which the judge approved in lieu of specific performance. P appeals the damage judgment, and D appeals the denial of specific performance.

Issue. May the buyer in a fixed price contract be excused from performance when the market price drops so as to render the contract unprofitable for the buyer?

Held. No. Judgment affirmed.

♦ The force majeure clause in the contract allows P to stop taking delivery of coal if a civil authority's orders prevent it from utilizing the coal. P argues that the PSC's economy purchase orders prevented it from using the coal. However, these orders did not prevent P from using the coal; they merely did not allow P to shift the cost of its bad business deal to its ratepayers.

♦ The PSC acts as a substitute for competition because the electric utility market is naturally monopolistic. If the market was fully competitive, P would not be able to pass on the extra cost of buying coal to produce electricity because the customers would buy cheaper electricity from P's competitors. While the contract assured P a steady supply of coal, it also presented a risk that the price would fall below the minimum agreed price, leaving P with an obligation to buy coal at higher than market rates.

♦ The force majeure clause would apply if the PSC ordered P to close a plant because of a safety or pollution hazard. However, the force majeure clause does not allow P to avoid the consequences of the risk it assumed when it agreed to a minimum price, fixed quantity contract. The judge should not have even submitted the issue of force majeure to the jury.

- The judge did not submit P's defenses of impracticability and frustration to the jury. Under U.C.C. section 2-615, delayed performance is not a breach if it is infeasible, as long as the promisor did not create the infeasibility. This section applies specifically to sellers; because a buyer usually only has a duty to pay, his performance is rarely impracticable or impossible. Instead, the concept of frustration is applied to buyers. Frustration is similar to impracticability. It means that something happened to make the performance for which he would be paying worthless to him.

- As a buyer, P is really claiming frustration. Although the judge ruled that Indiana does not recognize frustration as a defense, that issue need not be decided because this case is not within the frustration doctrine.

- The frustration doctrine is intended to shift risk to the party who was in a better position to prevent the risk from happening or who could better insure against the loss. The risk is shifted in accordance with the parties' presumed intentions, however. When the contract expressly allocates the risk to one party, that risk cannot be shifted to the other through the frustration doctrine.

Comment. As to D's claim for specific performance, the court held that continuation of uneconomical production was not appropriate, and that although D's employees would be adversely affected, they were neither parties to the contract nor third-party beneficiaries.

---

7. Destruction of Thing Which Was to Be Done--

Young v. City of Chicopee, 72 N.E. 63 (Mass. 1904).

Facts. Young (P) contracted with the City of Chicopee (D) to furnish materials and to do repairs on a wooden bridge on a public highway. The contract required P to assemble the materials on the site prior to beginning work, and P complied. After part of the work had been completed, the bridge and some of P's materials were destroyed by fire without fault of either party. P sued to recover the value of the materials destroyed by fire and the value of the work he had done prior to the fire. The trial court allowed recovery of all damages requested, and D appeals with respect to the value of the materials which had not yet been incorporated into the structure when destroyed by the fire.

Issue. When an object upon which work is being performed is destroyed without fault of the parties, may the party performing the work recover the value of his work as well as materials purchased in contemplation of performing the work?

Held. No. Judgment affirmed as to materials and work on the bridge but reversed as to materials damaged by the fire but not yet incorporated into the bridge.

♦ D assumed the risk of loss of work and materials incorporated into the bridge, but P retained title and possession of the materials assembled for work and could have exchanged or removed them without being liable to D, so P had the risk of loss as to those materials.

Comment. *Young* states the general rule with respect to repair contracts, *i.e.,* the risk of loss for materials and work incorporated in a repair project prior to the project's completion is on the owner. However, the general rule is otherwise for building contracts. In building contracts, the risk of destruction of the structure before completion is, in the absence of agreement to the contrary, on the contractor. However, this risk is usually covered with builder's risk insurance, which may be written in the names of both the builder and the owner.

X. THIRD PARTIES: RIGHTS AND RESPONSIBILITIES

A. THIRD-PARTY BENEFICIARY CONTRACTS

1. **Introduction.** Two persons may validly contract for a performance to be rendered to a third person. The question normally raised is whether that third person, who was not a party to the contract and gave no consideration for the promise, may enforce the promise which was made for his benefit.

   a. **Example.** For example, if A offers to paint B's house, if B will promise to pay $1,000 to C, can C enforce B's promise? (Here B is the promisor, A is the promisee, and C is the third-party beneficiary.)

   b. **Common law.** The common law rule was that the third party could not enforce the promise since he was not in privity of contract.

   c. **Modern law.** The modern rule is that the third party may normally enforce the promise made for his benefit.

2. **Classification of Beneficiaries.** Once it is known that a contract was made primarily for the benefit of a third party, that party's status as a beneficiary must be determined. Many courts draw a distinction between a "creditor" and a "donee" beneficiary when considering questions about vesting of third-party rights. A modern approach is to determine whether the beneficiary is "intended" or "incidental."

   a. **Creditor and donee beneficiaries.**

      1) **The test.** The test is whether the promisee intended to confer a gift on a third party (donee beneficiary) or to discharge some obligation owed to the third party (creditor beneficiary).

      2) **Creditor beneficiaries.** If the promisee's primary intent was to discharge a duty he owed to the third party, then the third party is a creditor beneficiary. [Restatement (First) §133(1)(a)] The older view was that there actually had to be a debt owing to the third party. The modern view is that the test is whether the promisee intended to satisfy an obligation which he believed was owed to the third party (even though there might not actually be such a debt).

      3) **Donee beneficiaries.** If the promisee's primary intent in contracting was to confer a gift upon the third party (*i.e.,* to confer some performance neither due nor asserted or supposed to be due from

the promisee to the third party), the third party is a donee beneficiary. [Restatement (First) §133(1)(b)]

    4)   Restatement (Second) position. The Restatement (Second) substitutes the term "intended beneficiary" for both creditor and donee beneficiary, the purpose being to eliminate the distinctions which presently exist between the vesting of rights for creditor as opposed to donee beneficiaries. But most states still recognize a difference and use the old terminology.

    5)   Creditor beneficiary--

Lawrence v. Fox, 20 N.Y. 268 (1859).

Facts. Holly loaned $300 to Fox (D), with instructions that D was to repay by giving the money to Lawrence (P), Holly's creditor. P sued to recover the sum from D and won. D appeals.

Issue. May a third-party beneficiary enforce the contract of which he is the beneficiary but not a party?

Held. Yes. Judgment affirmed.

◆   The consideration for D's promise to pay P was Holly's loan to D. It is a long-recognized principle of law that once a promise is made to one for the benefit of another, he for whose benefit it is made may bring an action for its breach. Although this principle has been applied to trust cases, it is not exclusively applicable to that type of case. The rule applies even where there is no privity between the promisor and the third-party beneficiary.

Dissent. The general rule requires privity, with exceptions where a trust or agency is involved. These exceptions do not apply here. D's promise created an obligation in favor of Holly, not P; D could have discharged his obligation by paying Holly, or Holly could have designated a different payee. P has no right to sue on D's promise.

---

    6)   Donee beneficiary--

Seaver v. Ransom, 120 N.E. 639 (N.Y. 1918).

Facts. Decedent's wife was dying, so he drafted her will, providing that her home was to go to him. The wife wanted the house to go to Seaver (P), her niece, so the decedent promised her that he would leave enough in his will to compensate P for the loss of the house. Decedent did not leave anything to P, who sued Ransom (D), the executor of decedent's estate, as a third-party donee of the wife-decedent contract. The lower courts held for P, and D appeals.

Issue. May a third party for whom a gift was intended enforce the contracting party's obligation to make the gift?

Held. Yes. Judgment affirmed.

♦   Contracts made for the benefit of a third party may be enforced by the third party. It is just and practical to permit the person for whose benefit the contract is made to enforce it against one whose duty it is to pay.

Comment. Early cases involving donee beneficiaries required some family relationship between the donee and beneficiary, but later cases removed this restriction.

---

b.   **Intended beneficiaries vs. incidental beneficiaries.** In order to enforce the promise, the third party involved must be more than a mere "incidental beneficiary." [*See* Restatement (Second) §302]

   1)   **The test.** Unless the contract is made primarily for the benefit of the third party, he is only an incidental beneficiary and cannot enforce the contract. Therefore, to be enforceable by the third party, it must appear that a major purpose (although not the only one) of the contract was to benefit the third party.

   2)   **Factors considered.** In making the determination as to whether the third party is an intended beneficiary or merely an incidental beneficiary, the courts attempt to determine the intent of the promisee (that is, did the promisee intend the promisor's performance to be rendered to the third party?). The following factors are looked at:

      a)   Is performance to be rendered directly to the third party?

      b)   Do express provisions of the contract purport to create rights in third parties?

      c)   Are third parties specifically named in the contract?

      d)   Is there a close relationship between the promisee and the third parties?

   3)   **Intent to confer a gift.** In *Detroit Institute of Arts Founders Society v. Rose*, 127 F. Supp. 2d 117, the Detroit Institute of Arts

("DIA") claimed to be the owner of Howdy Doody, a puppet that had been in a long-running children's television show. When the show went off the air in 1960, Rose, who was a puppeteer and a caretaker for many of the puppets, kept Howdy Doody. In 1967, NBC, which owned the puppet, agreed to pay Rose for past storage and maintenance of Howdy Doody, and Rose agreed to send the puppet to the DIA. However, Rose did not do so, and after his death, the DIA sued his family for possession of the puppet. The district court found that there was a contract between NBC and Rose, under which Rose was required to turn the puppet over to the DIA, the third-party beneficiary. The court stated that two parties may enter into a contract to benefit a third-party beneficiary, who is then entitled to enforce contractual obligations and may sue the obligor for breach. Although there need not be express language in the contract creating a direct obligation to the third-party beneficiary, both parties to the contract must have intended to create a direct obligation from the promisor to the third party.

4) Beneficiary of parallel contracts--

Rathke v. Corrections Corporation of America, Inc., 153 P.3d 303 (Alaska 2007).

Facts. Rathke (P) had been convicted of a crime in Alaska and was sent to Arizona to serve his sentence in a prison operated by the Corrections Corporation of America, Inc. (D). While there, he was disciplined for using marijuana, based on a drug test that showed levels illegal in Arizona but legal in Alaska. D operated pursuant to a contract with Alaska that was parallel in many respects to the "*Cleary* FSA," a settlement agreement between Alaska and its inmates, which was incorporated into Alaska's contract with D. P sued D, claiming that he was a third-party beneficiary of D's contract with Alaska. P also sued the drug testing company, PharmChem, on the same theory. The trial court held that P was not an intended third-party beneficiary, and so could not sue D. P appeals.

Issue. Is P a third-party beneficiary of the contract between Alaska and D?

Held. Yes. Judgment reversed.

♦ The key issue in a third-party beneficiary case is the objective motive or intent of the parties to the contract. The intent to benefit the third party is clear if the promised performance is rendered directly to the beneficiary.

♦ The trial court held that P was not a third-party beneficiary because the *Cleary* FSA was between the state and its inmates, while D's contract was between it and the state. However, the *Cleary* settlement is incorporated by reference into

Alaska's contract with D, and many provisions of the two agreements are virtually identical, including portions of the disciplinary section.

♦ Therefore, P and other prisoners are third-party beneficiaries of the portions of D's contract that are taken directly from the *Cleary* FSA. Otherwise, P could sue under the *Cleary* FSA but not under the identical provisions in the state's contract with D, even though D is charged with the care and discipline of inmates such as P.

♦ On the other hand, D's contract with PharmChem does not refer to inmates. Although it does refer to specimens to be tested, this contract does not suggest that either party intended to give P the benefit of the promised performance. Thus, P is not a third-party beneficiary of D's contract with PharmChem.

Comment. P also sued D's employees individually, but the court dismissed this claim on the ground that an employee cannot be held liable for his employer's breach of a contract between the employer and another party.

---

5) Student's claim under teacher's employment contract--

Verni v. Cleveland Chiropractic College, 212 S.W.3d 150 (Mo. 2007).

Facts. Verni (P) was a student of Dr. Makarov (D) at the Cleveland Chiropractic College (D). D reported that P was selling copies of an upcoming exam, and P was dismissed from the college. P alleged that D breached his employment contract with the college and violated standards of the faculty handbook. P sued D, claiming that he was a third-party beneficiary of the employment contract. The jury returned a verdict for P. D appeals.

Issue. Is a student a third-party beneficiary of his professor's employment contract with the college?

Held. No. Judgment reversed.

♦ Where a contract lacks an express declaration of intent to benefit a third party, there is a strong presumption that the third party is not a beneficiary and that the parties contracted to benefit only themselves.

♦ The employment contract in this case required the college to pay D a salary and D to perform certain duties, but it did not clearly express any intent that D was undertaking a duty to benefit students. The contract also required D to comply with the policies and procedures stated in the faculty handbook. P alleges that D violated the handbook's requirement that faculty members treat students with courtesy, respect, fairness, and professionalism. Even if the faculty handbook was a binding part of the employment contract, its language does not change the strong presumption that the parties entered the contract solely for their own benefit.

♦ Although P and the other students are incidental beneficiaries of employment contracts between the college and faculty members, not everyone who is benefited by a contract may sue to enforce it. Only third parties who are clearly intended beneficiaries are third-party beneficiaries with standing to bring suit to enforce the contract.

_____

6)   Intentions of both parties to the contract required--

Grigerik v. Sharpe, 721 A.2d 526 (Conn. 1998).

Facts. Grigerik (P) offered to buy a piece of undeveloped property from Lang for $9,000. P agreed to pay $16,000 based on Lang obtaining approval of the property as a building lot. Lang contracted with Sharpe (D) for a site plan for drainage, including the design of a septic sewage-disposal system. Lang told D that the site plan was necessary for him to get the land approved as a building lot. Lang obtained the approval, and P paid for the property. However, P's application for a building permit was denied by a new inspector on the ground that the property was not suited to a septic system. P sued D, claiming professional negligence and breach of contract on a third-party beneficiary theory. The jury found for P. The appellate court reversed, holding that the trial court incorrectly allowed P to recover as a foreseeable, rather than an intended, beneficiary of the contract, but also incorrectly required that both parties, rather than just the promisee, intended to benefit P. The appellate court ordered a new trial on the breach of contract count. P appeals.

Issue. May a third-party beneficiary relationship arise based solely on the intent of the promisee of a contractual obligation?

Held. No. Judgment affirmed in part.

♦ The jury found that P was a foreseeable third-party beneficiary. However, the correct rule confers third-party beneficiary status only where it is intended by the parties to the contract. Foreseeability is a tort concept and does not give rise to third-party beneficiary status.

♦ The appellate court held that the third-party beneficiary status could be created solely by the intention of the promisee, but this is contrary to the traditional test. The Restatement (Second), section 302, provides that a third-party beneficiary status is recognized where appropriate to effectuate the intention of the parties and where the circumstances indicate that the promisee intends to give the beneficiary the benefit of the promised performance. This means that the intent of both parties determines whether a third party received third-party beneficiary status.

♦ In this case, the jury specifically found that P had not proven that he was an intended beneficiary of the contract. Lang's intention alone would be insufficient. On remand, the trial court must render judgment for D on the breach of contract claim.

Comment. In *Lucas v. Hamm*, 364 P.2d 685 (Cal. 1961), the court imposed liability on a lawyer to beneficiaries of a will who lost their testamentary rights because the lawyer failed to properly draft the will. This rule is widely, but not universally, followed.

---

7) Only one party intended to benefit third party--

Septembertide Publishing, B.V. v. Stein & Day, Inc., 884 F.2d 675 (2d Cir. 1989).

Facts. Septembertide Publishing, B.V. (P) was owned by Harry Patterson, who wrote the novel *Confessional* under the pseudonym "Jack Higgins." P granted exclusive licensing rights to Stein & Day, Inc. (D), a New York publisher, to publish a hardcover edition of the book in the United States. D had also entered a paperback agreement with New American Library ("NAL") to publish the paperback edition of the novel. P terminated D's rights for failure to make the final hardcover payment and requested that NAL send all of its future payments to it instead of to D. NAL refused, and P sued. The court found that P was a third-party beneficiary of the paperback agreement.

Issue. May a party be a third-party beneficiary where only one of the original parties to the contract clearly intended to benefit the third party?

Held. Yes. Judgment affirmed.

♦ P's third-party beneficiary rights depend on D's intent when it made the two contracts. D entered both the hardcover and paperback agreements at nearly the same time. Both contracts mention P by name, suggesting that D intended to use NAL's payments to satisfy its obligations to P under the hardcover agreement.

♦ It is not clear that NAL had an intent to benefit P, but NAL should be charged with knowledge of the fact that P was to benefit from the paperback agreement. Consequently, P is an intended beneficiary of D's paperback agreement.

---

3. **Rights and Liabilities of the Parties when the Promisor Refuses to Perform.**

   a. **The third-party beneficiary's rights against the promisor.** Once the beneficiary's rights have vested, he can sue the promisor on the contract for failure to perform.

   b. **Defenses of the promisor.**

      1) The beneficiary takes subject to the defenses of the promisor assertable against the promisee.

      2) The third-party beneficiary is not subject to defenses which only the promisee can assert against him. For example, if A paints B's house and B promises to pay $1,000 to C, but B fails to pay, when C sues B, B cannot assert that the $1,000 is for a debt A owes C on which the statute of limitations has run (*i.e.,* only A, the promisee, can assert this defense).

   c. **Right to retain the promisor's performance.** If the promisor has rendered the performance to the beneficiary, she cannot force the beneficiary to repay it even if she discovers that she had a right to rescind the contract with the promisee (unless the beneficiary had notice at the time of performance of the facts allowing the promisor to rescind).

B. DELEGATION OF DUTIES

1. **Introduction.** This section deals with problems that arise when one or both of the original contracting parties seeks to transfer to another party some right arising from the contract, and/or some duty of performance created thereby. The assignment of rights and/or the delegation of duties may be distinguished from other three-party concepts.

   a. **Third-party beneficiary contracts.** In third-party beneficiary contracts, the original contract contemplates that performance will be made to a third party by the promisor. Assignment or delegation occurs where the original contract did not contemplate performance to a third party, but where one of the parties seeks (by acts subsequent to the original contract) to achieve this result.

   b. **Novation.** A novation involves a three-party agreement whereby the promisee agrees to discharge the original promisor and accept another in her place (*i.e.,* it is a substitution of parties to the contract). An assignment does not have this effect since the original contracting parties remain liable for performance.

c. **Assignment of rights.** An assignment is a transfer of a contractual right or benefit which operates to extinguish the right in the transferor (the assignor) and to set it up exclusively in the transferee (assignee). [Restatement (Second) §149]

   1) **The effect.** The effective assignment of a contractual right operates to give the assignee a direct right against the promisor under the contract.

   2) **Real party in interest.** The assignee is the real owner of the right transferred; she alone may enforce it against the promisor.

d. **Delegation of duties.** A delegation of contractual duties is really not a transfer of such duties since the delegating party remains liable for the performance thereof if the party to whom the duties are delegated fails to perform. Rather, a delegation is simply an appointment given by the promisor (A) under the contract to another party (B) to perform her contractual duties. The delegating party (A) is called the "delegant," while the party to whom the duties are delegated is the "delegatee."

   1) As part of a delegation of duties, the delegatee (B) may expressly or impliedly promise the delegant that he will perform the duties owed by the delegant (A) to the other party to the contract (C). This is the typical assumption agreement and it is a third-party creditor beneficiary contract since it gives the other party (C) a right of action directly against the delegatee (B).

   2) Rights under a contract can be assigned without any delegation of duties; or, conversely, duties can be delegated but rights retained. However, the more frequent cases involve attempts to assign rights and delegate duties at the same time.

      a) If this intent is clearly manifest, there are no problems. Often, however, there is simply an "assignment of the contract," with no express agreement by the assignee to perform obligations still due from the assignor to the promisee under the contract.

      b) The question is whether the courts should imply the assignee's obligation to perform from the fact that he has accepted benefits under the contract. There is no easy answer; the courts are split on this issue.

e. **The U.C.C.** The U.C.C. has drastically altered the common law rules on assignment of rights and delegation of duties.

2. **Delegation of Duties and the Sale of a Business.** As indicated previously, a delegation is the appointment by a party to the contract of another person to perform some duty owed by the party under the contract.

a.   **What duties are delegable.** Any contractual duty may be delegated to another, unless the obligee has a substantial interest in having the original obligor perform personally. Thus, except in those cases where performance by a delegatee would vary materially from the performance promised by the obligor, the duty may be performed by some agent or servant of the original promisor (or an independent third party) without constituting a breach of contract. [Restatement (Second) §150; U.C.C. §2-210(1)]

1)   **Applications.**

a)   The principal example of a nondelegable duty is the performance of *personal services*. Where the contract requires performance by a painter, author, teacher, lawyer, etc., in his professional capacity, this duty obviously cannot be delegated to another—no matter how competent—without the obligee's consent.

b)   Most other contractual duties *are* delegable—*e.g.,* duties to pay money, to manufacture or deliver goods, to build or repair buildings, etc.

2)   **Effect of restriction on delegation.** Provisions in a contract limiting either party's right to delegate duties to another are almost always strictly and literally enforced. They evidence the parties' intent that the services involved are personal, so that performance by another would not constitute the bargained-for consideration.

3)   **Effect of attempt to delegate nondelegable duty.** Since the original promisor (delegant) remains liable for performance in any event (see below), his mere attempt to delegate a nondelegable duty does not amount to a breach of contract. If, however, he indicates to the obligee that he is delegating his duties to another and will not perform personally, this may be a sufficient repudiation of his obligation to constitute an anticipatory breach of contract. Performance of a nondelegable duty by another is never sufficient to constitute a tender of performance under the contract (unless knowingly accepted by the obligee in discharge of the original obligor's duty).

b.   **What constitutes a valid delegation.** No special words or formalities are required. All that must appear is a present intent by the obligor-delegant to authorize another to perform the duty. (The word "delegate" need not be used; the more typical wording "assign all rights *and duties*" is clearly a sufficient delegation.)

c.   **Effect of valid delegation of duties.** A valid delegation of duties does *not* excuse the delegating party (delegant) from his duty to perform. It merely places the primary responsibility to perform on the delegatee (who becomes the principal debtor). The delegant becomes secondarily liable (as surety) for performance of the duty promised.

1) **Compare—assignment of rights.** Contrast this with the effect of a valid assignment of rights, which operates to *extinguish* the rights in the assignor and set them up entirely in the assignee. This distinction is critical in the frequent cases which involve *both* an assignment of rights and a delegation of duties. In such cases, the assignor-delegant is cut off from any benefits under the contract, but still remains potentially liable for its performance.

2) **U.C.C.—right of obligee to demand assurance.** In contracts for the sale of goods, the very fact that duties of performance have been delegated entitles the obligee to demand assurances of performance from the delegatee.

d. **Rights and liabilities of the parties following valid delegation of duties.**

1) **Where delegatee has expressly assumed the duty.** If the delegation arises out of a transaction in which the obligor-delegant bargained to have someone take over her obligation, she may have extracted an express promise to perform from the delegatee. For example, A sells her business to B, and as part of the transaction obtains B's promise to pay off all the existing creditors of the business (to whom A was personally liable). Where the delegatee has expressly assumed the delegant's obligations to the other contracting party, a third-party creditor beneficiary contract exists—*i.e.,* the typical "assumption agreement."

a) Thus, in the event of nonperformance, the delegatee is directly liable to the obligee (creditor beneficiary).

b) Moreover, the delegatee is also liable to the delegant (original obligor) for breach of the assumption agreement. The delegant (now surety for the obligation) has the right to an equitable decree of specific performance to compel the delegatee (as principal debtor) to perform. Or, in the event that the obligor-delegant has been forced to perform himself, he can hold the delegatee liable in damages for breach of contract.

2) **Where delegatee has not expressly assumed the duty.** If the delegation is made apart from any assignment of rights under the contract, and there is no express assumption of contract duties, the delegatee's only liability is to the delegant.

e. Limiting assignment rights--

Sally Beauty Co. v. Nexxus Products Co., Inc., 801 F.2d 1001 (7th Cir. 1986).

Facts. Best became the exclusive Texas distributor of hair care products made by Nexxus Products Co., Inc. (D). Sally Beauty Co. (P) purchased Best, and D canceled the distribution agreement. P was itself owned by a hair care products manufacturer that competed with D. P sued for breach, but D claimed the contract was not assignable. The district court granted summary judgment for D on the ground that the contract was one for personal services. P appeals.

Issue. May a party to an otherwise assignable contract prevent assignment to its competitor?

Held. Yes. Judgment affirmed.

♦   The sales aspect of the distribution contract was significant enough that the U.C.C. applies to this case. The trial court erred in holding the contract was for personal services instead of for the sale of goods.

♦   Under U.C.C. section 2-210, delegation of performance and assignability are normally permitted. However, the other party to a contract may prevent assignment if it has a "substantial interest" in having the original promisor perform the contractual duties. This case involves the delegation of Best's duty of performance. D did not accept P's substituted performance; D had promised to refrain from supplying other distributors in Texas in return for Best's promise to use its best efforts to sell D's goods. D should not be required to accept P's best efforts when those efforts are subject to the control of one of D's competitors.

♦   Unlike Best, P is a subsidiary of one of D's direct competitors. P's competitive position gives D a substantial interest in not having P perform the exclusive distribution duties. D may not be forced to assume the risk of an unfavorable outcome in the event the interests of P's parent company conflict with those of D. Thus, the duty of performance under an exclusive distributorship may not be delegated to a competitor in the marketplace.

Dissent. It is not uncommon in business for companies to do business with competitors. P carried hair care supplies made by many different companies that compete with P's parent as much as D does. It is not very likely that P's acquisition of Best would hurt D. The other competitors would not continue to allow P to distribute their products if P favored its parent's products. If P failed to use its best efforts, it would be liable in damages to D for breach.

C. ASSIGNMENT OF RIGHTS

1. **General Rule.** The general rule is that all contract rights are assignable, subject to certain exceptions. These exceptions involve policy factors that outweigh the general policy of free alienation of contract rights. The Restatement (Second) provides that a right may not be assigned where it would "materially change the duty of the obligor, or materially increase the burden or risk imposed on him by his contract, or materially impair his chance of obtaining return performance or materially reduce its value to him." [Restatement (Second) §149; *see also* U.C.C. §2-210]

   a. **Rights which if assigned would materially alter the obligor's duty.** Rights may not be assigned where the assignment would require the obligor (promisor) to render something material that he previously did not have to provide.

   b. **Rights which if assigned would vary materially the risk assumed by the obligor.** Wherever an assignment would require the obligor to assume a materially different (even if not increased) risk than that originally contemplated, the right is not assignable. For example, where personal credit is involved, any substitution of debtors varies the risk and hence no assignment is permitted.

2. **What Constitutes an Effective Assignment.** Any manifested intention of the obligee under a contract to make a present transfer of his rights to another will constitute an assignment. The obligee must intend to vest in the assignee a present (rather than future) right to the thing assigned.

   a. **Formalities.** No formality is required; absent a statute to the contrary, an oral assignment is just as effective as a written one. (Note that lack of writing does affect revocability.)

   b. **Statutes.** By statute, most states require that certain specific assignments be in writing to be effective (such as assignments of interests in land).

   c. **Consideration.** Consideration is not required for an effective assignment. Lack of consideration does, however, affect revocability.

   d. **Words manifesting present interest.** The only other requirements for an effective assignment are that the right assigned be adequately described and that present words of assignment be used. Of course, the word "assign" does not have to be used; the test is whether the language used manifests an intent by the assignor to divest himself completely and immediately of the right in question and set it up in the assignee.

3. **Revocability of Assignments.** Once an assignment is "irrevocable," the assignor does not have the "right" to revoke it or make a subsequent assign-

ment of the same right to another party. However, the assignor has the ***power*** to do so. Any assignment for consideration is irrevocable.

4. **The Legal Effect of a Valid Irrevocable Assignment.** An effective assignment extinguishes the assigned right in the assignor and sets it up in the assignee. Thereafter, the assignee alone is entitled to performance from the obligor.

   a. **Right of assignee against the obligor.**

      1) **Right of direct action.** An assignee can enforce his rights by direct action against the obligor.

      2) **Effect of notice to obligor.** Once the obligor has knowledge of the assignment, he is only protected by paying or performing to the assignee.

      3) **Defenses available to the obligor.**

         a) **Real and personal defenses.**

            (1) **Real defenses.** These are defenses that show that no valid contract was formed in the first place, *e.g.*, the obligor's signature was forged. All assignees take subject to all real defenses.

            (2) **Personal defenses.** These defenses admit the formation of a valid contract but assert some bar to its enforcement (such as failure of consideration, etc.). Assignees of token choses who qualify as "holders in due course" cut off all personal defenses of the obligor. But all other assignees (not "holders in due course") take subject to personal defenses to the extent explained below.

         b) **Defenses assertable against assignees other than holders in due course.** Assignees other than holders in due course take subject to all real defenses and subject to the following personal defenses:

            (1) **Obligor's defenses against the original obligee (the assignor).** Any defenses (real or personal) which the obligor has against the original obligee may be asserted against any ordinary assignee or subassignee (even a bona fide purchaser), provided the defense existed prior to the assignment or arose prior to the obligor's being given notice of the assignment.

(2) **The obligor's defenses against intermediary assignees.** Suppose A and B enter into a contract where A promises to pay $1,000 for goods to be delivered by B. B assigns her rights to C. C then borrows $500 from A; then C assigns to D, who seeks to enforce A's obligation to pay $1,000.

   (a) **Traditional rule.** The traditional rule was that a defense (such as A would have had if C had enforced the contract right) which the obligor acquired against some intermediary assignee could not be asserted against a subassignee (D) who is a bona fide purchaser (pays value for the assignment and takes without notice of the defense).

   (b) **Modern rule.** Under the U.C.C. and the Restatement (Second), a subassignee is treated no differently than the original assignee; if the obligor has or obtains any defense against an intermediate assignee, he can assert it against all subsequent assignees. [*See* U.C.C. §9-318]

b. **Action against assignor's attorneys--**

Herzog v. Irace, 594 A.2d 1106 (Me. 1991).

Facts. Jones was injured in a motorcycle accident and retained attorneys Irace and Lowry (Ds) to represent him. Before recovering any money for the accident, Jones was injured again. Herzog (P) performed surgery to repair Jones's new injuries. Jones could not pay for the surgery but gave P a letter stating that he requested that payment be made directly to P from the settlement of the motorcycle accident. P notified Ds that Jones had assigned the benefits from the motorcycle accident and was told by Ds' employee that the assignment was sufficient to allow Ds to pay P's bills when recovery was made. Jones received a $20,000 settlement for the motorcycle accident. He instructed Ds not to pay P directly but that he would pay P. Ds notified P that Jones had revoked his permission to have Ds pay P and they paid Jones the money. Jones gave P a check, but it was returned for insufficient funds and P was never paid. P sued Ds. The court found for P. Ds appeal.

Issue. May a party who makes a valid assignment later revoke the assignment?

Held. No. Judgment affirmed.

♦   Once a valid assignment is made, and the obligor has notice of the assignment, the fund is impressed with a trust, and the obligor holds the fund not for the original creditor, the assignor, but for the substituted creditor, the assignee. At this point, the obligor cannot pay the amount assigned either to the assignor or to his other creditors. If he does so, he is personally liable to the assignee.

♦ Jones's letter to P constituted a proper assignment of his future right to proceeds from pending litigation. P received a preference over Jones's other creditors through the assignment. Ds, therefore, were obligated to pay P, regardless of Jones's subsequent attempt to revoke the assignment.

♦ Ds claim that they were obligated by the rules of ethics to pay the proceeds as directed by Jones. However, the ethical rules do not affect a client's power to assign his right to proceeds from a pending lawsuit to third parties, and a valid assignment must be honored by the attorney in disbursing the funds on the client's behalf. Ds had no ethical obligation to honor Jones's instruction to disregard a valid assignment.

---

c. **Rights of the assignee against the assignor.** This problem may occur where the assignment is irrevocable but the assignor has nevertheless wrongfully exercised his power to revoke and enabled a subsequent assignee to prevail over a prior assignee. It may also arise where the obligor successfully asserts some defense he had against the assignor in an action brought by the assignee to enforce the obligation, thereby defeating the assigned right.

1) **Gratuitous assignments.** If the assignment is gratuitous (but irrevocable), then the assignee's cause of action is in tort for conversion (*i.e.,* the assignor dealt with the property right inconsistently).

2) **Paid-for assignments.** If the assignment was for consideration, then the assignee can hold the assignor liable in contract for breach of implied warranty (that the right as assigned exists and is subject to no defenses other than those stated at the time of assignment, that the documents given as part of the assignment are genuine, and that the assignor has the right to assign and will do nothing in the future to defeat the assigned right).

5. **U.C.C. Article 9.** Article 9 of the U.C.C. deals with secured transactions. Conflicts often arise when a debtor assigns accounts that are covered by security agreements. Because these issues are so common, it is important to understand Article 9.

a. **Basic terms.**

1) *Attachment* is the process by which the debtor and creditor create a security interest in the debtor's property that is effective between these two parties.

2) *Perfection* is the process by which the security interest is made effective against most of the rest of the world.

3) The *security agreement* is the contract signed by the debtor and creditor to create the security interest.

4) The *financing statement* is the document filed in the place mandated by U.C.C. section 9-501 which notifies the world of the creditor's interest in the debtor's property.

5) A *secured party* is the creditor who has a security interest, or the buyer in the sale of accounts or chattel paper.

6) A *debtor* is the person owing the obligation giving rise to the security interest, or the seller in the sale of accounts or chattel paper.

7) A *lien* is a creditor interest in debtor property. It may be: (i) consensual, or created by agreement, such as an Article 9 security interest; (ii) a judicial lien, or one created by judicial proceedings; or (iii) a statutory lien, which is created by statute or common law for specific unsecured creditors.

b. **Creation of a security interest.** A security interest in a debtor's collateral is created by the debtor and the creditor. The interest becomes effective between the parties through attachment; it becomes effective against other parties through perfection.

1) **Security agreement.** A security agreement is a contract between the debtor and the creditor that sets forth the rights and duties of the parties. It is separate from the financing statement which contains certain information about the creditor's secured interest. The security agreement is usually used to perfect the security interest by filing in the appropriate place.

2) **Attachment.** Under U.C.C. section 9-203, a security interest attaches when it becomes enforceable against the debtor with respect to the collateral. Attachment occurs the moment all of the three following requirements are met, regardless of the order:

   a) The debtor has rights in the collateral;

   b) The parties have a security agreement containing a description of the collateral; and

   c) Value is given by the secured party.

3) **Perfection.** The process of perfection is a set of actions which, when accomplished, give the secured party priority over certain

other classes of the debtor's creditors in the exercise of the security interest. Perfection may be accomplished by filing [U.C.C. §9-310], by possession [U.C.C. §9-313], or by automatic perfection in certain transactions.

4) **Rights in the collateral.** The U.C.C. does not define the term "rights in the collateral," but it refers to some ownership interest or right to obtain possession on the part of the debtor. The term "rights" does include remedies under section 1-201(36). The concept of "title" is irrelevant to secured transactions under section 9-202.

c. **Scope of the security agreement.** A security agreement must contain a description of the collateral involved. The description is sufficient if it reasonably identifies what collateral the parties intended the security interest to cover. Description problems arise in two contexts: (i) the description in the *security agreement* must cover the particular loan and collateral involved; and (ii) the description in the *financing statement* must be adequate to perfect a security interest in the particular collateral and loan involved. The first situation involves interpretation of a private contract, but the second requires that a public document be construed.

d. **Assignments.** Article 9 applies to an assignment of an "account" as collateral for financing. An account is any right to payment for goods sold or leased or for services rendered. Under U.C.C. section 9-404, the rights of an assignee are subject to all the terms of the contract between the account debtor and assignor and any defense or claim arising therefrom, and any other defense or claim of the account debtor against the assignor which accrues before the account debtor receives notification of the assignment.

6. **Successive Assignments of the Same Right.** Even where an assignment is irrevocable, the assignor retains the power to effectively revoke it by assigning the same right to another who may under certain circumstances (discussed below) prevail over the original assignee. Of course, where a token chose is involved, delivery of the token chose destroys both the right and the power to make a subsequent assignment.

a. **First assignment revocable.** If the first assignment is revocable (*i.e.,* it was oral or gratuitous), then any subsequent assignment revokes the first assignment and the subsequent assignee will always prevail.

b. **First assignment irrevocable—common law rules.**

1) **Where one of the competing assignees has a stronger equity.** Wherever one of the competing assignees has a recognized posi-

tion or equity which the other does not have, he will prevail. For example, the later assignee may have had actual knowledge of the earlier assignment (thus the earlier assignee will prevail), etc.

2) **Where the assignees have equal equities.** Where both assignees are innocent purchasers for value to the same assigned right, the courts are split as to who prevails. Some hold that the assignment first in time wins; others that the first to notify the obligor wins.

c. **The U.C.C. rules.** The U.C.C. has changed the rules on priority between competing assignments of contract rights. The Code requires the public filing of a "financing statement" by any person claiming an interest in a contract right. [U.C.C. §9-310] Such filing gives constructive notice of the interest claimed to all other persons; and in many cases the filing is mandatory in order to "perfect" the interest. While detailed rules govern priority as to specialized types of contract rights, the basic rule is that assignments are protected in the order of their filing. [U.C.C. §9-322] There are certain exceptions in which the common law rules still apply (for example, certain assignments which are not routinely used for commercial purposes, such as the assignments made as part of the sale of a business).

d. **Remedy against the assignor.** Regardless of which assignee wins, the losing assignee will have a cause of action against the assignor. [*See supra.*]

7. **The Effect of a Contractual Prohibition Against Assignment.**

a. **Introduction.** Traditionally such provisions were enforced. However, Restatement (Second) section 322 adopts a strong rule of construction against such provisions and U.C.C. section 9-406(d) renders such provisions ineffective to prevent assignment of the right to payment, whether or not it has already been earned by performance.

b. **Assignment despite noncompliance with written consent requirement--**

Bel-Ray Company v. Chemrite (Pty) Ltd., 181 F.3d 435 (3d Cir. 1999).

Facts. Bel-Ray Company (P), a manufacturer of specialty lubricants, entered agreements with Chemrite (Pty) Ltd., a South African company, to allow D to blend and distribute P's products in South Africa. Lubritene Ltd. purchased D's lubricant business, including its rights under P's contracts. P subsequently sued Lubritene for fraud and breach of the contracts. P obtained an arbitration order based on an arbitration provision in its most recent contract with D. Lubritene appeals, claiming the contract was not binding because it required P's written consent to any assignment of D's interests under the contract and P had never provided such consent.

Issue. Is an assignment ineffective where the assignor does not obtain the other party's written consent to the assignment?

Held. No. Judgment affirmed.

♦   A court may only compel arbitration where the party has entered a written agreement to arbitrate. Lubritene can be compelled to arbitrate only if the contract between P and D providing for arbitration was effectively assigned to Lubritene.

♦   The Restatement (Second), section 322, provides that a contract term prohibiting assignment of rights gives the obligor a right to damages for breach of the terms forbidding assignment but does not render the assignment ineffective. This distinguishes between a party's power to assign and its right to assign.

♦   A party's power to assign is only limited where the parties clearly manifest an intent to limit that right. This requires a provision in the contract stating that non-conforming assignments are void or invalid, or that the nonassigning party shall not recognize any such assignment. In the absence of such language, a provision limiting or prohibiting assignments is merely a covenant not to assign or to follow specific procedures before assigning. Breach of such a covenant may make the assigning party liable for damages, but does not affect the validity of the assignment itself.

♦   In this case, P's contract with D does not contain the requisite clear language to limit D's power to assign the contracts, so D's assignment to Lubritene is enforceable.

---

8.   **Gratuitous Assignments.** An assignment which is not for consideration is ordinarily revocable at any time by the assignor.

   a.   **How revoked.** An assignment may be revoked by any of the following:

      1)   *Successive assignment* of the same right to another assignee;

      2)   *Death of the assignor*;

      3)   *Bankruptcy of the assignor*;

      4)   *Notice of revocation*; or

      5)   *Acceptance by the assignor of payment or performance directly from the obligor.*

b. **How made irrevocable.** Any of the following makes a gratuitous assignment irrevocable:

    1) **Delivery of a token chose.** If a token chose is assigned, delivery of the token makes even a gratuitous assignment irrevocable (*example*: delivery of stock certificates).

    2) **Writing.** Putting the assignment in writing makes it irrevocable.

    3) **Estoppel.** If the assignee has detrimentally relied on a gratuitous assignment, the assignor may be estopped to revoke.

    4) **Performance.** If the assignee has received the performance, the assignment is irrevocable.

    5) **Novation.** If the assignee, assignor and the obligor all agree that the right should be transferred to the assignee, it is irrevocable.

9. **Obligors and Assignees.**

    a. **Assignee assumes assignor's position--**

Delacy Investments, Inc. v. Thurman & Re/Max Real Estate Guide, Inc., 693 N.W.2d 479 (Minn. Ct. App. 2005).

Facts. Delacy Investments, Inc. (P) factored receivables from real estate agents. Thus, a real estate agent could assign or sell his future receivable or commission to P in exchange for immediate funds. Thurman was a real estate agent who entered into a security agreement with P, granting P a security interest in all of his accounts receivable. This made P an assignee and Thurman an assignor. About 15 months later, Thurman entered into an independent contractor agreement with Re/Max Real Estate Guide, Inc. (D) that provided for payment of commissions to Thurman only if they exceeded Thurman's past-due financial obligations to D. This agreement made D an account debtor, possessing the potential right to receipt of what Thurman assigned to P. P factored a $10,000 receivable for Thurman. Before it was collected, D terminated Thurman, who owed D over $11,000 at the time. D refused to pay the receivable to P because Thurman was not entitled to it. P demanded payment. When D refused to pay, P sued. The trial court granted D summary judgment. P appeals.

Issue. Are the rights of an assignee subject to the terms of an agreement between its assignor and an account debtor?

Held. Yes. Judgment affirmed.

    ♦   Thurman was not entitled to collect the $10,000 commission because his past-due financial obligations to D exceeded the amount of the commission. The trial court held that P could not obtain a greater right in the commission than Thurman himself had. Under U.C.C. section 9-404(a)(1), the rights of an assignee are subject to all terms of the agreement between the account debtor and assignor. This means that P is bound by the agreement between Thurman and D.

♦ An assignee of a claim does not take greater rights than the original assignor. P could have contracted otherwise, but it did not. Therefore, P's rights are limited to those of Thurman.

♦ P claims that under U.C.C. section 9-201(a), its perfected security agreement is effective against creditors. This is true except as otherwise provided in the U.C.C. U.C.C. section 9-404(a)(1) does provide otherwise, so it governs.

---

b. **Financing consumer credit.** Most purchases of automobiles and durable consumer goods are consummated through use of a financing arrangement enabling the consumer to pay for the purchased items over time. Because the sellers are primarily in the business of selling goods and not making loans, they usually have a working relationship with a finance company. Pursuant to the financing arrangement offered by the seller, the consumer can obtain credit directly by means of secured loans from a finance company or bank or the seller can assign the contract of purchase to the finance company for cash (or an equivalent line of credit) at a price discounted from the consumer's purchase price. If the purchase contract is assigned to a finance company, the seller may act as the finance company's collection agent or the consumer may be informed that the purchase contract has been assigned to the finance company and that all payments are to be made directly to the finance company. While there are many variations on the methods used by sellers of consumer goods and finance companies to facilitate the sale of consumer goods to consumers who are unable to purchase the goods other than on time, these methods are generally geared toward establishing "holder in due course" status in the finance company, in order to protect the finance company from defenses the consumer may have against the seller.

1) **Holders in due course.** U.C.C. section 3-302 defines a holder in due course as one who takes a negotiable instrument for value and in good faith, without notice of any defense or claim against it.

2) **Rights of a holder in due course.** U.C.C. section 3-305 provides that a holder in due course takes the instrument that he holds free from all claims to it on the part of any person, and free from all

defenses of any party to the instrument with whom the holder has not dealt except for those based on:

a) Such incapacity, duress, or illegality as makes the transaction a nullity;

b) Misrepresentation which induced the party obligated to sign the instrument with neither knowledge nor reasonable opportunity to obtain knowledge of its character or essential terms;

c) Discharge in bankruptcy; or

d) Any other discharge known to the holder when he takes the instrument.

3) **FTC Notice Rule.** The FTC requires a notice provision in certain contracts providing that the holder of a consumer credit contract is subject to all claims and defenses which the debtor could assert against the seller. One court held that the main purpose of the rule is to preserve the consumer's right to refuse to pay, but other courts take the position that the rule permits consumer claims of assignee liability.

4) **Truth in Lending Act ("TILA").** The TILA requires lenders to provide statements containing specified disclosures, including the amount of the finance charge and that amount expressed as an "annual percentage rate" or APR.

c. **Waiver of defense clause--**

Chemical Bank v. Rinden Professional Association, 498 A.2d 706 (N.H. 1985).

Facts. The Rinden Professional Association (D), a law firm, leased an office phone system from Intertel for an eight-year term, with the option to buy the equipment at the end of the term for one dollar. Intertel desired to sell the payment rights to Chemical Bank (P), but D had to agree to the terms. One of the terms stated that D's obligation to pay P was unconditional and that D promised to pay notwithstanding any defense, set-off, or counterclaim whatsoever which D might ever have against Intertel. D signed the assent form and Intertel assigned the lease to P. Three years later, the phone system had to be replaced because it malfunctioned. Intertel had gone bankrupt, and D stopped paying P. P sued. The lower court found for P and D appeals.

Issue. May a waiver-of-defense clause be enforced against a nonconsumer?

Held. Yes. Judgment affirmed.

♦ This lease is a security agreement under U.C.C. section 1-201(37)(b) because it gives D the option to buy the goods for nominal consideration. Security agreements are governed by Article 9. Under U.C.C. section 9-403, a waiver-of-defense provision is generally enforceable.

♦ If a buyer who is not a consumer agrees to waive the defenses against the assignee, the waiver is valid if the assignment was made (i) for value, (ii) in good faith, and (iii) without notice of a claim or defense. In this case, D is clearly not a consumer.

♦ P gave value when it paid $8,800 to Intertel for the assignment. D claims P was not a good faith purchaser because P and Intertel were too closely connected, but all the evidence shows that the two parties had an arm's length commercial relationship and did not give or receive favorable treatment. The fact that P checked D's credit rating and insisted on the waiver-of-defense clause does not show lack of good faith either, as these are normal procedures when a bank provides credit. There is no evidence that P had notice of a claim or defense when it took the assignment.

♦ D claims that it did not receive consideration when it signed the waiver-of-defense agreement. Under section 2-209(1), however, a modification does not need consideration. The waiver-of-defense clause is not contrary to public policy. A policy of the U.C.C. is to encourage the credit supply by protecting the lender from lawsuits over the quality of the goods.

---

        d.   **Commercial credit.** In general, the rules pertaining to commercial credit are more relaxed than the consumer credit provisions. The theory is that commercial parties are better able than consumers to protect themselves because they are more sophisticated and have more comparable bargaining power.

10. **Assignees and Third Parties.** For an assignee, an effective filing of a "financing statement" under U.C.C. Article 9 is an important protection. Where there are multiple secured creditors, perfection of an Article 9 security interest is crucial to collection.

        a.   **Failure to perfect.** In *U.S. Claims, Inc. v. Flomenhaft & Cannata LLC*, 519 F. Supp. 2d 515 (E.D. Pa. 2006), U.S. Claims, Inc. had purchased from a law firm, Flomenhaft & Cannata LLP ("Flomenhaft"), attorneys' fee interests in pending legal claims. However, U.S. Claims did not file financing statements for these purchase agreements. Subsequently, Flomenhaft entered into a financing agreement with the Stillwater Asset-Backed Fund LP ("Stillwater"), in which Flomenhaft pledged all of their assets to Stillwater in exchange for a monetary advance. Stillwater did file a financing statement. U.S. Claims brought an action, claiming that its rights in Flomenhaft's assets were superior to those of Stillwater. U.S. Claims relied in part on U.C.C. section 9-309(2), which provides that an assignment of accounts that does not by itself, or in conjunction with other assignments to the same assignee, transfer a significant part of the assignor's outstanding accounts is perfected when it attaches. The court found for Stillwater, explaining that U.S. Claims failed to show that the contingency fee agreements collectively did not transfer a significant part of Flomenhaft's outstanding accounts. Moreover, the court stated that section 9-309(2) would not likely help U.S. Claims, even if it adequately pled that section's applicability, because the official comments make it clear that section 9-309(2) is not intended to apply to assignors like U.S. Claims, since its purpose is to save casual or isolated assignments from invalidation. A purchaser such as U.S. Claims, which was in the business of purchasing attorneys' fee interests, should file a financing statement.

TABLE OF CASES
(Page numbers of briefed cases in bold)